# A Higher Purpose

## Three Rules of Conscious Leadership

**By Arturo Cuenllas**

*To Carlota and Elena*

# Author Bio

Conscious Coach, Consultant and Speaker
Professor of Leadership and Human Behavior in the International Master in Management at the IE Business School and IE University. Director of the Master of Hospitality Management at Ostelea School of Tourism. MBA Professor in Sustainability and Management at City University of Seattle and York St. John University (BHMS campus Lucern, Switzerland). Global MBA Professor in People Management and Organizational Behavior at ESDEN Business School. Associate Professor in International Master in Hospitality and Tourism Management in Sustainability, ESCP Europe Business School.
Over 19 years leading teams and executive positions: Hotel General Manager in several hotels and hotel chains for more than ten years in Galicia, Madrid, Balearic Islands and the Canary Islands. Nine years of international experience in management of hotels in Mexico, France, Dominican Republic, Germany, and the Philippines.

Executive Master in Tourism Business Management from IE Business School. Executive Development Program by IESE Business School. Graduated in Hotel Management from Glion Institute of Higher Education, Switzerland.

## TABLE OF CONTENTS

# CHAPTER 1: A HIGHER PURPOSE

## THE TRAP OF INERTIA

The definition of inertia in the Cambridge dictionary deals with the force that causes something not moving to tend to continue not to move. Inertia is also the situation in which there is very little activity or interest, or when people are unwilling to make an effort to change.

People often function by inertia in our day-to-day. We work without finding a deeper meaning in our jobs, above fulfilling our responsibilities, deserving our bosses' recognition, or letting ourselves be carried away by our tasks' hectic activity. Companies also operate by inertia, not just people. The inertia of a company is transferred to its management systems, its policies, or its routines. It is the usual way of doing things. This inertia of a company is usually determined by the sector in which it operates.

The inertia of an organization usually dictates the essential priorities we work for, which are usually reduced to two factors. First, the work needs to go ahead. At the top of every manager's priorities is that workflow or operations go smoothly: the assembly line has to work, planes have to take off and land on schedule, dishes from a restaurant kitchen have to reach the tables, projects in organizations must eventually end, and patients in a hospital have to be taken care of.

The second priority is making money. Money is necessary because otherwise, there wouldn't be any business or jobs. Nevertheless, there is a difference between placing the benefits of a company as an end in and of itself and doing it as a consequence of pursuing a higher purpose. When money is at the top of the equation, executives who run by inertia prioritize everything in terms of numbers and maximize the profits in the short-term. Management practically simplifies everything to figures and ratios. It is what the market demands. In this way, the main goal which the company stands for basically boils down to making more money (at least in the mindset of many shareholders, executives, and entrepreneurs). Customers matter, but products or services are often offered through a process of inertia as well.

However, work activity per se and making money are not goals that can give meaning to work. It is possible that maximizing profits in the short term may be a motivating factor for some people, including shareholders, but companies are not only made up of shareholders. There are other business stakeholders, such as customers, employees, suppliers, the local community, even the environment. These different stakeholders are also part of the central nucleus of any organization. Even shareholders are not the stakeholder group that matters the most, although the markets' inertia leads us to believe otherwise.

Therefore, this inertia happening in companies creates work situations with neither great significance nor a sense of purpose in our jobs. The status quo poses a trap because it reduces our vision and creativity. Just as fish are not aware of the water they live in, markets can fail to consider another way of doing things. If companies that function by inertia are pure activity, they do not offer greater meaning in their jobs, nor do they produce a stronger impact on society and customers. My case is an excellent example of this. A large part of my professional life has been dedicated to the hotelier sector. Although the essence of my work should have consisted of better serving clients and getting the best out of employees, the reality is that I prioritized everything to meet budgets and to improve financial ratios. It's what my bosses had taught me. The priorities that always focused my duties as hotel director were profits. Inevitably, this led me to neglect other interest groups.

When everything is prioritized in terms of numbers, employees become parts of a machine. That machine has to 'grease' them well to work efficiently; they are mere human resources. Managers expect employees to work with discipline and commitment. And although companies talk about motivation and talent management, the truth is that they are not capable of getting the best out of them.

Customers also become mere numbers. We all talk about how important they are to the business, but we offer them value out of sheer inertia. Although the market has evolved and is now more difficult for us to retain them, we continue to provide them with a sanitized service. Why? Because the people who should be serving them are not inspired or trained to do better because they do not share corporate values or a business purpose that motivates them to do it any differently. So, when they have to serve the customer, they are usually more concerned with replicating instructions and procedures than generating unique value experiences. They can't do better because financial priority also sacrifices the customer. Customers are objectified and become an entity, a figure, or a ratio.

Society and the environment are not part of the purpose of most companies either. Today, many companies claim corporate social responsibility actions, but they often trade its initially good intentions at the CSR office for short-term profits. Although markets have evolved, and new laws now force companies to be more responsible, their social and environmental goals continue to happen by inertia. Its corporate social responsibility actions are lacking in ambition and consistency.

Inertia makes us work with the autopilot on. Our professional career can be a compelling reason that moves us to strive; we want to be successful, get promoted, and take on more responsibility. Our career plan is a purpose that gives meaning to our work. Titles, knowledge, power, and money can be potent motivational factors, but they also stop fulfilling us at some point. Suddenly, at some point in our life, we can ask ourselves: What is the meaning of my work? Can I get the passion back again? Can I contribute to the greater good? I'm not going to be here forever, so how would I want to be remembered? What can I tell my children that I do with pride?

## In times of Covid-19: Higher Purpose and Shared Values

Purpose is created when we believe that what we do matters. To whom? To us, to other people and society. This purpose is something very personal. Different concerns move to each one of us. Although to all of us, our life purpose can offer more meaning to what we do. It inspires us to try harder. According to Victor Frankl, life can provide purpose and meaning, but it cannot "promise" happiness or well-being. The purpose we pursue is above both. Ultimately, happiness stems from purpose.[1]

Organizations can share a purpose with customers, employees, shareholders, suppliers, and other stakeholders. This purpose could help them escape from the trap of inertia. At the root of any company's purpose is its reason for being. You start by asking yourself: *Why? Why do we do what we do?* In their Conscious Capitalism proposal, Raj Sisodia and John Mackey mention the need to bring forward a purpose that goes beyond making money [2]. This would be a higher purpose that would unite the organization with all its stakeholders, starting with the customers and employees. It is a journey that guides us all in the company. And to that purpose we have to add the corporate values. Values, ultimately, are derived from the organizational purpose. The problem for many organizations is that company values are no longer credible. Nobody believes in them, even if they appear on the corporate website because they do not translate into behaviors. Values say one thing, but bosses do another.

A higher purpose has a dose of idealism. It ceases to be practical and realistic, although not for that reason. Answer questions like:

- What impact do you want to make on the world?
- What do you believe in?
- How can our company make a difference?

This book presents a higher purpose focused on three areas: employees, ourselves, and other stakeholders. The proposed purpose is not at odds with the benefits. The three areas of work presented in the book seek the same goal: to make people and the company better. When we talk about organizational learning, corporate identity, knowledge, or competitiveness, we always refer to people. Motivation, love, the pride of belonging, effort, degree of responsibility, talent, creativity, and synergies between teams originate in our employees. These things do not happen by mandate, nor spontaneous generation. However, the origin of these factors is the purpose and the values that move the organization. All this, in the end, will pay off.

In such turbulent times of uncertainty, fear, and economic crisis after Covid-19, it is even more necessary to work for a company that pursues a higher purpose. Such a business purpose should answer the questions posed and provide a set of values that can unite us all with the brand. After this pandemic, so deadly for lives and the economy, it is a very human impulse to attend to the pyramid's lowest needs. It is tempting to focus solely on the financial bleeding, all the while neglecting the purpose. Any form of purpose would seem like a superficial and frivolous luxury in the face of that which is most urgent. But this dichotomy is false. The purpose and values of the organization are not incompatible with urgency.

On the other hand, sooner or later, these economic and health crises will pass. The questions we should ask ourselves then are: how will we emerge? Stronger or weaker? This is not the first crisis we have suffered. It won't be the last either. But the facts show that those companies which do not have a shared purpose or values suffer more in troubled times. For example, in times of crisis and uncertainty, it is more necessary than ever to count on our employees' commitment and best efforts. Nowadays, there is also a lot of talk about the concept of 'resilience.' Resilience refers to people's ability to get up after an adverse situation. In psychology, it is associated with optimism, tenacity, and confidence in our abilities. Well, resilience is more comfortable to acquire when we pursue a purpose that matters to us.

A few days after starting to write this chapter a complaint of a famous businessman in the hotel sector went viral. It was a rebuke of his workers for not wanting to join their jobs during the provisional labor adjustment plan 3. His anger was ever-growing because this company put a measure in place: for workers not to lose money, the organization decided to supplement government salaries. "Gentlemen, you are not on vacation!" "You are in a temporary downsizing plan" - the hotelier's frustration was at a maximum. In turn, social networks were at fever pitch for and against his statements: "He is right." "It is outrageous that employees do not value the companies' efforts. Where are the unions?" "This is how the country goes." "I'm looking for a job; where should I send my CV?" However, opinion on social networks was also positioned against him, while making it a political issue. But, at the expense of our common prejudices, we should ask ourselves: why? Psychologists warn about the fear of returning to a job after such a long confinement period. And yet, at the root of the problem, there is a lack of commitment and responsibility of some employees to the company.

In these situations, we can glimpse a lack of purpose, a shortage of shared values, and a sense of belonging. Maybe some employees are not the right ones because their sense of responsibility and work ethic are very low. The nirvana of motivation does not exist and, no matter how well things are done, there will always be ungrateful people who do not value the company's effort. But it is also possible that workers do not appreciate the employer's goodwill, perhaps after having suffered a history of disagreements with their bosses and the organization. This brings us to two new causes. Employees can simply be adequate, or suffer under the management of bad bosses.

Similarly, people's sense of belonging to their companies can be null as a by-product of a dysfunctional organizational culture. For the employee, everything is boiled down to a simple labor transaction.

I do not know what the organizational climate of this particular hotel company is. Personally, I think it would be unfair to attribute causes that I have not been able to analyze more rigorously. Now, our work's motivation and commitment failures often happen because there is no emotional connection to the company. This emotional void can also occur with clients.

Barry Wehmiller is a company that has an overall profit of about 1,500 million dollars annually and has 7,000 employees. This organization manufactures technological components and provides consulting and engineering services. Bob Chapman is the CEO of this company of more than 130 years of history, and he will tell you that the primary purpose of their business is not the equipment, the services, or the products they manufacture. Barry Wehmiller's purpose is people. What do they produce? They produce extraordinary people. In 2002, twenty people came together for an introspection exercise to explore their belief system. Out of these meetings came his guiding leadership principles: the company values. They measure success based on the impact they have on other people, starting with their employees, extending to their families, suppliers, customers, and the community.[4]

Bob Chapman talks about people, purpose, and performance. Everything is interconnected and produces synergies. Bob also tells us about his managerial experience and the inertia trap: "I was raised in an environment where only maximizing shareholder value mattered. Profits were the metric of success. I had a management position, and I got a business degree. And what did I do? I managed people. But I was never really aware of the incredible responsibility of leading others. "5

# A HIGHER PURPOSE: 3 RULES OF CONSCIOUS LEADERSHIP

A rule is a principle imposed or adopted to direct the conduct or the correct performance of an action. Rules are necessary for the proper development of an activity. Leading people involves following rules. The problem is that the focus on priorities of shareholders, the inertia of the markets, and many companies' management has confused the rules. But we have already seen that shareholders are not the only stakeholder. This book presents a higher purpose through three rules. These rules, in turn, make up a conscious leadership:

1. Enhance the power in others
2. Enhance the power in yourself
3. Enhance the value among all stakeholders

## Rule # 1: Enhance the power in others

The first rule is about others. Leading other people is about making them better. Period. Make them do their jobs better and, in turn, make the organization better. So easy to understand, yet so challenging to execute. Because for this to happen we not only have to have suitable employees, but we also must have appropriate bosses at all levels. We must provide people with adequate leadership. And the setback is that most bosses are mediocre.

In **Chapter 2**, we will talk about the leadership crisis that threatens companies. When evaluating bosses, you usually get mediocrity ratings. A mediocre boss is unable to get more out of people and their teams. Throughout the chapters, I will explain why such mediocrity levels are commonplace. The leadership crisis is also the consequence of a lack of appropriate values. Companies say they have values, but they do not work credibly with them.

In **Chapter 3**, I will analyze a business's culture as a source of competitiveness (or vice versa), as the reason that explains dysfunctional behaviors and low performance in many working environments. An organization's culture begins with the belief system, the personal values and the motivations of the executives. It starts with the founders' character. Organizational culture is an extension of the nature of the business leaders. Going deeper, we can analyze two antagonistic belief systems that answer the following question: What is the potential we do see in people?

Then companies must articulate their values. It is an opportunity to do it from the beginning: in the business plan. **Chapter 4** will present a series of values that could be defined as universal and make up a conscious enterprise. They are guiding principles of conscious leadership that can refer to many companies. These principles will be developed throughout the book. Once the values have been articulated, both managers and directors have to work on them daily. This chapter will discuss five essential working areas.

**Chapter 5** presents excellence as a conscious leadership goal. The path to excellence has no end; it is a continuous journey of improvement, an improvement that begins with the employees. However, it is unrealistic to speak of excellence if we do not start treating our employees as workers of knowledge. Coined by Peter Drucker long ago, this term needs to be updated and adapted to new generations and to our times.

Empowering others is to do so in your team. A conscientious boss is a team coach. The reality is that many groups are in a conflict phase. When this happens, not only are synergies not generated, but the net sum of the parts is negative. **Chapter 6** will analyze the areas that every team leader must attend to in order to take it to the most advanced stage in its development: the high-performance phase.

However, any team is made up of individuals. A good boss has to attend to the interests of the team as well as to the shared goals. But you should also dedicate yourself to each person on the team, listening to their specific needs. The conscientious leader has to deal with the strengths and vulnerabilities of each team member. **Chapter 7** will expand the vision we normally have regarding the boss-coach or coaching. The conscious leader is a multiplier boss who brings out the best in people because he invests his time and dedication. He knows how to recognize work but also to give negative feedback if the situation requires it.

## Rule # 2: Enhance the power in yourself

For the first rule to be fulfilled, we have to attend to the second rule in parallel. It is not possible to bring out the best in other people if we cannot update our internal operating system. Leading others also means doing it for yourself. **Chapter 8** will talk about the character of the leader: his internal operating system. To be more effective, we have to attend to every conscious leader's vital competencies: self-awareness and emotions. Both competencies are usually undervalued, but the interesting thing is that they always affect the rest of the skills that could be defined as *hard*.

**Chapter 9** will explain how to update one's internal operating system. For this, an ancient technique will be presented: meditation and mindfulness. Science has been trying and testing its benefits, both physical and psychological, for more than two decades. It is time to start incorporating these methods into management practices.

## Rule #3: Enhance the value among all stakeholders

The last rule of conscious leadership looks to the rest of the stakeholders. But it focuses on three of them: customers, society (communities) and the environment.

**Chapter 10** will present a higher vision of service: an exceptionally human service. Such a level of service is unlike a commodity or bureaucratized service. Companies can offer these higher levels of service and even measure them. To enhance the value that we provide to our clients through use, we must work in four strategic areas.

Finally, conscious leadership enhances value in society and the environment. **Chapter 11** proposes a vision that goes beyond corporate social responsibility. The United Nations Sustainable Development Goals (SDG) for 2030 provide an opportunity to direct our efforts. These are 17 goals with 169 targets that all UN Member States have agreed to achieve by 2030. This chapter also introduces the entrepreneur or social enterprise. Altruism and business are compatible. What are the common characteristics shared by the most sustainable companies?

**Special Note: clarification of the 'boss' concept.**

The boss concept will be used a lot throughout the book. Nowadays, 'the boss' could seem a pejorative term whereas the more appropriate term might be leader. But the reality is that we all have a boss and, for better or for worse, it is a practical, familiar word. In descending order, companies have exceptional bosses, good bosses, mediocre bosses, bad bosses, and terrible bosses. Ultimately, there are even psychopathic bosses. The latter is likely a tiny percentage, but the damage they cause to others and the organization is devastating.[6]

## My purpose

Eight years ago, I wondered what the point of my work was. I remember the conversation with my wife after picking her up one day at her company. At that time, I had been looking for a job for more than nine months. It was a time in which my motivation and confidence were cracking. The economic crisis had affected us all. It was a desperate moment because not only did you have the financial pressure on you, but you also suffered an inner emptiness, finding yourself without direction or purpose. That day, two questions changed the course of my life and provided my escape from inertia. My wife asked me: "How is it possible that you don't make your talent worth more?" "Why don't you start working for yourself?"

Since then, I have regained my sense of purpose. In my case, it did not come suddenly, but little by little. Every year that I have spent on this new professional stage, I have seen it more straightforward. This book is the culmination of all these years.

My purpose is crucial to me because it has awakened a passion and energy that, until then, I had not appreciated in my life. This is also important for other people, such as my MBA and MiM, university students, and many other individuals who seek to improve their leadership skills. But it also provides value to society since my lessons aim to improve the quality of leadership in companies. I would have liked to have these things in mind when I was a first-time boss. The path to being an exceptional boss requires a lifetime, but it is a purpose worth pursuing. My tiny contribution seeks to raise awareness, showing that there is another more conscious way to lead a team or a company.

All these years, I have been focused on analyzing successful case studies and best practices in leadership. This book has taken four years of work, and its value lies in its proposal of synthesis. Although many concepts are might be new, I have not discovered anything that has not really been told before. I have not come to anything first, nor have I had doctoral research that has led me to a pioneering discovery about something in particular. Everything has already been seen. However, creativity and originality also lie in forming a new concept or a new idea, bringing together different elements that were scattered. Therefore, the value of the book lies in the way it presents the ideas and vision it offers. I don't limit myself to citing only the best management practices, but I also bring my own experience in leading teams. So, I will share my mistakes and successes in different stories throughout the book.

Authors like Raj Sisodia and John Mackey speak of higher purpose, stakeholder integration, culture, and conscious leadership. This work also presents these concepts, but from a different perspective. It also delves into where the authors did not go. In a way, it complements their book.

## Why write this book?

I have not stopped asking myself this question. Writing a book is a very long and laborious process. At least in my case. It is also frustrating because blocks, doubts, laziness, anxiety, procrastination arise in the process. Although the opposite also happens, there is nothing that beats a flowing creativity. It is an essential work of learning, necessary in putting ideas in order.

Is it worth all the effort? There are millions of books, and leadership books number in the hundreds of thousands. Will it be read? Will it be valued? All these doubts always appear, but in the end, the purpose always wins. My students are the main engine: they are my purpose because they are the future leaders.

We may still not understand what it entails to be a leader after thousands of articles, books, seminars, videos, and stories on leadership. The concept has been tampered with so much that it has lost its value. The same thing happens with the term leadership as with the idea of democracy. People continually mention these concepts to convey a positive notion that is on everyone's mind. But in practice, people's intentions and actions are opposite to what the idea represents.

All these years of learning and mastering have shaped my purpose: to write a book that explains and reinforces conscious leadership. The questions this book will solve are: What does the concept mean? What does conscious leadership imply? How can conscious leadership contribute to companies and people? And, even more importantly: how can we get it?

Bill George is the Henry B. Arthur Professor of Ethics at Harvard Business School. He has also been named among the most influential CEOs when he ran the healthcare giant Medtronic. Bill proposes that his students and future leaders to ask themselves three questions.[7]

We should first ask ourselves: What kind of leader do we want to be, and how will we use our leadership talents? The response we make will define our leadership priorities. This question, in turn, raises other questions: Are you going to prioritize yourself or others? How are you going to channel your energy and passion? What are you going to spread to others with your leadership?

The second question is about you: How are you going to develop as a leader? The answer, however, does not focus only on the technical-professional level. Obtaining professional degrees or just knowing more is not enough to answer this question. We also have to be able to work and develop our interior, our character. This question is crucial because it is necessary to banish the concept of heroic leadership that has been implanted in the collective subconscious. Leadership skills are developed; they are not given. An exceptional leader is not a person chosen by the gods, capable of pulling the sword from the rock. It takes work. Lots of work. An exceptional athlete is a person who works very hard to improve. An excellent boss presents the same effort mentality as an elite athlete does physically.

The third question is about the impact you will make on others and society: What difference do you want to make in the world with your leadership? This question may seem idealistic, but it is very close to our reality. The answer to this question is measured through the impact of your actions on other people (your team, organization, clients, and society.)

This book answers the three leadership questions that Bill George asks.

# Part I: Enhance the power in others

# CHAPTER 2: A CRISIS OF LEADERSHIP

## MEDIOCRITY IS COMMON

### The mediocrity of bosses is one of the leading causes of the low level of employee engagement

Managers often talk about employee engagement, and executives encourage their leaders to motivate their employees, but motivation is a feeling that cannot be imposed. Like it or not, employees have complex inner lives of emotions, perceptions, and motivations. Teresa Amabile and Steven Kramer warn in their book *The Progress Principle* about the inner lives of employees. People rarely reveal their feelings and motivations. And just like an iceberg, emotions such as frustration, demotivation, anxiety, resentment, or negative thoughts about our bosses, usually remain hidden.[1]

Studies and research on motivation make reasonable the hypothesis that many of us have been maintaining: the main factor of commitment and motivation of people at work is the company's quality of leadership. The employee's private life also explains the gap between bosses' and subordinates' perceptions, as we will see later.

The quality of leadership is mostly found at levels of mediocrity. It is what most studies conclude. When employees can evaluate their bosses, the results are usually not positive, and the research does not distinguish between sectors, generations, or nationalities. For example, Linda A. Hill's research concludes that most organizations have few managers who can be classified as excellent, while some are good, with a horde of mediocre managers, along with some which are bad, even terrible! [2]

More global studies, such as a Gallup poll on motivation, reveal low levels of commitment among employees to their companies and their jobs. Globally, the percentages of employees who are defined as committed to their jobs are very low. Gallup found that only 13 percent of people were engaged in their jobs. So, the remaining 87 percent were employees at different levels of motivation, somewhere at the lower scales. These levels could be the same as that of David Sirota and Douglas A. Klein: moderately satisfied, neutral, and dissatisfied. People committed to their jobs could be defined in enthusiasm levels above the group of moderately satisfied employees in their companies. [3]

Blame could be shared between organizational policies and the direct bosses; however, Gallup concludes that immediate bosses have the most significant impact on people's motivational states. And above all, we tend to abandon our jobs because we suffer from bad bosses [4]. And this is obvious; who hasn't quit a job because the direct boss they had was bad?

The truth is that any boss can create a sub-culture within his team, different from the company's prevailing culture. This could happen positively or negatively. For example, let's take the case of a manager who, despite the dysfunctional organizational culture and policies in his organization, brings out the best in his employees. Perhaps the internal climate in this company could be one of the continuous labor conflicts, a lack of confidence, a lack of commitment, or low motivation levels. But this boss seems to have created a microclimate that protects his employees. Despite the internal pressures, he has established specific values and appropriate behaviors within his team. People give their best, primarily because of their boss. Their work is more productive and results improve.

However, this situation could also change from one day to the next. The team might get the bad news that the manager they admire so much is leaving. He or she may be tired of fighting the rest of the organization to do a good job. In this new scenario, the incoming boss is more aligned with the rest of the executives. Like them, the new boss now prioritizes everything by the numbers so that the work goes ahead - no matter how. He or she neglects the relationships with his collaborators. The human aspects that his predecessor had nurtured so much is now secondary. From one day to the next, the motivation and commitment of that team plummet.

It is a contradiction that executives do not focus their strategic priorities to ensure leadership quality in their companies. Enthusiasm and commitment are necessary to move towards higher levels of productivity. As we will see in the following chapters, these higher performance levels are superior customer service, continuous work improvement, better ideas, creativity, and better team business problem-solving.

## I've been a mediocre boss. But many others too...

The following is a confession that I make out loud in my classes and seminars: "In my professional career of more than 20 years leading teams in different countries, I have been a bad boss at first, then I improved, but I stayed at levels of mediocrity for a long time. And only in my final stage as a manager could I define myself as a good boss. In any case, I'm not sure I was an exceptional boss. Probably not."

The shocked faces are priceless. Some student uses it against me in his evaluation of the teacher, when for some reason he did not connect in my classes: "He teaches us leadership, but he admits that he has been a lousy leader. What a bad example!"

The truth is that if such confession is made in a selection process, the chances that you would end up being hired would also be slim. By the way, this makes me wonder how much the typical interview question can turn against you: "What would you define your areas for improvement? What are your weaknesses?" When I hear these questions, I always think of the scenes of police officers in arrests: "You have the right to remain silent: anything you say can be used against you." Above all, the people asking the question may not be prepared to hear an honest and self-critical answer.

Why then would I define myself as a mediocre boss? Because mediocre is average. To the same people who are surprised, it is possible that they are also mediocre, like the people who would be doing the interview, as well as the managers who throw their hands in the air when they hear this statement.

## Mediocrity is limited to complying with the job

When Max DePree, founder of successful furniture and design firm Herman Miller, was asked in a presentation seeking investors: "What is the most difficult area you would say you need to work on?" The audience had the same surprised faces that I did in my classes.

Max DePree replied: "Fight against entropy" 5. Although this is a very technical term that defines the second law of thermodynamics in physics, its banal interpretation is explained by the tendency of the entire universe towards disorder. Murphy also explained it in his law that says: "If something bad can happen, it will."

My honesty is also explained through the vision of Max DePree. If someone asks me, 'what is the most challenging thing in your role as a director?' My answer is: to be able to get my team out of a habitual state of complacency. Why? Because it is always easier to improve things when they deteriorate, implement new ways of working or priorities to focus on, make people improve, and even get results. **But the most challenging thing is getting to the next level. Getting people out of their state of satisfaction and success, raising the pressure level without burning out your team. Preventing them from relaxing.**

All of this has to start from within yourself. My mediocrity is explained by the fact that, despite having improved a team, at some point, a state of entropy began to creep in. That moment happens when you least expect it, usually because you are celebrating the results and perhaps thinking about how good you are. Herb Kelleher, the legendary executive and driver of Southwest Airlines' unparalleled success, used to warn that companies were more at risk in those stages of success. Herb said that a company [or manager] is most vulnerable when it is at its highest levels of success. "A company is never more vulnerable to complacency than when it's at the height of its success." And he kept warning: "The number one threat is us! We must not let success breed complacency; cockiness; greediness; laziness; indifference; preoccupation with nonessentials; bureaucracy; hierarchy;

quarrelsomeness; or obliviousness to threats posed by the outside world." [6]

**I continue to stress the warning that the tricky thing is to induce more pressure without burning out the people you lead.** The type of pressure I'm talking about is positive stress. Unfortunately, what we often see is the easiest and most common thing: to stimulate negative pressure. For example, the words of the founder and CEO of one of the largest tourist groups in Spain may reveal the preference towards this type of negative pressure: "The employee must feel the pressure of some objectives to perform at their best. If he relaxes, if he feels comfortable, he enters a state of torpor that drags down the rest of the organization "[7]. While it is true that most people perform better at levels of moderate or positive stress (eustress), we must be careful not to cross the line into negative stress (distress). If so, people's performance will decline [8].

Throughout all these chapters, I will articulate the vision of a conscious leader as an exceptional boss. 'Exceptional' is above mediocre and good. We can also see that excellence is a goal that has no end. It is a work philosophy of continuous improvement that begins with you. A conscientious leader has to raise the bar, but without losing talented people along the way. He must fight against mediocrity and entropy, be demanding with people, and show a more human and intimate side with his collaborators. Testing the person and caring about him or her is not mutually exclusive. Caring about someone but being honest and straightforward for this person to improve can be defined as *radical candor*, or tough love.

# 8 REASONS THAT EXPLAIN THE MEDIOCRITY OF LEADERS

Having clarified that mediocrity is indeed common, now I would like to explain the causes of this mediocrity among bosses.

## #1. First managerial experiences are not easy

I suppose that my professional development is not far from the trajectory of other people who have had the opportunity to lead teams. In my case, the first time I had the chance to lead a team, it was a disaster. It happened in France. Back then, I believed that you just had to have experience and technical knowledge to be a good boss. My thinking was elementary: "now that I have the boss title, people will be easily organized and coordinated. They will do what I tell them". Before being a boss, you think things are easy, and you keep thinking about how much you would change and fix if you were in charge. It's easy to see yourself as the conductor of an orchestra: leading to the beat of your baton and waiting for everyone to respond to you in perfect harmony. But this analogy that we usually hear, often attributed to Peter Drucker, is not very realistic. [9]

Professor Henry Mintzberg, in his book *Managing,* warned us of a very different scenario: the conductor can feel like a puppet. This other vision of Sune Carlson demystifies the image of heroic leader and makes him more vulnerable. In his metaphor, he presents us with the figure of the leader as a puppet, because he is subject to pressures from different interest groups, including his employees. [10]

That's how I felt, like a puppet, especially in my first stage as a manager. It was a time when I was mostly confused and vulnerable.

But the usual thing is to see yourself lacking in inner confidence when assuming a new position. You also don't have a track record to support you in your new role. And here is a paradox: despite feeling more vulnerable, most of us act as if we are sure of what we do; we want to project security. We are the complete opposite of what could be defined as an authentic boss because we hide our vulnerabilities. Often, this is not just because of our lack of inner confidence, but because we find ourselves in a work environment lacking the psychological security to do so. It is the necessary climate of trust that allows us to show our weak areas to our colleagues and bosses.

Things can get even uglier. When it comes to pretending that we are in control, some of us can make the mistake of replacing our insecurity with authoritarianism: we listen less and confuse our collaborators' expectations. What expectations are these? First, employees do not expect you to have all the answers to problems that arise at work or decide everything without consulting them.

It is also very possible that the people who report to you may decide that they will not follow your orders. Or maybe they can understand that there are other priorities to take care of, other than those you think are more important. They do not have to express it openly, but there are many hidden ways to boycott a boss's intentions. Your illusion soon falls apart, and your dreams of being the boss can turn into a nightmare.

This was my short experience in France as a first-time boss. Within three months of assuming my position, I was fired. My authoritarian style, the product of a lack of self-confidence, turned my entire team against me. The truth is that I was not prepared to lead a team.

Linda A. Hill, Professor of Leadership and Management at Harvard Business School, wrote a very successful article about this situation that happens to many of us when we are bosses for the first time 11. The step from being a good worker, even a model worker, to being a boss can be more complicated than we think. It is a stage that we tend to underestimate. New bosses rarely realize that it's not about them. Now, the team they have to lead and the objectives matter more. But many new bosses are still in the "me" when it comes to the "us." In essence, it requires having the ability to influence others to do their jobs better. But influencing others is not that easy. Linda Hill points out that new executives are surprised to learn that the skills and methods for being successful as individual employees are markedly different from those required for a boss. 12

Therefore, there is often a gap between your initial capabilities and the requirements of the new position. If your success depends on your experience and personal actions in previous jobs, now, as a manager, you realize that you no longer rely so much on yourself but others. We believe that the title and position in the organization chart are accompanied by a formal power of having authority, but this is not usually the case. To have 'power' means having the capacity to influencing others, and the questions you should ask yourself are: how will I be able to influence my collaborators to do their job? Or even better: how could I influence my team to produce more in their jobs? It is also about having the right amount of power to influence your colleagues and bosses.

## #2. Paradoxically, gaining confidence in ourselves can impede continued improvement

As you accumulate experience leading teams, you also gain more inner confidence and power. This is necessary on your way to being a good boss. The results accompany you, a formal and informal recognition on the part of your bosses, employees, or work colleagues. **But be careful; being a capable boss does not mean being a good boss**. Or a good leader. Simply, you are recognized as prepared in the technical area of work and qualified to provide solutions to problems that arise on a day-to-day basis. Your experience as a manager or executive also makes you gain more confidence. You may already know the answers to problems that arise every day because you have lived them in the past.

Similarly, you also seem more confident in turning things around and contributing to ideas. But is this enough? Is it enough to know a lot about your professional area to be a good boss?

The answer is no, it's not enough. This is the professional stage in which many directors and managers get stuck. It is a phase of mediocrity, and not because we are bad bosses (although there certainly exist bad, even toxic ones), but because we cannot bring out the best in people or generate more knowledge in our team. **But it is also a phase in which we can get stuck because we forget that leading others is a parallel path to leading ourselves. Not only do we have to grow technically, but we also have to do it personally**.

Many managers and directors stagnate in this period of their professional career because accompanied by these results they believe that they have reached the top in their professional development. It is another way of being affected by entropy since this prevents us from expanding to other improvement levels.

Why?

Because now, it's about defending the image of an efficient professional that you have carved for yourself, staying in your comfort zone, enjoying your successes, and congratulating yourself on your ego. Many professionals get stuck here without knowing it. Carol Dweck, a psychologist, and professor at Stanford University, defines this *fixed mindset* - as opposed to a *growing mindset* - very well in her research and her best-selling book *Mindset* 13. Your self-image as a great professional who does your job well, which provides solutions and does not usually fail, will prevent you from moving forward because it is an image that you will protect at all costs. Any negative feedback that threatens that image will be rejected.

However, new adversities could challenge you and take you out of your comfort zone and reveal your vulnerabilities. The challenges I am talking about could be a new job, another demanding boss, or a more complex project. All this will involve doubling your efforts and feeling more vulnerable. At this point, two types of thinking will help or harm you. The fixed mindset will make you walk away from these challenges because they expose your vulnerabilities and the self-image you have created. The growing mindset will make you appreciate the challenge and accept that, in this new venture, you will have no choice but to deal with your inconsistencies. It is difficult because it takes you out of your comfort zone and exposes your weaknesses. It can break that image of Mr. or Ms.'Perfect' that you've made for yourself.

Furthermore, a growing mind is necessary to move to the next level 14. Are you ready to take it on?

## #3. Results matter, but the obsession with sticking to the numbers puts off other necessary qualities of the leader

A mediocre or even harmful manager can get the job done, with the accompanying results. You might also achieve brilliant results one particular year, but that's not the point. The questions that we should ask ourselves are the following: At what price? How sustainable are these results?

Companies that focus their priorities almost exclusively on improving quarterly or annual financial results miss other leading indicators that are also critical to maintaining, or even improving, those results. By focusing only on quantitative performance results, it is always easier to overlook behaviors that could be undermining people's engagement and productivity.

Many organizations often show evident blindness because in their obsession to maximize their profits in the short term, they lose their way in what matters most, namely the personal and organizational capacity to generate those benefits. **We cannot forget that money is always a by-product of excellence**. Aesop's famous fable of the *Goose and the Golden Egg* reminds us of this priority. In our obsession with the short term (the golden eggs), we can undermine employees' engagement and capacities (the goose).

## #4. Many companies have not established a necessary list of qualities that define their talent and their bosses' superior quality.

Typically, companies base their selection and promotion criteria intuitively. The problem is that according to research, we tend to be very biased in our decisions 15. For example, managers often focus their hiring or promotion decisions on qualities of the candidate that are similar to their own. Similarly, most of the interviews are decided unconsciously in the first few minutes, or even seconds. This strong inclination of the mind is called confirmation bias, which is nothing more than the tendency of a person to favor the information that confirms their own assumptions, preconceived ideas, or hypotheses, regardless of whether they are true or not. We often decide on hiring based on the candidate's track record when the future and context may require different skills.

But how could this process be better structured? What do we define as an exceptional boss? Intelligence? Professional knowledge? Google is a company that discovered through rigorous internal research and better data management that extraordinary bosses affect the bottom line of their teams even more than they initially believed. But to reach this conclusion, they first decided to reinvent the wheel and find out for themselves.

Google is a company founded by engineers and with an internal culture that reflects the mindset of engineers. It is an overly analytical and objective organization guided above all by data, with very autonomous and decisive people. At Google, bosses have always been seen as a necessary evil at best, or problem at worst. So, in 2009 a Ph.D. team within their personnel department called PiLab, decided to launch the following hypothesis: Are bosses necessary?

In its research called "Project Oxygen" 17, Google discovered that managers who were evaluated above the average, with general scores above 86 out of 100 (an evaluation that was determined by several factors, but above all, between the opinions of subordinates and their direct bosses) impacted their teams more.

These managers were fairer, work happened more efficiently, the results were better, people were more engaged, and voluntary leave levels were reduced. This last point is vital for a company that prioritizes its strategy to attract and retain the best talent. Between one and three million resumes a year arrive at Google, but only 0.25 percent make the cut. It's 25 times more difficult than getting into Harvard 18. This research concluded that good bosses at Google met eight common attributes. And these attributes became the basis by which they began to measure and shape managerial talent.

What was the surprise?

That the last attribute, number 8, referred to as 'technical skill' of the boss, was the lowest priority. It is undoubtedly necessary for any boss, but it was the last of seven other attributes sought by their direct bosses' subordinates. Employees at Google previously valued other qualities such as *#1. Is a good coach; # 2. Empowers team and does not micromanage; #3. Expresses interest/concern for team members' success and personal well-being; #4. Is productive and results oriented; #5. Is a good communicator; #6. Helps with career development; #7. Has clear vision/strategy for the team.*

So Google focused its priorities on measuring bosses on these criteria, but above all, offering them the necessary resources to improve in those areas where they were weakest.

You don't have to be Google to come up with a list of attributes that determine and evaluate your company's leader quality. The first step should start by considering what you understand as an exceptional boss: what are the skills, knowledge, and human qualities that we should measure in our leaders at all levels?

It is a necessary roadmap in any company and defines employees and managerial talent. But it also marks the training needs and leadership programs required in the organization. For example, when the Carlson-Rezidor hotel group determined its bosses' talent in seven dimensions, the next step was to evaluate more than 300 hotel managers and 3,000 department heads on those competencies they decided common to all. In this way, they also knew how to prioritize their training needs in their Corporate Business School. [19]

Finally, I should note that any talent roadmap worth its salt must consider people's values to fit into the company culture. In the following chapters, we will see the importance of culture and how to enhance it. We will understand that values are a set of beliefs and motivations that are translated into daily behaviors. Therefore, talent not only has to measure challenging areas or hard-skills, but also the incorrectly labeled soft areas or soft-skills expressed in the organization's values or principles.

## #5. The perception gap between employees and bosses is accentuated by not applying a 360º evaluation to employees

Interestingly, when managers and executives are asked about their leadership qualities, the quorum is above average [20]. But wait: didn't we say that most of them were mediocre?

This self-awareness deficit is due to a perception gap between what the bosses think and what their collaborators think. This evaluation discrepancy is even more accentuated in those companies where employees' opinion of their bosses is not measured. **The first reason for this discrepancy is justified by our inability to generate self-awareness. People are not very objective when it comes to self-evaluation. As we will see in the leader's inner area later, self-awareness is one of the most critical competencies that we must develop**.

I should add that many bosses are not good at interpreting the employees' inner lives mentioned in the opening chapter. This inner life comprises opinions, feelings, perceptions, and motivations from our bosses and our job [21]. It is a form of 'hidden life' that we usually keep out of view.

No one wants to be ineffective or a lousy boss. But, despite the years of experience we have and the right results we have obtained, we can always be surprised by what our collaborators can perceive of us in upward evaluation - or 360º evaluation. Such an assessment allows subordinates to give an opinion on their bosses. It is then that the results can fall on us like a bucket of ice water. Suddenly, as bosses we are not as good as we thought. One can say that such a perception is wrong, unfair, or out of date, but what matters most is the perception that employees have about us.

Why? Because perception dictates reality; if the team members perceive in us that, in general terms, we are mediocre, or even bad bosses, that perception will be transferred in one way or another to their work.

Despite all this, many companies distrust the opinion of their employees. The only form of evaluation that has been implemented is top-down. The boss values the subordinate, but not the other way around. This balance happens once or twice a year and measures the annual performance of the worker. The point is that, since only the boss evaluates, this system can promote dishonest behavior; with those above, everything is pleasantries, open-mindedness, and availability. For those below behaviors differ; now we find rude answers, the imposition of orders, lack of attention and sour faces. Hence it was always easier to deceive the boss than the collaborators.

## #6. The leadership myth: the boss must have all the answers

Another reason for such mediocrity is a myth that has done a lot of damage to management. Jack Stack reminded us of this in his book *Open Book Management* 22. It's the myth that the boss has to have all the answers.

Before, I have commented that this is a common confusion among many managers. But, as Jack Stack recalled, this myth can quickly undermine credibility. It is unrealistic to think that the boss always has the solution to all problems, especially if you are surrounded by competent people. Furthermore, this also isolates you from your team.

I want to add that a boss who shows this outdated vision fails in his or her first goal: to make the team better. Getting the best potential out of a team happens by attending to the strengths and weaknesses of each member of that team. For this, you need the right qualities as a head coach.

This myth also has micromanaging built-in, the obsession with dictating orders and controlling everyone's work details. Micromanaging undermines the trust of your employees. Some organizations may expect this from their bosses. When they do, they do their company's talent a disservice.

## #7. To lead is also to lead yourself: The leader's internal operating system

When we talk about a boss's skills and qualities, we tend to focus on what, *a priori*, is most important: that the work goes well and that our numbers are met. For this reason, we give more importance to those competencies related to the more technical skills and knowledge of the job. Similarly, companies prioritize this area when selecting, promoting, or evaluating their managers and directors.

Obviously, without technical skills, the job would not go well. Just as I've said before, that it is a myth that the boss has all the answers, I also have to clarify that a boss is expected to have many solutions to the problems that will arise at work. People expect our bosses to be smart and prepared.

Now, is that all? Maybe for a mediocre boss or a bad boss, covering the technical aspect is enough. However, from a good boss we must ask for more.

If it has been said before that an exceptional boss can bring out the best in us - as individuals and as a team - for this to happen, he has to inspire us somehow. When Mandela (Morgan Freeman), in the movie *Invictus*, asked Francois Pienaar (Matt Damon), captain of the South African rugby team: "How can we make them better than they think of themselves?" Mandela kept pondering: "Inspiration, maybe." But how do we get inspired by greatness when there is no alternative? How do we inspire everyone around us? "

The character of the leader is the unknown area of leadership. Mary Crossan, Gerald Seijts, and Jeffrey Ganz of the Ivey Business School reflected on the leadership crisis and the morally questionable behavior of many executives in the aftermath of the financial crisis. In the summer of 2009, and after the subprime crisis, this group of authors brought together more than 300 executives (CEOs and Level C) from the public and private sectors. Dominic Barton, McKinsey CEO, reflected. "When we talk about leadership, we usually focus on what leaders do, but we don't spend the time necessary to know what those leaders are like, in other words their character [23].

In the second part of this book, we are going to see that character and emotional intelligence are decisive in the performance of a leader. They can be seen as our internal operating system. Just as it is necessary to have more advanced software on a computer to download the most up-to-date programs, leaders also need to have an adequate internal operating system to get the best out of equipment. The character of the leader impacts the culture of the company. For better or for worse, your value system will resonate with the organization. Therefore, if companies intend to increase their competitiveness levels, they must also attend to their leaders' operating system—especially the higher-level ones on the organizational chart. Ultimately, the effectiveness of an organization is measured by the collective operating system of its bosses.

The leader's character works on our internal qualities such as humility, responsibility, temperance, responsibility, collaboration, determination, courage, humanity, judgment, justice, and integrity. Our character is made up of different dimensions and elements that form a mixture of values, skills, virtues, and talents. And it is essential to overcome the barrier in which many bosses find themselves stuck. It is also a way to achieve higher levels of emotional maturity, which is necessary to be more effective in directing people and achieving better results.

## #8. We learn from mediocre bosses

Have you ever wondered if the boss you admire so much is the best example to follow?

We may idolize him because he is attentive, patient, and close to us. But perhaps it is only so with a few, excluding the rest. Similarly, it is convenient to ask yourself the following questions: Is he fair, working in equanimity with all the team members or only with you? Is he able to bring out the best inner energy and commitment from each of the team members? Is he able to make the team communicate better and resolve conflicts effectively?

Additional questions: Is a leader capable of generating self-awareness in himself and others? Is he or she a role model?

Is he or she authentic by acknowledging his blind spots and fearlessly exposing his vulnerabilities? Does he or she know and manage his emotions well? And those of others?

Albert Bandura, a Stanford professor, is one of the most-cited authors. He is probably also the most influential and recognized in the psychological field. Bandura shows his work on social learning that people learn new behaviors by observing others. Just as children learn many things by observing and imitating their parents, we also acquire many of our skills by observing our bosses. That is why we would define practices as bad or mediocre and incorporate them into our management kit. For example, we observe our bosses and the most influential managers in the company and how they conduct meetings, manage conflict, prioritize, delegate, communicate, etc. In this way, it is easy to assume their decisions and behaviors as the best way of doing things.

**It is then expected that mediocrity feeds more mediocrity. If organizational learning experts estimate that much of our learning happens to work, learning from our bosses occupies a significant area within this process**.

I imagine you are thinking: "No, I can discern between good and bad, and apply my best common sense leading my team." However, it is not that easy. First, because you may have many blind spots that need attending to, and second, the corporate pressures to meet deadlines, objectives, or make decisions will add a layer of difficulty. So, it is possible that we unconsciously implement those behaviors from our bosses which we hate.

Throughout this book, we will reflect on all these assumptions. The leadership crisis can be reversed through more conscious leadership. Nevertheless, leading is also management, administration, and control. Management and leadership are two sides of the same coin, as Henry Mintzberg reminds us [24]. You cannot manage a company or a team without leading, nor can you lead a team without implementing discipline, rules, control, or targets.

# CHAPTER 3: EVERYTHING STARTS WITH THE CULTURE

## OUR SYSTEM OF BASIC BELIEFS AND ASSUMPTIONS

### The gap between intentions and realities

In my MBA classes, I usually do a brief survey with my students (all with work experience), asking the following question:

"Could any of you define the values of your organization for me?"

I always start my seminars on organizational cultures and values with the same question. In the six years that I have been doing it, with probably more than 600 students, there are always few hands that are raised, sometimes none. On other occasions, some students can indeed explain the values of their companies. From there, I ask the second question:

"What do those values you mention mean?"

This is a timely question because often values are empty words or corporate clichés such as: "Excellence," "Integrity," "Customer Service." If that's the case, I move on with:

"How do you translate the integrity you speak of into action?"
"What does 'excellence' mean to your company?"

There is usually little or no clarification. However, it is my last question that rarely makes the cut:

"Could you say that the managers and directors in your organization are a mirror of those values?"

Faces of skepticism ...

Values, therefore, become scrap paper. "In my company, they say that integrity is a fundamental value, but my boss is the first one who is not sincere with us," comment some resigned students. "They talk about customer service, but they always cut corners in quality to save costs." "They entrust us to show passion for our work and, in truth, I do not know how this is possible, if the morale of almost everyone is in the gutter," confess others with faces of frustration.

These statements that I hear, unfortunately often repeated, reflect the gap between what is said and what is done. **This gap between intentions and realities explains why attempts to make the company more productive and competitive through culture fail. And this is also a reason that explains why there is so much skepticism about a company's culture. Many executives view culture as a formalism that has no impact on company productivity.**

This situation also reveals the organizational perception gap between managers and employees: the managers' statements do not agree with those of the employees. Some executives believe that it is enough to write corporate values and publish them on a website or require the Human Resources department to make presentations of the culture in their orientation and training processes. However, reality shows that it doesn't matter what business executives preach; the employees' beliefs and perceptions which they consider to be accurate will determine the culture. **Ultimately, values materialize in general behaviors. The first ones that have to reflect these behaviors are those at the top. In this way, those at the bottom will be able to trust that behavior and replicate it. In the end, they will be the ones who will establish it throughout the company. For this reason, the organizational culture must be constantly evaluated. Explicitly reflecting the organization's values is essential, but it is only the first step in a long journey.**

## A journey of a thousand miles begins with a first step: the personal values of company executives

Lao Tzu, one of the most influential philosophers in China's history, said that a journey of a thousand miles began with a first step. You must get moving and attend to the first thing. But when we talk about a company's culture, what is the first thing we should attend to?

**We need to evaluate our intentions first; we must identify how close or far they are from reality. Thus, when we think about designing our organization's culture, the first task will be to review our belief system.**

For better or for worse, leaders set the tone. Deep within the culture of a company, as James Heskett noted, is the belief system and fundamental assumptions of its executives [1]:

• What do I believe?
• How do I think a company should be run?
• What potential do I see in people?
• What is the most important stakeholder group that we should prioritize?
• What should be the primary purpose of our company?

Only when these variables have been defined should we make our values explicit; since it is precisely our values, behaviors, and beliefs that we will transfer to the rest of the company.

## Bridging the gap between intentions and reality

The gap between the intentions and realities of many companies happens, and usually unconsciously. Entrepreneurs and executives have wishes that they would like to manifest in their companies. They highlight that their workers must be honest and show a high level of commitment and motivation in their jobs. They want their employees to be flexible, respectful, creative, proactive, open-minded, disciplined, attentive to customers, etc. However, these aspirations often turn into frustrations, as such behaviors do not occur in a consistent and thorough way in the company. This scenario reveals the gap that exists between what managers want and what employees experience. Companies can publish their values, but if employees don't honestly believe in them, they won't speak out.

**Values are manifestations of principles, qualities, and virtues that we assign to the world we believe in. They are part of our meaning system; a mix of attitudes, behaviors,**

**beliefs, motivations, and talents. Just as they are part of people's character, values also make up an organization's character. They are the DNA of any company culture.**

Therefore, if we cannot believe in our values, there will be no way to convince others. For example, most companies urge their employees to provide good service to their customers. These businesses can invest in courses to teach them techniques to serve better or resolve customer complaints. They can also do quality inspections, even force them to smile in front of their customers. The problem is that employees do not share this reality and recognize such intentions as hypocritical. People might see that managers only care about costs or revenue and not so much about customers. They can see that managers deny vital resources needed to do a quality job. They may even think that corporate policies are inflexible when it comes to compensating customers. The company's procedures and bureaucracy have become an end in and of themselves, preventing them from being creative and proactive in serving customers.

Similarly, these same managers could also encourage their workers to be more responsible and show more commitment to their jobs. But people see that executives are always designing internal rules and policies, which treat them as the typical suspects because there is no real trust. In the end, companies lack shared values.

## Checking our belief systems: Red or blue pill?

The red pill and its opposite are symbols of popular culture that represent the choice between two paradigms. In the movie *The Matrix*, Morpheus proposes Neo choose between two alternatives: "This is your last chance. After this, there is no turning back. You take the blue pill—the story ends, you wake up in your bed and believe whatever you want to believe. You take the red pill—you stay in Wonderland, and I show you how deep the rabbit hole goes. Remember: all I'm offering is the truth. Nothing more." **Each of these pills represents a different belief system that will manifest itself in our decisions and actions through future regulations, corporate policies, our strategic priorities.**

The most profound assumption that will determine the values we adjust to our company answer is: *What confidence do we have in people?*

When I refer to 'people,' I include employees and the rest of the interest groups (stakeholders), such as customers, suppliers and even the local community in which we operate.

Douglas McGregor, a professor at MIT, and who was influenced by his friend Abraham Maslow, explained in his book *The Human Side of The Enterprise* that there are two ways of looking at people and understanding their work. Depending on the vision we adopt about these people, the management style, and the way we organize ourselves would change 2. From this, McGregor presented a couple of theories about the two options of perceiving employees: they are known as *Theory X* and *Theory Y*.

Both theories shape our managers' beliefs and assumptions; they also dictate their mental models and, therefore, influence their motivations and behaviors. **The type of model used will determine the culture of any organization.**

Douglas McGregor's Theory X promotes an authoritarian management style. **Micromanagement and efficiency are his axioms.** This alternative is based on the main idea that workers cannot be trusted without first establishing strict orders and controls. For the most part, people act on extrinsic factors such as retribution or fear of sanctions and avoid taking on greater responsibilities and making decisions. **The basis of motivation centers on the *carrot and the stick*.** The business cultures most influenced by this belief organize their processes around policies and regulations that must be followed with discipline.

The mantra of theory X is a Tayloristic management system, promoted by Frederick W. Taylor in the early 20th century. **His workers' system and vision limited his activities to just following instructions and rules, thus cutting out opportunities for development and self-actualization in the jobs.** Although the organizations that assume this theory claim the opposite, the truth is that employees' productivity is more limited since it inhibits their opinions, to the extent that it prevents them from being more proactive. It also reduces employees' level of responsibility and motivation. **It is an unfortunate way to squander people's talent and potential.** I have to confess that I have seen entrepreneurs and managers lean more towards this vision in much of my work experience.

The reality is that there are people who, perhaps, can be more comfortable in this way of working. They are more relaxed receiving orders and doing a good job, based on clear and rigid instructions. Similarly, there are very mechanical jobs that are organized based on this Tayloristic management approach. For example, working in a call center involves repeating simple steps and instructions.

An X-minded person will be comfortable working under this system. But are most people like that? Is this the best way to go for individual companies and industries that seek, above all else, to be more productive and offer more value to their customers?

Theory Y is at the other extreme. **Inspired by the more humanistic part of psychology that contemplates human potential and self-esteem, it promotes a more participatory management style.** Workers not only can, but must, acquire greater responsibility. This theory assumes that people view work as a form of self-fulfillment and not as an obligation. **McGregor entrusted companies to adopt this vision because they could only achieve higher levels of productivity and competitiveness.** This was the secret of Procter & Gamble during the 1960s. The company organized the company into teams that would take on more skills, learn to manage themselves better at work, and innovate more. [3]

This theory believes more in people's potential; it is the paradigm that best suits our times. We don't have to limit the job to a routine of tasks, which happens from Monday to Friday and provides us with a livelihood, rather it should be a space to grow as people and professionals, where we can expand our capabilities and, at the same time, bring improvements to the company.

Theory Y is the basis of more conscious management because it turns manual employees into workers of knowledge. As we will see in the following chapters, a worker of knowledge can also be found in operational positions, such as in a supermarket, hotel, restaurant, call center, or in an assembly line in a factory. People who fit into the environment AND are more committed to their work are more proactive and show greater responsibility in meeting goals. They are even capable of improving the company's financial results.

## The Pygmalion effect: we create our reality

The most interesting aspect of both theories is found, as James Heskett warned, in a self-fulfilling prophecy that is generated 4. The initial beliefs will be more reinforced with any of the paradigms they assume. If we take the red pill, we will reaffirm ourselves in the paradigm that it shows us. It will happen because our expectations will determine the reality that we will obtain. If we take the blue pill, we also reaffirm ourselves in its paradigm. Psychologists call this process the 'Pygmalion effect,' which refers to the influence that positive or negative beliefs exert on the definition of performance that we create for ourselves or in others. We influence the performance of people based on the expectations we have of them. It is us who make the reality that we find ourselves.

On a small scale, we can see this idea in the following way: if I have a boss who believes in me, supports me, has patience (though he or she might often challenge me), shows a positive attitude towards my present and potential qualities and creates an environment in which I can grow, chances are high that his expectations are met. **It is very likely that I will try harder to meet his or her expectations, resulting in positive results.**

From a macro perspective, we can see the same example. Now, it would no longer be just a situation of trust between a boss and an employee, but between many managers and the majority of workers. The result would also be positive.

## The usual skepticism of an X-mindset

Y theory makes sense, and businessmen would imply that they empower their employees. However, reality depicts a different picture. Again, there is a gap between intentions and actions. There is a general skepticism about the potential of workers and job descriptions. In this way, organizations tend to put controls, thereby limiting jobs to their essential functions. So, this scheme raises the following questions:

"Shouldn't we be clear about whether we can trust our employees?"
"Shouldn't they demonstrate, in advance, that they can be trustworthy?"

These questions are sensible because they show a particular caution and essential truth: not all people can be trustworthy. However, this scheme creates a bottleneck since it raises skepticism from the start.

What came first, the chicken or the egg? Trust is born from either side because it is a mutual feeling. Nevertheless, managers' responsibility is to break this paradigm and trust other people first. Somehow, the trust conundrum puts the person who's trusting first in a vulnerable position. That's why doing so requires courage. However, it is not about applying an open bar that distributes continuous shots of confidence without control. Still, it does require starting from the following presumption: "I will trust you, from the outset, until you show me otherwise."

Furthermore, this presumption makes more sense if we have designed a rigorous selection process; if we select a person to work in our company, we assume that we have seen inherent qualities of trust in that person. If then he doesn't follow our vote of confidence, it will be his or her problem. Not ours. Our initial beliefs in trusting people, in any case, are not going to be affected because of a few bad apples.

On the contrary, if my basic presumption is based on a principle of distrust towards my employees, I will probably validate it over time. If I think that the level of performance is limited to mediocrity, I will undoubtedly get mediocrity.

I have often seen this self-fulfilling prophecy come true. In a Spanish hotel resort where I worked as a manager, located in the Dominican Republic, the assumed principle was maximum distrust towards all employees. I still remember my first interaction with the hotel director: the first thing he did was give me a bunch of keys, and he told me that everything should be locked, even the drawer of pencils and paper. I felt like the lord of the dungeon. The executives had established an inferior compensation policy at this company - the local salary was meager, and our hotel complex paid even less. This scenario caused local talent to go to other hotel resorts that provided better salaries; the best did not work with us, instead there were many employees who should not have been hired in the first place. As you can guess, the selection process was anything but rigorous.

I also remember that this hotel resort general manager ruled like a little dictator. His mere presence conveyed fear. This executive toured the facilities in his 4x4 car and, if he saw any worker with a suspicious attitude, he would fire him on the spot. Quick and without explanation. I could have been training my team, developing their talent and, overnight and without prior consultation, receive the news that the CEO had fired one of my employees because he did not see him at work. It didn't matter if he was on his day off or maybe running an errand; nobody argued with the CEO. He applied the sentence despite the summary judgment. Seeing his car from afar, one had the same feeling as seeing *Christine*, the car from the famous Stephen King movie.

I have said *ad nauseam* that the boss sets the tone, and, for better or worse, this tone begins with the top executive. In this hotel complex, the executives started from a mistrust mindset base that demanded continuous control of all staff. However, it seemed that the more controls they put in place and the more audits they performed, the more problems arose.

The exciting thing is that when you get to the root of the problems by asking *why* many times, explanations are clearer. In contexts such as the one described, we can see that people's belief system at the top is the one that is producing behavioral problems and irregularities. These managers did not understand that the root of many issues lay in the company's dysfunctional culture. This culture manifested itself in the form of fear of bosses, mutual mistrust, and low pay. This atmosphere alienated the excellent workers and left us with the bad ones. It resulted in continuous deficiencies in customer service and episodes that reflected a lack of ethics in some team members.

What did the executives think of all this?

"The origin of the problem was in the lack of control!" They exclaimed.

According to the managers, we did not do our work well. Therefore, their reaction to correct all these deviations was limited to imposing even more controls.

Managing the factors mentioned above is essential for managers' belief systems to comply with the first rule of conscious leadership: getting the best out of people. The level of trust we have on people will influence the result they can bring to the organization.

## A COMPANY CULTURE CAN MAKE US BETTER OR WORSE PEOPLE

Herb Kelleher, co-founder, CEO, and eventually president emeritus of Southwest Airlines, was the leading promoter of this airline's unique and competitive culture. Southwest has been the only profitable airline business in its more than 45-year history. Everyone has copied its business model, but few have been able to replicate its culture. Kelleher used to say that a company's culture is how people behave when the bosses aren't looking.

## Culture manifests itself through daily actions.

Let me tell you a couple of stories. These are two service situations of two well-known airlines that occurred at the same time, between 2011 and 2012. Both stories reflect the culture of each organization very well. In both cases, the client is the protagonist. However, the employees' behavior dealing with customers differs radically.

### Story #1. A Ryanair case: Police take the passenger off the flight

The scene was known on social networks and even captured some media's attention a few years ago 5. At the plane's gate, a desperate woman argued with a police agent who was about to expel her. This passenger wanted to board with an object that looked like a rolled-up poster in a plastic bag, thereby violating airline policies. Ryanair, at that time, limited cabin luggage to a single bag; therefore, it could be assumed the client evaded paying extra for the item.

Based on their policies, the airline staff demanded an additional payment of €50 from the passenger for these items. It is not clear if the woman directly refused to pay the amount or did not have money, but she tried to get on the plane anyway.

The situation reflects the inflexibility of the airline staff concerning its policies. We can imagine the passenger's complaints after allowing a modicum of flexibility and empathy. On the other hand, impassive and perhaps accustomed to some customers' shouts, Ryanair staff decided to call the police to remove the passenger from the plane. Meanwhile, at the door, where the scene took place, the other passengers shouted indignantly: "Arrest the one in yellow!" referring to a Ryanair employee. "What a shame!" "But tell him the truth!" Other passengers offered to carry the lady's articles inside their suitcases. However, it was too late; the decision was made: the woman would not be boarding the plane.

If you look closely at the scene, you can see a flight attendant passing in front of the camera. It is a rapid image, but you can perceive the total indifference of this airline's personnel at that time. As we are going to see, working in this organization or other companies can transform you in some way. Often businesses are obsessed with being more efficient and thus prioritize rules and standards over customers. The problem is that they divert attention to what matters most: customer service.

For this reason, it is essential to distinguish between efficiency and effectiveness. Efficiency is doing things well; meanwhile, effectiveness is doing the right thing. Many companies focus on improving efficiency by saving costs, reducing errors, increasing the time to do a task, etc.

59

Although all of this is important, they should ask themselves if they are also being effective. Are they prioritizing what customers value? For example, the low-cost approach would cease to be effective if the cost reduction is pushed too far, as when, in their obsession with increasing income through complementary services, they create a feeling of discomfort and rejection among clients and employees. The fact that Ryanair has conceived cost-cutting as an end in itself may lead many customers to decide not to fly with them anymore. Likewise, it can produce conflicting relationships between employees and executives that would increase the number of strikes with unions and workers, affecting flight planning and leading to cancellations. Finally, it can affect the brand's image due to bad press [6]

## To question the qualities of culture and levels of empathy

It is also essential to ask whether the culture is enhancing organizational performance or employee and customer engagement within a company. We must ask: Is the culture effective when the company does not show empathy for its customers' problems? Can an organization be successful when its employees view the customer as a depersonalized routine or even a hindrance?

The obsession with being efficient and prioritizing procedures, rules, and shareholders will influence the people who work in the company. This adaptation, caused by the organization's culture itself, stimulates frustration and indifference among employees when it comes to solving customer problems. When clients are polite, pleasant, and submissive, all goes smoothly in service; but what happens when customers prove challenging or difficult? Then they are as classified as subversive, typical suspects, or conflictive personalities.

I must confess that it is very human to lose the gift of empathy with the client, even if it is one of your most vital qualities. There is a form of acculturation that can turn you over to the dark side.

My case is an example:

I chose the hospitality and hotel industry because I was fascinated with the stories I read in a Philip Kotler Service Marketing book. For me, it was terrific to see empowered front-line staff solve customer problems, or anticipate their needs and surprise them. I was excellent in that part of my job! Unfortunately, we don't always work in those companies that best match our talents and personal values. As a hotel receptionist, I had an attitude and ability to make a great impression on clients and address their problems. But my proactivity and enthusiasm always clashed with bureaucracy and regulations, which focused on maximizing benefits over customer value.

I remember an occasion when I worked, as a manager, for a Spanish resort in Cancun that had a very perverse standard and unethical policy. It went something like this:

*"If the client breaks something in the room, he must pay the price of the object in question, plus a 300 percent surcharge."*

What should be a moment of leisure and pleasure, in some cases, could turn into a nightmare for our clients. For example, in this hotel complex, we had rooms on the beachfront, with spectacular views of a turquoise Caribbean Sea. Any client would be willing to pay more to stay there.

However, these rooms also had a problem: if the front door was not closed, there was a risk that it would slam shut, aided by a draft coming through the terrace window. The doors, which were of low quality, would crack from top to bottom after the door slammed. When this happened, the customer, surprised, came to the reception to report the mishap. It was then that the receptionists called me, as they anticipated a conflict:

Customer: "Excuse me, are you the front desk manager?
Me: Yes, Sir. How can I help you?
- We had an accident in the room. The door slammed on its own and cracked open with force.
- Umm ... I understand. But did you read the sign in the room that warned you of this possible problem?
- Not really. We are on a relaxing vacation, and we have not noticed any placards.
- I see. However, if you had read the sign on the door, you would have known not to leave the terrace door open in order to prevent the draft from coming.
- Well, yeah, but that's not our problem.
- Actually, it is. We warn you that if a mishap happens, you will take care of the damage.
- Excuse me?! This cannot be happening. You are not going to make me pay for the door.
- I'm afraid so.
- What are you saying?! And how much is that?
- 300 dollars.
- What?!

Zero empathy whatsoever. It is sad to say, but one can get used to these rules and working methods. This happens because the vision and the culture of the company you work for are contagious. The system of beliefs and assumptions, represented through these norms, becomes something familiar. Although unethical, norms and procedures can be accepted as a good standard. It is the culture part of the business. At first, it may negatively surprise you. Indeed, I remember that I couldn't believe that we made clients pay for these types of accidents, not to mention the 300 percent surcharge! At times like this, your values collide with those of the organization. I remember that I used to argue strongly against this rule, but I must admit that my proactivity to combat it quickly changed to submission. As soon as they told me clearly: "Arturo, we have not brought you from Spain to criticize our norms, but to defend them. You must reflect on whether our organization conforms to your principles. In any case, we need a manager who knows how to protect our organizational policies".

### Story #2 The Southwest Airlines case: We must do everything possible to get the passenger to the plane!

This second story is very different. The driving force of employees at this airline is empathy, common sense, and an unmatched service culture. At Southwest Airlines, they believe that leadership is not just about titles. Anyone can show leadership attitudes in their day-to-day lives if they live the company's values.

Like Ryanair, Southwest Airlines is a low-cost company. Ryanair replicated Southwest business model 7. And yet, what Ryanair could never replicate was its most significant competitive advantage: Southwest Airlines' organizational culture. The difference between Southwest employees and Ryanair employees lies in their willingness, training, and freedom to interpret the rules and offer their customers the best possible service. Employees at Southwest are empowered to break the rules, if necessary, except if their decisions put security at risk or violate moral or ethical precepts.

Colleen Barrett, President Emeritus and former Southwest Chief Operations Officer, tells the following story.

It all starts with a phone call. In this episode, our protagonist receives tragic news from his daughter while traveling to a convention. His grandson is in critical condition. He has been shot. He had to return immediately to his home city 8. However, the man, who could not support himself from the anguish, did not have a return flight scheduled for that day, nor was he flying with Southwest Airlines. Despite this, he immediately took a taxi to the airport and called the Southwest reservations number to tell them about his emergency and desperation situation. He asked them which plane was leaving soonest for his destination. The booking agent on the other end of the line told him the next flight departs in 40 minutes but due to new security restrictions after 9/11, reservations were not allowed after 45 minutes before departure. However, he encouraged the client to go to the airport and meet with the ground staff. She would talk to them, and they would try to do something.

The operator, aware of this exception, contacted another Southwest Airlines agent at the airport who took charge of the situation. The agent at the airport also informed her supervisor of the problem. "Okay, let's do something special with this man. It would help if you had her last name and ID and a credit card number to make the reservation and generate a boarding pass." replied the supervisor. However, the airline agent at the airport only had the customer name. She did not even know her last name, and, of course, she did not have any ID and credit card data.

The airline agent wanted to do the right thing for the customer and decided not to give up. So, he came up with the idea of buying a ticket with her credit card and putting it in her name. Also, she classified the boarding pass as "person with special needs"; this way, you could walk the man to the gate and get through security faster.

The check-in agent contacted the agent at the gate who, in turn, ran for the boarding ramp to tell the pilots. The commander also took charge of the situation and informed the passengers of the problem. She said to them that they were waiting for a person who had received the sad news that his grandson was in the hospital, in critical condition, and that he needed to catch the first plane to meet his daughter. He explained that the passenger was on his way (they were not sure when exactly he would arrive). The response from the passengers was very positive. They even applauded the commander for his decision.

At this point, you have to consider how difficult it is to decide to wait and delay the departure of a plane, even for minutes. Southwest Airlines is one of the most punctual airlines in the US, and all its workers work stubbornly to maintain that attribute. A delay of 15 minutes would be enough to lose the takeoff turn and delay the flight's arrival even more.

Considering all of this, the captain left the plane and decided to wait for the man at the boarding gate - he imagined how emotional he would be. When he finally arrived, he hugged him and comforted him. He also told him that all the passengers were praying for his grandson. The man thanked the captain from the heart for waiting for him and expressed his surprise at his having stopped the plane. "The plane was not going to leave without me, and I was not going to leave without you," replied the pilot. When he reached his

65

destination, another Southwest employee was waiting to take him immediately to the hospital. Unfortunately, his grandson ended up passing away.

Southwest Airlines executives learned of this event because of the press. At first it wasn't known because the pilot didn't claim personal credit. Nor did the ticket agent claim a refund. This story was made public because the deceased son's grandfather spoke of it at the funeral, and the press reported it.

## A CULTURE OF SERVICE AND TRUST IN EMPLOYEES

Could the story have gone wrong? Could the flight have been delayed longer than it should have, affecting customers and subsequent flights? What if the man's story was a sham? Worse still, what if he had been a terrorist? All of this is possible. There is no doubt that Southwest employees made bold decisions that day. After all, this company has a principle concerning security: 'Employees should always follow standard operating procedures.' However, this airline staff firmly believed that they were doing the right thing because that is how they had been trained. Workers are genuinely empowered to do the right thing based on the company's values. Values that promote behaviors such as: 'be bold', 'follow the golden rule', 'never give up', 'put others before yourself' and 'be fair', among others.

The truth is that these types of organizations, which empower their service employees to such a level, have something in common: an obsession to learn from mistakes. The mistakes have to be shared and analyzed; only then can continuous improvements be made. However, this is only possible if a culture of psychological safety can recognize operational failures and provide reasoning tools that result in real solutions.

## Same industry: two planets

These service anecdotes are different regarding the performance of the staff. At Ryanair, ground employees only care about enforcing the rules. At Southwest Airlines, employees skip the rules, paying attention to context, and using their best judgment. There is no flexibility or room for interpretation in the first case, but rather a rigid manual and procedures that must be followed. In the second, even with processes and procedures, they do not represent an end in and of themselves. They are a guide to follow, but not always followed in every situation, especially if they are of common characteristics.

Southwest Airlines sees the customer as a priority. Shareholders are also essential, but they are not at the top of the stakeholder group. Since its inception, this airline has codified the belief that both customers and employees are the most critical stakeholders. Although Herb Kelleher always claimed that employees go first, the truth is that one element cannot go without the other. It's a fruitless debate, as Doug Raug, former Trader's Joe president, stated "... they are like two wings on the same plane; you need both to fly". 9

Southwest executives prioritize delivering more value to their employees and that they, in turn, can return it to customers. This airline considers its passengers as people who should receive humane and professional treatment. This premise has become the company's strategic priority and value proposition.

## Flexibility and accountability go hand in hand - you need skilled employees

Any airline indeed has to design regulations and policies (mostly related to safety). And some norms can never be violated. However, Southwest has appropriate staff who can interpret some regulations depending on the situation.

Ultimately, at Southwest Airlines, there is a fundamental factor in being more productive and achieving higher service levels: the ability to be flexible and not die trying. Flexibility and responsibility must go hand in hand since both are necessary when breaking a rule. Under what criterion of the greater good can you decide to be flexible with a corporate policy? What can be the consequences of breaking a particular norm? Southwest expects employees at all levels to apply the right judgment to make decisions putting in balance security, the customer, and the company.

So, is the customer always right? What do we do with those customers that want to profit from our goodwill and flexibility? Although there will always be disrespectful or unethical customers, companies shouldn't design their policies around them. If an unwanted episode occurs, the employee must explain company policy with great patience and empathy. Assertiveness to defend a norm and compassion to understand the client's situation are not mutually exclusive. Showing kindness does not mean that we agree with everything the user says. For this reason, we must have employees capable of efficiently explaining the details of a situation while remaining extremely respectful. In these scenarios, the rules are to be met, but they are also to be circumvented if necessary.

However, breaking the rules can be dangerous if you don't have the right people. It is necessary to have trained workers in whom we will place more trust. These are the type of employees I will refer to as *knowledge service workers* in Chapter 5. At Southwest Airlines, most employees are prepared to do so because they are in a characteristic Y-mindset culture. Not at Ryanair. This is an X-mindset environment that sees employees as *manual service workers*.

Ryanair's business decisions are not focused on its customers and even less on its employees. The priority is the numbers and short-term benefits. There is no trade-off between the long and short term because everything is seen based on the quarterly or annual results. At Ryanair, both the customer and the employee are a generic resource that must comply with corporate rules and policies. As long as they offer customers low prices, punctuality, and security, they are willing to sacrifice other things. Therefore, the rules and the systems that support them are above everyone else. Being flexible is not possible unless authorization to skip a procedure comes from above. Besides, the people who work in this company do not have the same level of preparation to take on a challenge of this nature.

Imagine that all of a sudden, the CEO of Ryanair has a revelation. In this hypothetical situation, Michael O'Leary suddenly changes his belief system and thinks that the company must prioritize its customers and employees over shareholders. In his dream, Mr. O'Leary has seen how more productive and empowered employees can further improve the company's profitability and competitive advantage. His vision is clear: the organizational culture must change since it is not only about adding value to customers through a safer, more efficient, and reliable service, but also more humane. These attributes would be guaranteed while still offering

69

lower prices! So, overnight, he decides to apply the same management philosophy as Southwest Airlines.

The question is: could Ryanair workers adapt to this new situation of greater responsibility, from one day to the next? Would they be able to display the same competencies as the Southwest staff just by being more confident? The truth is: no. Many workers will not feel secure enough to do so, and many others will not make informed decisions. It would take time to do this because it is not part of their culture.

However, it is not impossible. The process by which a company can establish or modify its culture to increase its competitiveness will be what we will study in the next chapter.

# CHAPTER 4: HOW TO DEVELOP A CONSCIOUS CULTURE

In the last chapter, we saw that an organization's culture is an extension of the founders' beliefs, assumptions, values, and behaviors in a company. Why is this so important? Because at its root, any culture can enhance a company's competitive advantage or, on the contrary, it can give rise to many dysfunctional, toxic behaviors that undermine its performance. Business cultures are based on different values that make up the character of the organization. However, its roots are in the principles of its founders and its closest management team. For this reason, it is necessary to review the belief systems of these first people internally. Otherwise, the actions and decisions will not follow their words, and skepticism will spread.

This chapter will explain how to work the culture of a company; what values and behaviors could define a conscious culture that increases people's productivity, motivation, and performance. And, therefore, make the company more competitive.

By developing a series of steps and strategic actions, we will be able to mark the path that leads us to enhance the culture, values, and behaviors of an organization that allows it to be better and to grow.

Once the executives have reviewed their belief system, the next step is to define the values to be implemented in the organization. It's always easier to do it early on than having to change already entrenched behaviors and mindsets. However, companies can indeed change their cultures. Only it will take more time as it implies dedicated change management.

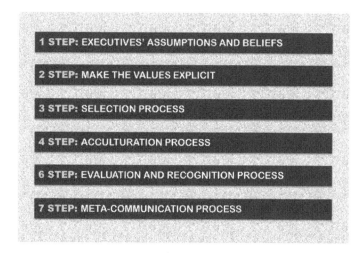

Once the beliefs and assumptions of the founder and extended team are clear, the next step is to articulate the values or organizational principles.

## STEP #2: MAKE THE VALUES EXPLICIT

### Culture in the business plan

It is always easier to define the values that we would like to implement in our organization and make them explicit *before* hiring people. It makes sense to start our business projects by working on the values from the beginning. Therefore, any business plan should address the market opportunity, the unique value proposition, the financial projections, the expansion plan, and the behaviors that are desired for the organization.

Such behaviors are manifestations of people's values. Thus, the hiring process should be based not only on skills, knowledge, or experience, but also on the candidate's values. In this way, the business plan should incorporate the intentions of the partners and executives concerning this point:

• What kind of people do I want to work with me?
• What behaviors would I rather not see happening in my company?
• On what principles do I have to guide my hiring decisions?

It is also important to translate values into explicit behaviors to everyone. Otherwise, we will risk that employees might not understand their role and view those values with skepticism.

In her book *Built on Values*, Ann Rhoades, former executive vice president of personnel at JetBlue Airways, clearly explains the process for building a competitive culture capable of impacting a company's performance. Rhoades asserts that it is the leaders, founders, and senior executives of a company who must determine their organization's values. These values must be linked to behaviors; the latter will determine culture and company performance [1].

JetBlue Airways went through this process. For two weeks, David Neeleman, founder and then CEO, along with Rhoades and other executives, met to define the values that would help the airline to be better 2. From this debate and reflection sessions, five core values emerged: 'Safety,' 'Caring,' 'Integrity,' 'Fun,' and 'Passion.' These principles were later translated into comprehensible behaviors for all people: "Exhibits a Sense of Humor and the Ability to Laugh at One's Self." "Champions Team Spirit." "Commits to 'Safety First'." "Demonstrates Honesty, Trust and Mutual Respect," among others.

## Four factors to take into account when deciding our values

In specific industries or contexts, companies often use similar principles. However, what is essential to one company might not be so in another. For example, humor is a crucial behavior for some companies that seek to be closer to the customer and thus reinforce the service experience; but this does not apply to all organizations. Excellence doesn't have to be a priority for everyone, either. Differences and similarities are expected in these cases. However, the values must be unique in each organization since they define a non-transferable identity.

These values must be credible. On the one hand, managers are the first to behave in accordance to them. On the other, important business decisions will be made with those values in mind. This synergy is what makes culture a decisive factor for the competitiveness of the company.

Thus, when we reflect on the values that we would like to implement in our company, we must answer the following four questions:

1. Will they improve the competitiveness of the company?

2. Will they improve people's productivity?
3. Will they contribute to improving the levels of motivation and commitment of the employees?
4. Can such values connect with customers and other stakeholders?

## Explicit values of the conscious service company

Next, I will explain the values, beliefs, and behaviors of a conscious company. They do not claim to be unique; they seek to illustrate a very close reference to the belief system that this book intends to communicate.

While before I said that each company has to find its values and define them with its words, now I would like to present a series of 'universal' values capable of representing a conscious company's image. They are values that fall within a company's DNA paradigm, of a *Conscious Company,* associated with a more social and competitive organization.

**A conscious company's mission is to offer more value to customers and improve the contribution of the people who work there through a management system of trust which brings out the best in them. This type of company is also more conscious because it seeks a higher purpose. Therefore, this company mission highlights a series of values that answer the four questions that we have posed. Simultaneously, they can be seen as a cluster of general behaviors that complement specific values, capable of providing a more practical sense in day-to-day work.**

*Superior customer service*

All companies take service for granted, but very few stand out in execution. Offering a superior service does not mean that we have to increase our costs or that we have to locate ourselves somewhere on the luxury sector. Being a low-cost company and providing excellent service are compatible categories. Companies like IKEA, Amazon, Mercadona, Southwest Airlines and more, prove it every day. Amazon, for example, has as its leadership principle (value) the 'Customer Obsession.' No one can question Jeff Bezos' commitment to serving the customer, so much so that it has even postponed short- and medium-term benefits in the company for long periods of time, in exchange for better results in customer service. Today, Amazon's leadership is irrefutable; one of its main factors is its obsession with providing more value to users, whether with lower prices, variety, punctuality in deliveries or immediate response to problems.[3]

Providing a superior service means that the company's strategy puts the customer first. The customer has a vacant chair on the board of directors. Any decision that is made always starts with the same question: how will users' value this?

In hotels, restaurants, airlines, the retail sector or other service companies where human contact is crucial, superior service begins with the customer-employee interaction. So, having the capacity to provide an outstanding human service is a key factor, as we will see in the last part of this book. To fulfill this superior service, workers must possess high levels of empathy and authenticity. Besides, they need to be proactive in anticipating potential customer needs. Finally, it is essential to have people who know how to do their job very well and make appropriate decisions to correct any errors or problems during the service.

*X factor:* to provide a service that surprises customers with its quality, managers must give workers more autonomy and empowerment.

### Knowledgeable people

A knowledge worker assumes higher levels of responsibility, shares values, and is more committed to the goals and objectives of the organization. The conscientious company gives more confidence to its employees and is more generous in remuneration, as long as the objectives are met. If the company wins, the employees also win.

A knowledge worker shows an entrepreneurial spirit and is able to fully understand their work. bringing continuous ideas to improve it. Likewise, he is able to see beyond individual and even group objectives. His vision is panoramic. This profile of people is based on the 1 = 3 paradigm: contributing three times more value to work.

In order for people to better understand how their daily work impacts the mission of the company, they also need to receive more information. For this reason, transparency is a fundamental principle in the conscious company. It serves to create an environment of greater trust.

### Tough Love and Candor

Caring about a person is essential for developing trust; however, the caring component needs to come together with accountability. It is not realistic in a job -or for any manager- to attend to the performance side without listening to the human side. Demanding that people behave as good professionals is essential, but it will not be a realistic aspiration if we don't consider people's feelings, perceptions, and motivations as well.

Tough love and candor are the best ways to balance the human side with the performing area. Bosses have to bring out the best in their employees, challenge them, and continually grow them to accomplishing higher results. But this will never happen if they are not also close or don't attend to their collaborators' personal and professional problems. For this reason, a boss must not only promote results; he must also inspire his workers.

A climate of tough love and honesty also applies between co-workers and between subordinates and bosses. To do this, you have to accept what is known as *positive conflict* and make a distinction with the negative one. Positive conflict involves the confrontation of opinions, ideas, and the constructive criticism of others to improve. Focusing on this discussion, Tal Ben-Sahar, a doctor and professor of psychology at Harvard, explained in an interview the idea of 'beautiful enemy', proposed by the American philosopher Ralph Waldo Emerson.

What he wrote in his essay on friendship is that "a friend does not seek a lot of concessions, a person who agrees with him in everything he says; what you are looking for is a person who challenges you, who pressures you, who is a beautiful enemy who helps you reach the truth. What do you look for in a friend? Are you looking for someone who will say yes to everything? Sometimes we need a pat, someone to tell us that we are great, despite everything. But in the long run, we want someone real to tell us when they disagree, challenge us, help us reach the truth, be better people, be more successful, and be happier. That's the real friend," [4]

### Creativity and innovation

Creativity and innovation are two sides of the same coin. The conscious company sees creativity and innovation as a natural way of working and not as something reserved only for managers, marketing and R&D departments, or technology industries. Any job and person can apply creativity to their jobs, even in small proportions. This process can be done in two ways: (1) Spontaneously: for example, a creative response from a service worker to a specific customer problem. (2) Planned: a group of rank-and-file employees from different departments and their managers can develop a new idea that improves the customer experience. This structured creative process needs a certain level of autonomy and collaboration.

A conscious company aiming to enhance creativity and innovation as part of any job believes that all employees, no matter what position in the company they occupy, can improve the job and enhance its performance.

### High-performance team

Good teams help you grow professionally and also personally.

Teamwork is often taken for granted, but reality indicates that not all people who work together can be defined as a team. To be able to work in a high-performance team, people must show essential skills such as: generosity, an open-mind, flexibility, work ethic and accountability, integrity, and humility.

Excessive egos or eagerness to look above the rest can affect the good work of a team. This does not mean that we cannot defend and fight for our ideas. Great teams understand the challenge of coming up with high-quality ideas or finding solutions for attending to root problems. For this, it doesn't matter who came up with the best ideas or who has a more accurate opinion. What matters are team and company goals: what is best for the company.

The difference between large and mediocre teams is their ability to generate synergies that provide better solutions to problems. The good ones solve a large part of their conflicts as a team and stimulate a climate of positive pressure between them.

### *Humility and self-confidence*

An example of a company that makes humility a fundamental behavior in its internal culture is Bridgewater Associates. Ray Dalio founded this investment management firm in 1975 and it is considered one of the world's most successful funds. Bridgewater manages a portfolio of about $150 billion. Executives at this company have always been very concerned about analyzing and systematizing all of their decisions. There is a fundamental leadership principle in this firm, which states: *keep the ego from getting in the way of finding the truth*. For Ray Dalio and the rest of the company employees, being aware of what you do not know is even more important than your current knowledge.

The moments of success are the most dangerous; when you are riding the wave's crest, celebrating, it becomes more challenging to generate analysis and self-criticism [5]. Therefore, you should always keep improving. Why have we achieved more profitability than the expected value in the market? What should we learn from it? Companies' standard practices are to analyze and draw conclusions when they have not met the expected profitability, but not so much when they exceed it.

However, humility and confidence should always go hand in hand. The balance between both is essential. Humility helps us be more open-minded; to recognize mistakes; to be more objective and honest with ourselves and others; to keep learning; to listen to others and change our opinions. But we must also be decisive when it comes to defending our ideas and conclusions. In other words, being able to defend our beliefs and, at the same time, to have the capacity to change our own opinions when data, compelling facts or better reasoning prove otherwise.

One of the most important principles at Bridgewater Associates mentioned by Ray Dalio is: be assertive and open-minded at the same time 6. This value demands a high level of maturity since it is common for people's ego to generate resistance to criticism, which weakens the discussion.

### *Transparency and Honesty*

There are many degrees of transparency; for example, companies like Bridgewater Associates or Netflix are higher on the spectrum of internal transparency. At a lower level, we would find Google - even though it is a very transparent company. The conscious company's standard mode is to share the most significant amount of information unless it could not be shared for exceptional reasons. Why should we be so generous in sharing information? Because this provision empowers the commitment and knowledge of the employees. Sharing information is also the best remedy for preventing employees from developing a narrow vision.

However, behaviors and beliefs related to transparency are often the most missed in companies. The lack of transparency between managers and workers limits knowledge and commitment to improving the latter's results. Besides, it also produces perceptions and feelings of injustice, which affect their motivation.

Transparency not only applies to within but also outside the circle. A conscientious company must be as transparent as possible with the rest of the interest groups such as investors, customers, suppliers, public opinion, and the communities where it operates. Sharing information with the stakeholders is a fundamental principle in a sustainable company. External transparency responds to questions like: What are we doing to reduce environmental impacts? What do we do to increase our social footprint? How are we meeting these goals? What are our successes and flaws in these areas?

All these questions entail answers that businesses need to communicate with different stakeholders through a continuous communication process.

### Sustainability or responsible company

A conscious company is a company that seeks to be more sustainable. Yvon Chouinard, the founder of Patagonia, a textile and retail company, is well known for his commitment to the environment. Arguably, the company prioritizes reducing environmental impacts and creating great products at the same time. Yvon explains that the total sustainable enterprise does not exist. According to Patagonia, businesses will always be net pollutants because they produce environmental impacts in some parts of the value chain, either directly or indirectly.

In any case, a conscientious company makes a firm commitment to improving continually, credibly striving to reduce its environmental impacts throughout the life cycle: in product design, operations, supplier selection, etc. A conscientious company also seeks to increase its social footprint to offset adverse environmental impacts ($CO_2$, water, energy, waste, etc.). Therefore, sustainability is a corporate value within the culture that integrates benefits for humanity, the planet, and the business itself. Critical business decisions have to meet this triple goal. Likewise, all employees are jointly committed to the sustainable process. For example, everyone is indirectly responsible for reducing waste, water consumption, or energy in the business operations or throughout the supply chain. People working in a company can also enhance social impacts by volunteering, fundraising, collaborating with NGOs and other foundations, etc.

The strategic priorities must seek synergies between all stakeholders. For this to be possible, it is necessary to change our way of viewing the relationship between stakeholders. As John Mackey and Raj Sisodia imply in their book *Conscious Capitalism*: to create synergies, you need to develop a more innovative system of thinking that finds opportunities where others see problems. [7]

Throughout the book, I will develop each of these values that make up the conscious company.

## STEP #3: SELECTION PROCESS

Once the core values or leadership principles have been defined, and the management shows a firm commitment to make them real at work, a third essential process must address the candidates' selection. The problem is that companies rarely focus their hiring on the candidate's values.

The interesting thing is that no matter how skeptical you are of the idea of strengthening your internal culture, if you do nothing, a sort of culture will still develop despite what you think. Culture haunts like a shadow. We can work on it expecting a positive outcome, or we can forget about it. What does not change is its existence. Are we going to control the process or leave it to be random? And yet, we should worry about not managing the process of building our culture. Like weeds, the developed behaviors might not be the most appropriate, especially when there are people who should not have been selected in the first place. We are talking about companies where the behavior of some people is dysfunctional and is infecting the rest. Often, many dysfunctional behaviors end up spreading and covering the culture of a company. For example, when the relationships between bosses and employees are not the most appropriate, when there is no clear commitment to the company's goals, objectives, or combating conflicts between workers and departments, productivity will decrease exponentially.

Imagine in the job interview you are asked the following:

• "What attracts you the most about our organizational culture?".
• "With which of our values do you identify yourself the most? And why?"
• "Why do you think you can fit into an organization like ours?"

Most candidates would not know what to answer unless they had analyzed the company beforehand. Many applicants apply for a job, focusing on their responsibilities, salary, or brand recognition. They seldom do it thinking about the culture and values of the company. I have made this mistake several times; blinded by position or salary, I didn't bother to research the company's culture I was applying for. I hadn't thought much about my values back then. And neither do many companies.

Companies need to be concerned with making it clear upfront that they are not just looking for professional experience and knowledge, but for the right people who fit their culture. Or better yet, those who help to strengthen it. In 2009, Netflix published a PowerPoint that quickly went viral: the 125-slide presentation has been slightly modified over time but remains, basically, the best tool for learning about the company's culture 8. Netflix indicates that it is not enough to be smart, have the best degrees or to know how to do the job; you have to fit into the culture and the company's way of doing things.

Hiring someone is easy. It is enough to be guided by intuition after reviewing a candidate's file and conducting several interviews. Companies and headhunters establish their hiring criteria in many selection processes, almost exclusively based on technical skills and work experience. These criteria are defined by the candidate's knowledge and career path, professional education, and qualifications. However, hiring the right people also means focusing on their values and characters. These are just as important as technical knowledge; in some companies, they even have a higher value.

Ritz-Carlton distinguishes between selection and hiring 9. This hotel chain claims that it does not hire, rather it selects people. The selection process is more rigorous and analyzes the technical worth of the candidate and his character and values in a more structured way. Companies of this type know that hiring decisions cannot be focused exclusively on professional experience or academic degrees. Interviews should also focus on the person's attitudes and values. That is why the selection process is more thorough and usually takes more time. They cannot risk contaminating their culture by hiring the wrong person.

Ritz-Carlton and other companies that focus on values involve role model employees in the selection processes. A candidate for a management position, for example, goes through several interviews. In these interviews, different people are to assess the candidate; not only the hiring manager has a say in the selection process but also HR, manager peers, and even subordinates.

What is a thorough consideration of character and technical expertise? It will depend on the position, the level of responsibility, and the skills required. In any case, the values will always continue to weigh heavily in the final decision.

Organizations like Nordstrom, Southwest, Zappos, Whole Foods, The Container Store, Union Square Hospitality place more importance on the candidate's values and attitudes than on the more technical knowledge dimension - at least for rank-and-file employees. These companies seek personal values and attitudes, such as:

- Being open-minded.
- Having a desire to learn.
- Showing a spirit of improvement.
- Being a collaborator.
- Being positive.
- Showing passion and humility.

The reason is that these character traits are more difficult to teach and take more time to develop or change.

As a rule of thumb, companies must distribute selection decisions based on values and knowledge by 50-50.

## STEP #4: ACCULTURATION PROCESS

The job of developing a company culture doesn't end when we've defined our values and hired the right people. Culture is present in our conversations, meetings, problem analyses and decision making. The acculturation process comes after the selection because the new employee has to adapt to its way of doing things. It starts with the orientation but continues for a trial period.

Some companies extend the orientation through a mentoring process. The best way to learn the values is by living them. How to do it? By working with employees who best represent those values. At Southwest Airlines, for example, they assign a person who will be with the new worker for four weeks. Role model employees are the best candidates for taking care of the mentoring process. The new hire will have the opportunity to see the best behaviors from the start. [10]

Many companies delegate the care of culture to Human Resources, but this arrangement is inefficient and excessive. Caring and developing the culture in any organization should be everyone's job. Indeed, Human Resources can lead the process, but the rest of the managers and employees are equally responsible for promoting the culture every day. This is one of the factors most often valued by everyone, since a company's culture reinforces their sense of belonging and pride.

The acculturation process can be demanding for some employees. Companies like Bridgewater, Amazon, or Netflix require a lot from people; working in these companies is a significant challenge for which not everyone is prepared. For example, at Amazon, the levels of responsibility, sacrifice, and internal competitiveness are a filter [11]. At Netflix, the degree of responsibility and demand for delivering results is so great that workers assume the probability of losing their job at any time. Being at Netflix is like belonging to a high-performance sports team. You must produce to the maximum to keep your job. Otherwise, you will have to leave your place to someone who can [12]. At Bridgewater, its principles of honesty and radical transparency may not be comfortable for you. There are other companies, like Southwest Airlines, where relationships and dealing with others are what is essential. Not only do you have to serve the customer very well, but you also have to offer good service to your colleagues.

Each organization has its codes of behavior, vocabulary, symbols, explicit and implicit norms. And new employees have to adapt. It is not the company that adapts to the candidate, but the other way around. That is why the selection process matters: you must hire people who already share most of the values and behaviors proposed by the company. This encourages inertia in the acculturation process. People entering the organization will be infected by the symbols, company norms, or rituals of the people who are already in the organization.

There is a trial period for the selected candidate to determine their integration into the culture or their departure from the company. In Bridgewater, for example, it can take 18-20 months to adapt to their culture [13]. There is the case where people never feel comfortable. When this happens, it is best to leave the company.

This acculturation process is more effective than selection. Only when people can work and interact with others can we know them. No matter how well it is done, any selection process can never guarantee that the candidate will be the right one. For example, imagine that a company defends a significant value, such as humility. How is it possible to determine this in a selection process? It is always more difficult for candidates to lie about their technical qualities or knowledge related to the work; more than anything, because we can always ask specific questions related to the functions and make you go through technical tests or the resolution of a case study, etc. However, questions related to the character can be easily misrepresented. If I ask: How humble do you think you are? The usual thing is that you answer that you are indeed humble. But are you? Or is it false humility?

Tony Hsieh, CEO of Zappos, often says that the most important of his ten corporate values is humility. Or, at least, it is the value that ends up affecting your hiring decisions the most 14. At Zappos, another critical value involving service employees, customers, and the company value proposition is *WOW Service*. This company begins the acculturation process in the first weeks of orientation. Everyone, absolutely everyone, must spend the orientation period working and learning in their customer service department. For this organization, the people who answer the phone and take care of customers are paramount to the company strategy. What could be a call center with no value for the customer and little self-fulfillment for the workers has been transformed into a superior service department. In this area of the company, highly trained and motivated people work to surprise the client every day.

Zappos has an excellent example of how humility can be deducted in the process of the acculturation. They spent quite a while looking for the right person to fill an executive position, but they had to ask him to leave after a few days in his job. It turns out that the manager they had hired had a lot of trouble participating in their four-week orientation process in the customer service department. He did not understand why a professional of his level should devote so much time to such a primary job [15]. For Zappos, this department is strategic, and his attitude did not fit with its most important value: humility.

Like great teams, organizations can bring out the best in us. Sadly, they can also bring out the worst - acculturation happens both ways.

## STEP #5: EVALUATION AND RECOGNITION PROCESS

In my experience as a hotel manager, more than once I have asked myself the same question when I joined a new company: How is it possible that this department head or employee has been in the company for so long? I'm talking about people in continuous resentment and conflict with the company, and who poison the environment. Sometimes, such grievance is sustained by the unfair treatment he or she has received in the past. But is this provision justified when the company has been as fair as it could be? On the other hand, if a new manager demonstrates with his daily work that he or she wants to regain employee trust, motivation and change things for the better, should people's hostile resentment and toxicity still be justified?

The best answer to many dysfunctional behavioral problems is that often companies haven't established those red lines concerning certain behaviors. What is right or wrong is not clear. What are the attitudes and behaviors that should never be allowed in the company? The same is valid for working standards: Managers -and peers- must clearly define the standard level of performance that is expected.

The question is: how is it possible to measure all this? What tools are necessary to evaluate managers and employees?

Typically, companies assess performance based on their technical skills and results. However, what they do not usually measure are behaviors and values. Yet, when they can evaluate behaviors, they do so through annual or semi-annual performance reviews. This is the only time in a year that your boss sits with you and gives you feedback. The problem with this type of evaluation is that it has many flaws. Some people are experts in showing their best face when there are bosses around, and they save their 'true self' for colleagues or subordinates. John Mackey warned about this situation, saying that it is relatively easy to fool a boss (and even more so your boss's boss).

On the other hand, it is not so easy to deceive your colleagues. At Whole Foods, for example, the selection process is not as exhaustive as at other companies. They think that the best evaluation happens once you start working in the company. So, it will be your colleagues, those who best represent the organization's values, who decide if you remain a permanent employee after the trial period. The boss does not resolve it. At Whole Foods Market, you need to have two-thirds of the team votes to confirm your stay in the company. [16]

I would also like to add that it is tough for a boss to deceive his subordinates. For this reason, the best way to evaluate everyone is through a 360º evaluation. Some companies fear this process because they believe that employees could use it to their advantage and against their bosses or colleagues. Similarly, many executives reject this type of evaluation because they think it could detract from their power and firmness in their decisions. However, there is a small possibility of this situation happening. Research shows that the percentage of such dishonest cases is minimal. [17]

Nevertheless, this assessment tool works better when creating a context of psychological safety, honesty, and transparency. Employees must be honest and straight when evaluating their managers and peers. And yet, bosses must display the courage to share their results in front of others with an open mind, even if employees' opinions aren't favorable.

In short, protecting your culture consists of recognizing those behaviors that embody the values that you are trying to promote in your organization. This quality must be recognized. Companies that seek to protect their culture must evaluate their employees, managers, and directors; identify who is going in the wrong direction and who is in the right direction.

The best way to recognize a person's good work is often by promoting them. That is why internal promotion is the priority for three fundamental reasons: (1) It preserves your values. (2) It proves the success of your plan to develop internal talent in your company. (3) It motivates employees to keep growing. Now, not all people want to be promoted or promoted to bosses. In such cases, other forms of recognition must be employed—for example, explicit congratulations in public.

# STEP #6: META-COMMUNICATION PROCESS

The meta-communication process is not the last step but a continuous action that must be carried out every day in the company. It is a vital process to reinforce your culture and make it better. All employees participate in this stage - as in the acculturation process. We must bring out the values in our conversations and analyze our decisions with our values in mind.

There are several ways to do it:

## Storytelling

For example, Nordstrom creates campaigns to promote and recognize outstanding behaviors, which can serve as inspiration for the rest of the team. In a campaign titled *Heroes*, employees were encouraged to contact the Communication Department and report exceptional behavior that they witnessed. Employees would have to write the witness's story as an excellent example of displaying the company's values. Many role model actions were reported and went viral within the company. One of the stories involved a customer and the housekeeping department.

In this story, two workers from the cleaning department are the protagonists. It all began when a regular customer realized, arriving home the last minute, that she had lost her diamond. The stone had fallen from her ring. Fortunately, she remembered having seen it before entering the store. But it was too late to call, so the first thing she does the next day is go to the store to look after her diamond. Store staff found her desperately looking on the floor and approached her to ask what was happening. "I've lost the diamond in my ring, and I'm pretty sure I lost it here!" exclaimed the customer. However, by that time, they had already vacuumed the entire floor. Could it be that the diamond had been sucked in? At that moment, our two housekeeping operators decide to check all the vacuum cleaners. They opened the waste bags and searched for the diamond among the dust, hair and paper. In the end, they found it! [18]

Other companies like Ritz-Carlton have made Line-Up Meetings a ritual within their culture. More than 40 thousand employees, including senior management, meet every day for 15 minutes. A regular meeting of the coordination and follow-up teams turns into a training session and reinforcement of values. Hundreds of these meetings happen daily between departments, hotels and corporate [19]. In these meetings, stories that have occurred in a hotel are shared; they are selected actual episodes. As at Nordstrom, it is the employees who write and tell the stories. The Communication or Human Resources Department verifies them and shares them with the rest of the hotels. The most exciting thing about this practice is the conversation that happens after the story. These actions can be seen as a general training exercise since you have to reflect aloud on the values of service (Ritz-Carlton has 12 service values). What are the values displayed in the story by the employees and what are the motivations?

## Make a whole case study

Like a Line-Up Meeting, companies can make their problems, decisions, errors, or service milestones a continuous case study. Bridgewater is an excellent example of this. This company borders on an obsession of stimulating debate and encourage reasoning on daily matters. The most important thing about this action is the free learning it generates. It is also a more effective type of training than many external training alternatives.

There is work behind writing a case study, but it shouldn't take long. Most of the time, it is a mini-study case. Someone is to take over this role, and once the material is written, the document must be shared between departments and business units for all to learn about it. The goal is to create a learning moment that reinforces company values.

## Display your values at all meetings

It is not always necessary or possible to generate stories, videos, or develop case studies. The most important thing is that values are brought out every day and that behaviors are reflected in team interactions and with customers. One area to meta-communicate your values is in team meetings. Managers and employees can reserve a moment to talk about their values. Every decision or problem-solving situation is an opportunity to speak out loud about the values.

We should speak out loud about our values when reflecting on or evaluating our actions' consequences. For example, suppose bosses decided to let go of a worker who has systematically violated the company values. In that case, such an event can be translated into a case study. That is, as a point of reflection and debate for all.

If the first rule of conscious leadership seeks to enhance the power that exists in others, an organization's conscious culture is the beginning of everything. As a catalysis is a

95

substance that causes or speeds a chemical reaction, an organization's culture acts in the same way. In the following chapters, we will see how the conscious values I have described act as a catalyst for improving performance, drawing from the best versions of people for the company's benefit.

# CHAPTER 5: EXCELLENCE STARTS WITH KNOWLEDGE WORKERS

## FROM MANUAL TO KNOWLEDGE EMPLOYEES

In the movie *Modern Times*, Charlie Chaplin was a metal worker who was limited to tightening nuts, at a frenetic pace, on an assembly line. "Attention, foreman! Go to bank №5, check the production rate. The network is running slow at bank 5. Attention, foreman!" says a voice over. In the scene, Chaplin cannot keep up with the conveyor belt's speed since the simple act of scratching, due to an itchy armpit, prevents him from tightening the screws that keep running at a breakneck pace. The foreman threatens him. Before, it was a fly that prevented him from doing his work well. The job on the assembly line was simplistic, but it subjected the employee to fatigue and stress; it consisted of repeating the same movement, day after day, quickly and mechanically, with little rest. In the end, the operator ends up going crazy.

This film, written and directed in 1936, was a rebuke of the working conditions of the time of the Great Depression. In those days, workers had to cover productivity quotas by working as if they were robots, to the detriment of their mental and physical health. Taylor and Ford's working methods prevailed in companies and working conditions were inhumane. These systems had one purpose: to repeat tasks like automatons as efficiently as possible, following precise and clear instructions. The employees had no voice or vote and had to work without question.

"Why do I always have the whole person if I only want to hire a pair of hands?"[1] Henry Ford wondered at the time. The tycoon only asked for a disciplined workforce, but people insisted on showing up for work with their hearts and minds.

It was Frederick W. Taylor who inspired Ford and many other entrepreneurs with his "scientific" method to end laziness at work which he called "soldiering". They believed that people had a natural tendency towards laziness and needed to be put to work. For this reason, all these entrepreneurs were looking for a method that would ensure efficiency and productivity [2]. Bosses had to make sure that the workers carried out the tasks following the system that had been designed from the corporate offices.

Taylor viewed workers as "mute oxen." [3]. His ideas were far from trusting employees; he envisioned a standardized work system with inflexible methods and processes and a workforce that would have to be forced to adapt to the method. Peter Drucker defined them as manual workers.

## Voiceless manual workers still number in the millions

The reality is that the factory operator who tighten screws is not very different from the people who clean rooms in a hotel, the operator of a call center who takes calls, or the worker who handles orders in an Amazon logistics center. It is clear that there have been important labor advances, the product of relevant social development, but the truth is that in essence, the vision of these jobs remains the same.

An operator in a call center usually has to follow a script and stick to a stipulated time. In this work, the frenetic rhythm of incoming calls resembles the assembly line in Chaplin's movie. Supervisors are controlling time and productivity quotas like the foreman in Chaplin's assembly line. "If you have an interview with your son's teacher, they probably won't permit you to go. You are a number, a chair, a person who only takes calls," affirms a call center employee in an interview with the national press. [4]

Amazon's fulfillment centers would look even more like the jobs of that industrial age. The movements of an operator who walks the aisles in an Amazon warehouse are managed by software and controlled at all times by a GPS; the system tells them the time they have left to pick up the next item. They cannot go beyond the stipulated margin. This work has to be done by pushing a cart, with the added stress of meeting daily productivity goals. The average walking can be more than 20 km a day. They can collect 400 items in an hour, approximately one item every 10 seconds. [5]

A survey of workers at a logistics center in England revealed astonishing data: 74 percent of respondents were afraid to go to the bathroom to relieve themselves if this delayed them in their work and prevented them from meeting the quota [6]. On one occasion, a worker urinated in a Coca-Cola can to avoid wasting time due to the penalties he could receive for failing to meet daily productivity targets - only six negative points are enough to lose his job. The negative points can result for multiple reasons, not only for failing to meet the quota but also for being a few minutes late or missing work -even with a medical certificate, etc.

## *Las Kelly's*

Another group of workers suffers from the methods of those Taylorist industrial times. I'm talking about the maids who clean rooms in hotels and tourist apartments. Today we all know them as "Las Kelly's," and they have drawn attention for their fight for better labor rights in recent years.

Our hoteliers always saw chambermaids as factory workers tightening screws. So, to save costs, they decided to outsource this department. Many housekeepers saw their salaries drop by as much as 40 percent from one day to the next.

Some businessmen raised their voices, warning that the new working conditions could resemble a kind of slavery of the 21st century [8]. Cleaners have to undergo a hectic pace of work and earn less money. Depending on the hotel, they have to clean between 18 and 25 rooms a day, without help. They spend, more or less, between 15 to 20 minutes in each room. This is a very physical job that causes frequent muscle and back problems. To the physical effort is added the stress of meeting the daily productivity quotas. The cocktail is diabolical. It is common to see a high occurrence of sick leave in this group, cases of depression, or dependence on drugs (pain relievers) that help them continue working. [9]

In a meeting I had with the vice president of this association, Angela Muñoz, I was able to see how quality had dropped in many hotels. Sometimes the customer did not realize it, but the cleaning of the rooms and the bathrooms' sterilization left much to be desired. In some cases, hotels passed bills to the outsourced company for damages, such as scratches on the paint of the hallways or rooms caused by pushing cleaning carts or vacuum cleaners in the rush of the moment. These companies, in turn, deducted this charge from the payroll of their workers.

The contradiction is enormous: cleaning maids are expected to do a very physical job that always increases yet is poorly paid. At the same time, they are required to improve quality. Not even Taylor thought of such incongruity; at the very least, he would have noticed the need to pay the waitresses more money per job.

We imagine that these times of Covid-19, hotels will have no choice but to give more importance to this department: now it will become strategic.

## Motivation 2.0

What degree of motivation can a person develop in these jobs? What levels of commitment do these systems generate that conceive of people as manual employees without voices?

The problem is that most of us are not made to fit into these jobs naturally. Perfect efficiency can only be achieved by machines; until these functions are fully automated, the human component cannot be taken out of the equation. It was for this reason that Henry Ford complained when asking for a pair of hands. They were accompanied by feelings.

Employees' feelings, motivations, and perceptions play a crucial role in human behavior within organizations. Although we may be able to adhere to the instructions that are imposed on us with discipline, the reality is that we are not willing to be mute oxen who work without complaint. On the contrary, our intrinsic nature moves us towards higher levels of motivation. Even more so, when social, economic, cultural, and technological development accompanies the countries. When our most basic needs are met, we look for other needs further up the pyramid, such as the natural need to do a good job that makes sense and is recognized. We also want to participate in the script's design that dictates our work; we need to express our opinions and assert our voice. It doesn't matter our position on the corporate ladder; we want to voice our concerns, especially if we believe that we can improve things.

The system that relegates people to manual tasks limits their motivation and commitment; it only promotes extrinsic factors. Daniel Pink defines it as 'Motivation 2.0' in his book *Drive* 10. This idea refers to the ancient stimulus technique known as the 'carrot and stick': it is nothing more than the fear of being sanctioned or the ambition to obtain rewards - mostly financial - associated with doing a good job. But as Professor Edward Freeman often reminds us, while carrots and sticks can work to get a donkey going, human impulses are far more complex.

## Excellence begins by betting on the knowledge worker

Companies often speak of excellence very lightly. It's always tempting to pursue goals through shortcuts, especially when they require effort, investment, sacrifice, and persistence. How many times have we heard the word 'excellence' in corporate messages? The online travel agency and shopping website TripAdvisor gives certificates of excellence to hotels and restaurants. Tourism associations also reward their hotels when they achieve this distinction. And yet, we are referring to the same industry that has opted for outsourcing the room cleaning service, taking it out of its core competencies.

The reality is that excellence is not possible to achieve with a Taylorist mindset. Simple fixings don't work when it comes to achieving such a higher goal. Excellence starts with our employees, so companies need to stop considering them as *manual workers*. It is as if we wanted to connect to a Wi-Fi network with a Spectrum 48K or a Commodore 64.

Any organization that pursues excellence has to prioritize not only systems but people. Organizations that have made excellence part of their company purpose are aware that they need to include all their employees in their plan. Executives, managers and front-line workers must share values and behaviors, such as persistence to improve continually, effort, operational discipline, and a certain humility to maintain an advantageous student's attitude, always open to contemplating new ideas and opinions.

These companies know that excellence is not so much a final destination but a continuous journey in which they will always be learning. It is not possible to stand in front of everyone and say: "That's it, goal accomplished. We have accomplished our excellence goal!". Hence organizations pursuing excellence do not usually look at their navel and stop at only at the celebration; they know that the bar is continually rising. In their obsession to keep improving, they leave no room for minor distractions.

Nordstrom is a company known for its excellence in customer service. It takes humility to serve the customer. Erik Nordstrom's words sum up this idea very well. "You need to be humble to do service," said Erik. "The moment you think you're really good at it is when you're not really good at it. If you are connected to the customer, the customer keeps you humble because we're not perfect at it. If you are really looking to the customer, if you're really sensitive to the customer, and sensitive to the people on the front line, you are aware of your shortcomings. That keeps us focused on the things that are necessary in order to give customer service." 11

Excellence is both a way of being and of doing. It requires working obsessively for continuous improvement, at all levels, from the organization to the individual. When Toyota speaks of *Kaizen*, *Hansei*, *Jikoda*, *Just in Time*, or *Lean Thinking*, it is not only referring to a set of techniques, tools, and work systems but to a way of doing that begins with the workers. This company talks about *four Ps* or dimensions. 12

The first dimension is the philosophy of continuous improvement, in favor of excellence in the long term. The second dimension is about processes (process). Toyota encourages eliminating activities that do not add value. The third dimension is about people (people). This company strives to enhance the knowledge of employees and other partners -the suppliers. The last dimension focuses on problem-solving (problems). This last area is closely linked to the people dimension. It focuses on continually bringing issues to the surface to learn from them and continue to improve. Rank-and-file employees and managers must bring problems to the surface and analyze them in teams. The manual clerk tightening screws must evolve into a *knowledge worker* and add more value to the job. This is the philosopher's stone of organizational learning and knowledge. It is the only path to excellence.

## An elitist view of knowledge

Authors such as Thomas H. Davenport, knowledge management expert, professor, and chair of the information technology department at Babson College, argued that becoming a knowledge worker requires a college degree. However, he noted the exceptionality of cases such as Bill Gates or Michael Dell, who dropped out of university. [13]

But is it indispensable?

Peter Drucker, the forerunner of the knowledge worker vision, broadens the horizon and includes more people in this category. Drucker referred to those brain workers as 'executives,' managers or isolated professionals who, under their position or knowledge, make decisions that affect execution and overall results. [...] He said that the lowest-ranking employee could perform the same type of activity as the company president; that is, planning, organizing, integrating, motivating, and evaluating. However limited his sphere is, he is an executive in it. [14]. Drucker expanded his vision of the knowledge worker to all employees in a company.

Although Drucker did not stress the possibility of transforming all manual jobs into knowledge jobs, the point is that even today, millions of people could still offer more value to their occupations.

Davenport's and many executives' elitist view of knowledge is out of date, in my opinion. It is not typical of the times, for three reasons:

First, it does not fit with the social, economic, and technological development of our times. At present, there are many possibilities for an educational career without having to graduate from university. Similarly, the new Millennial generations, I or Z, are and will be even more intolerant of those tasks that are limited to lower levels of motivation. For these new generations, a job that makes sense matters as much as money. Although it is not a generational issue, most of us would like to have a job that fulfills us and gives us a purpose in life.

Second, the elitist vision of knowledge slows down the competitiveness of any company. For a long time, many organizations have realized that it is not possible to achieve higher levels of service without having more competent and proactive employees, able to work with more autonomy, solve service problems, or contribute ideas to improve work. Consequently, these managers have understood that it is essential to involve more people in the business's cognitive process to compete in more volatile, uncertain, complex, and ambiguous markets. These are called VUCA markets. Companies have no choice but to be more flexible; it is no longer enough to have disciplined employees who replicate processes like yellow minions without counting on their opinions. So, to compete better, manual workers must turn into knowledge employees. Blue-collar workers must apply more intelligence to their operations.

Lastly and most importantly, an elitist view of knowledge creates a self-fulfilling prophecy. If we cannot see people's potential and design jobs around that potential, the result we will achieve is lower productivity and engagement per employee. If we aim for mediocrity, we will undoubtedly get mediocrity.

## The productivity of the knowledge worker is measured by the value of what he or she can bring to work: 1 = 3

Fortunately, this self-fulfilling prophecy can also work in reverse. Organizations that have opted to turn manual functions into knowledge work have achieved competitive advantages, such as significantly increased productivity, improved customer service, and increased economic benefits. The success of companies such as Zappos, The Container Store, Nordstrom, Southwest Airlines, Whole Foods Market, Costco or Mercadona shows that people can assume higher levels of responsibility, commitment and become a fundamental pillar of the competitiveness of the company. In these companies, employees are expected to replicate processes and be able to think about the work itself to improve it. Manual tasks are still there, but they must be accompanied by more knowledge. Kip Tindell, CEO and founder of The Container Store, John Mackey, CEO and founder of Whole Foods Market, and Juan Roig, CEO of Mercadona, are executives who have seen how their employees have been able to assume more skills. It is a virtuous cycle; the people who work in these organizations are also more committed to improving economic objectives.

Kip Tindell summarizes his idea of a knowledge worker in the following simple equation: 1 = 3 [15]. A knowledge worker (salesperson), who serves customers in The Container Store shops, is three times more productive, for example, than an employee in a Zara store. Productivity in this company is measured not by sales per square meter and employees, but by the value (knowledge) that people bring to work to improve it.

## THE POWER OF MOTIVATION 3.0

There is another type of motivation that is more powerful than extrinsic motivation - or Motivation 2.0. This motive drives many people to work smarter and more committed. Daniel Pink calls it 'Motivation 3.0' [16]. It refers to the impulse that arises from the challenge that the same tasks impose on us, the learning we acquire. At the same time, we work toward self-realization by achieving objectives, having the feeling of growth and achieving mastery by demonstrating our worth. It is also a stimulus that arises when we perceive that our work matters and makes sense. And even more so if we are part of a project representing values with which we feel identified and proud.

According to Pink, motivation 3.0 seeks to develop better talents (Mastery) within an environment that offers the freedom to do so (Autonomy). And in doing a job that makes sense to us (Purpose).

## #1. Mastery: The New Knowledge Service Worker

What do we understand by Mastery? It is merely the desire that people have to improve and learn. It is the motivation that leads us to acquire new skills and use those skills that we already have. This drive makes us handle setbacks and roadblocks in our way since we all want to be more competent. For example, not having the necessary resources to do a good job irritates many employees. Often, companies deny training resources, equipment, or workforce, yet their workers still do their best to get ahead.

This happens because our jobs are more personal than we thought. People need to be effective; they want to show others how competent and accountable they are.

After several decades of asking employees questions in different countries, industries, and jobs, Gallup assembled a select group of researchers to analyze more than a million surveys. These data were analyzed to conclude what types of questions could best assess workers' motivation and commitment [17]. This mega study detected twelve aspects that affect people in their jobs. Today, the Gallup Q12 questionnaire is one of the most used tools in measuring people's commitment and satisfaction in many organizations, such as Ritz-Carlton, BBVA Bank, or Daimler Mercedes.

It is not surprising to see that ten of the twelve questions that this evaluation asks are related, directly or indirectly, to the desire to learn more, the desire to improve professionally, and the need to contribute more knowledge at work. It fits with the idea of Mastery. Some examples in this questionnaire are:

Q1: "I know what is expected of me at work."
Q2: "I have the materials and equipment I need to do my work right."
Q3: "At work, I have the opportunity to do what I do best every day."
Q4: "In the last seven days, I have received recognition or praise for doing good work."
Q6: "There is someone at work who encourages my development."
Q7: "At work, my opinion seems to count."
Q9: "My associates or fellow employees are committed to doing a quality work."

Q11: "In the last six months, someone at work has talked to me about my progress."
Q12: "This last year, I have had opportunities at work to learn and grow."

The Mastery dimension consists of knowing what to do and, above all, knowing how to do it. This last form of knowledge is developed in our jobs when we create the right working conditions, because organizational learning arises when all employees are involved in analyzing work and problems. In addition to replicating an operating standard, people have to get used to thinking. The Japanese call this process "Hansei." It falls within the philosophy of work known as "Total Quality," which includes Toyota's four Ps mentioned before. All employees are responsible for continually improving work (Kaizen).

For example, one way to do it is through mistakes and deviations. Ritz-Carlton has an acronym for this process: MR.BIV (Mistakes, Rework, Breakdowns, Inefficiencies, and Variations). According to Diana Oreck, vice president of global learning and head of the leadership center, how deviations, errors, inefficiencies, or inconsistencies at work are dealt with has become a routine dynamic.[18]

The difference between companies that expose problems and those that hide them is that the former know that mistakes often contain hidden pearls of knowledge. In this way, at Ritz-Carlton, they have removed the stigma from customer complaints or operational deviations that might arise on a day-to-day basis. Of course, nobody likes to fail, least of all Ritz-Carlton, an organization aiming to run its operations with zero failures. Still, realistically, there will always be errors or complaints due to clients' and employees' extremely variable nature and that they are people and not machines.

Ultimately, organizational knowledge is enhanced if workers are allowed to think about their tasks and are assigned more responsibility to the challenge of improving their work. But to improve your work, you must first be able to master the task at hand. That responsibility is in each employee's hands; a company responsibility is to train you for doing a good quality job and empowering you.

## #2. Autonomy and creativity: an opportunity to enrich jobs

Autonomy is not synonymous with anarchy and debauchery. It does not mean that people can do whatever they want. At the same time, it is not a concept incompatible with the observance of specific rules, norms, or work standards. Zeynep Ton, associate professor at the MIT Sloan School of Management and an expert in operations, explains in her book *The Good Jobs Strategy* how the most efficient and productive companies, such as Mercadona, Trader's Joe, Costco, or Quicktrip, combine rigorous standardized processes with significant doses of autonomy [19]. Flexibility and standardization are compatible. Companies like Toyota have always been sure that work cannot be improved without a standard that ensures the best way of doing things.

Often, companies claim that they empower their staff but really what they do is simply delegate tasks. Empowerment brings more autonomy, resources, and freedom to be more creative at work. For this reason, it is necessary to demystify the idea that we all have about creativity. When a company seeks that its front-line employees assume greater doses of autonomy, it accepts that they can make many decisions without continuously requesting authorization. After whatever decision they have made, there will always be an analysis to draw conclusions. This analysis should answer two questions:

1. Was the decision correct?
2. What can we learn from it to share with the rest of the team?

## How to apply creativity in the most operational work

At this stage, I would like to explain that creativity and innovation are two sides of the same coin. It is important, however, to dismantle the myth of the lone inventor. Although creativity happens individually, the generation of ideas is more fluid when done in teams.

Creativity represents the first step of any initiative. The next phase will imply working on the best ideas, making them commercially viable. Both processes require people's collaboration. Therefore, they must be developed in teams. Some have said that we all have insights and thoughts, so the idea generation is not the tricky part of the process. The real challenge is to make those ideas commercially successful. Four centuries ago, a comet streaked across the sky, capturing the attention of German astronomer Johannes Kepler. He noticed that the comet's tail seemed to spread out behind it. Sunlight, he thought, must heat the comet and free material from its surface. This astute observation spurred Kepler to think that sunlight might be a useful form of propulsion [20]. Johannes Kepler was the first human to think of traveling to the moon, but that dream was realized only 50 years ago when NASA launched its space program.

I should note that the innovation and creativity I mention are 'small' and 'incremental'. It happens through the continuous improvement of the work. Therefore, it is more accessible to everyone in a company. Anyone can be creative. Innovation and creativity don't need to be exclusively limited to specific jobs or industries, such as high-tech, Research and Development areas, or Marketing offices.

Let's imagine a standard scale for creativity in any job description. Such a hypothetical scale could measure creative ideas on a scale of 1 to 10. For example, Organizations like Apple, Disney-Pixar, or IDEO could reach the scale's upper levels, maybe getting top results of 9 or 10. On the other hand, imagine a team of hotel cleaning maids. What level of creativity can they offer in that same scale? Can these workers apply any creativity into their jobs? Can such creative efforts be included in the same scale? Maybe the creative outcomes from these workers could be measured at 1 or 0.25.

My point is that any worker, team, or industry can be creative and apply creativity to the jobs. I think it is essential to agree on this because if we focus on ideal models, such as those first three, many companies will deem creativity as unattainable. Therefore, it is more practical to place it on a less ambitious and more accessible plane.

We can all be creative. This is a fact. David Kelly, the founder of one of the most innovative companies in the world, IDEO, explains that creativity is a muscle; it is up to us to get accustomed to working it. The problem is that, in the most monotonous jobs, it is not allowed or exercised. The Spanish expression "piss out of the pot" refers to saying something irrelevant and doing something out of place. Many managers are too terrified to think that their employees can implement ideas for improving their jobs without asking for permission. But the truth is that you can always control risks and impose discipline on the creative process.

A work environment committed to excellence should take care not to inhibit creativity. Psychologists and experts agree that creativity is enhanced more in intrinsically motivating environments. Counterintuitively, any form of extrinsic motivation, which focus on rewards and punishments - "carrot and stick"- limit the creation of new ideas.

### *In operational jobs, there are two ways to apply creativity: spontaneous creativity and planned creativity.*

The first form of creativity responds to quick action when faced with a problem. It becomes evident in service because of a worker's ability to respond to a customer complaint or service failure. When companies rely on their employees' preparation to make decisions, the results of spontaneous creativity can increase.

Planned creativity responds to a calmer reflection process. It usually happens within a team. This is a form of the creative process related to incremental innovation. Planned creativity is necessary to improve processes or company standards. Employees must focus on the following questions in guiding their ideas:

1. Does your idea improve the costs of your working area - without affecting quality? (an example of a failed idea in a hotel: reduce water use by lowering the water pressure. Thus, reducing the experience of a pleasant shower).

2. Will your idea improve the income of your working area - without detracting customer value? (Example of a failed idea in a hotel: charge for the room safe or Wi-Fi).

3. Will your idea improve the customer experience?

Planned creativity must respond affirmatively to at least one of these factors. Therefore, it must present innovative and efficient alternatives that maximize performance and benefits.

## #3. Job Crafting: endowing work with purpose

How is it possible that people see the same job differently? The answer to this question has been attempted by Amy Wrzersniewski, Jane E. Dutton, and Gelaye Debebe in their research applied to different groups of workers [21]. A specific study analyzed two groups of employees in the cleaning area in the health sector. They were asked: "How do you see your work?"

A group of cleaners described their work as a set of tasks without much importance. Some also complained about the disorder and lack of respect shown by doctors and nurses, who often throw work materials on the floor and show no consideration. The most interesting thing is that another group of workers saw their occupation beyond their usual functions. These cleaners perceived their work with a greater purpose, associated with patients and their families' well-being.

The researchers noted that this more motivated and committed group of people had redesigned their jobs. In addition to their cleaning tasks listed in their job descriptions, they were doing new ones - and they even ran the risk of being penalized for it! Some cleaners spoke to patients and comforted them, especially when it came to people who did not receive visitors.

Amy Wrzersniewski recalls the case of a cleaner who decorated the rooms, changing the pictures of the place, so that the patients would not get tired of always seeing the same painting 22. This group of workers crafted their work, including new tasks, without the permission of the hospital. At the same time, they fostered their social relationships with patients and their families. These provisions gave more importance and meaning to their work, which consisted of improving people's well-being. Some of them came to see their jobs as part of the process of healing the sick, sterilizing the rooms of pathogens.

The purpose translates to the meaning or importance given to work. However, most manual employees often fail to see how their occupations fit into a general framework. Nor do they fully understand what their role is within the company's overall purpose. For this reason, the purpose of a company, and how a job fits into such purpose, needs must be communicated by managers regularly. I like the clock metaphor to explain this idea: there are no spare parts in a watch. All the pieces are there to meet the same goal: to make the watch function. If a single component is removed, the clock will stop. There may be more complex pieces, larger or smaller, but they are all critical for the functioning of the watch.

## TURNING A MANUAL JOB INTO A KNOWLEDGE JOB

## Backcasting: To imagine the future, it is essential not to be limited by the present

Professor and scientist Karl-Henrik Robert is the founder of *The Natural Step*. This non-profit organization reasons on the fundamental principles of economic, ecological, and social sustainability. Dr. Robert is a promoter of the Backcasting technique [23]. The usual planning techniques such as 'forecasting', which we use when making a budget or calculating an investment, consider present and past data. It's like looking in a rearview mirror. But this form of planning has its limitations: First, it sees the future by looking at current conditions. If you project the future starting from this type of data, creativity will be limited. Your ambitions will also be lowered.

On the other hand, the Backcasting technique shares similarities to the one that Jeff Bezos would use in his company. At Amazon, ideas have to be presented as future press clippings, outlining what the proposed innovation would look like. Bezos banned PowerPoint presentations long ago and replaced them with narrative models. A story can be six or eight pages long and takes time to write it, but it is a more complete and creative exercise. If a project team wants to present an idea or a business plan, it will always start from a narrative. Financial data can still be part of the annexes, but storytelling will be the way to present ideas [24]. "How would a journalist describe our new product or service once it has been successfully launched?" "What are customers feeling and thinking about the product?"

Backcasting broadens horizons and frees from many restrictions because, for seeing the future, it is necessary to imagine a new scenario. You start by devising your goal, and then you go back to the present moment. This provision is limitless compared to if you began at the starting box, planning how to reach the goal. Backcasting begins with the question: "What is the ideal state we would like to achieve? " So, our vision should not be subjected to the usual budget, training, knowledge, or investment constraints - elements of regular planning. Only when the ideal future scenario has been seen will you start working backward:

"What does it take to make it possible?"
"What are the deadlines?"
"What are the resources that will be needed?"
"What barriers will have to be overcome?"

## Backcasting Exercise: A High-Performance Team on Floors

Imagine this professional scenario in a backcasting exercise. This can also be seen as a storytelling or narrative example:

The events take place in a hotel. At this hotel, the flooring team is not outsourced. The chambermaids who clean the rooms do not have university degrees. Still, they all share appropriate attitudes and skills: a desire to learn and improve continually, open-mindedness, team player attitudes, willingness to assume higher levels of responsibility, adequate knowledge to do a good job, and motivation to serve the customer. Some of these qualities were identified in the selection process. But many of them were developed at work, in an environment of responsibility, trust, and continuous learning.

These chambermaids don't just limit themselves to cleaning rooms. They take on other responsibilities that have made

118

their jobs more productive. Productivity in this hotel is not measured solely by the number of rooms a cleaning maid can clean in a day. It is also measured by the ability each employee has in enriching his or her work. People must be active in participating in the company's cognitive system. For this goal, management would never intend to expand the load of cleaning rooms by looking only for quantitative criteria. Quality and quantity measures matter in the same way. They see the quality dimension as the process of cleaning a room properly. But also, as an employee's ability to add more value (knowledge) to their job description and, by extension, to the company's performance. It's not just about doing manual tasks like cleaning rooms well, but also in having the time to train further, come up with ideas to improve the job, and participate in analyzing operating procedures and results. These processes are carried out as a team.

In reality, we are not only talking about productivity but about bringing more meaning to work. In this hotel, most people do not see their work as a daily routine or as a simple means of making a living: it is more than a chore for them. And not only the chambermaids, but the rest of the workers assume it that way too. All employees are encouraged to voice their opinions and ideas constructively and participate in management decisions. Employees can grow in this company professionally and personally because jobs are more aligned with today's social development. Furthermore, it is a fairer job because it pays better for its variable part: if the company earns more, the workers also earn more through bonuses. If employees are expected to behave like entrepreneurs, they must be paid proportionally, consistent with these intentions.

Inspired by Mercadona's Total Quality Management philosophy, executives decided to copy variable remuneration models and distribute 30 percent of the profits at the end of the year, together with the rest of the hotel staff.

No one in the sector had ever appreciated this group of workers, beyond the essential functions that everyone already knew. Their tasks were limited to cleaning rooms or common areas, and their productivity was only measured by the number of places they could clean within their eight-hour schedule.

At the time, the director's decision was between outsourcing or reinventing the department. He eventually decided on the latter. Inspired by the case of other companies, such as Whole Foods Market, Zappos, Southwest Airlines, Quicktrip, or Ritz-Carlton, they chose to bet on this group of workers, as long as they were willing to assume higher levels of responsibility.

Knowledge functions were added to the manual task, so it was convenient for the entire department to show the same level of commitment towards this goal. The selection processes also became more rigorous. When it came to hiring new staff, a lot of attention was paid to finding candidates with the right attitudes and potential to expand basic job descriptions. The new job would become a little less physical but more cognitive. Like Toyota's assembly line operators, the cleaning maids would make fewer rooms but would have to get used to thinking more and adding more value to the job.

In this way and like the rest of the departments, the flooring team became a high-performance team with additional responsibilities like improving operational processes; analyzing teamwork with their bosses and providing ideas to reduce expenses of the department; improve the company's sustainability processes (saving energy, water, improving waste treatment or participating in the hotel's social actions); enhance the customer experience, among many others. The objective is that they become co-responsible for the organization's economic goals, reputation, and quality of service.

This hotel spent more money on training than other hotels. However, the employees' operational knowledge was enhanced mainly due to their participation in the analyses and discussions on solving operational problems. The hotel management was also consistent in the communication process. More information was shared to enhance employee knowledge, commitment to accomplishing company goals, and making them see the bigger picture. For example, they were always given the company's financial and strategic information and trained to understand how an income statement was managed - through a course called "Finance for non-financials."

The levels of commitment and motivation also increased considerably. Their new tasks and responsibilities allowed the development of 3.0 Motivation.

Increases in productivity, quality, and cost reduction happened as a consequence of these strategic decisions. Likewise, absenteeism and its intrinsic costs were also considerably reduced. For example, at times of peak demand, waitresses were willing to make efforts to reduce hotel costs. They agreed to work extra time if they were able to reduce expenses in indirect ways. They also reduced water and energy consumption by cleaning the rooms; for example, water and energy consumption was more efficient since they cared about using less water, or turning off lights, air conditioning, and other resources when not needed.

This projection exercise is more real and closer than we think. When organizations make the right decisions and take on the challenge, they can set up high-performance teams made up of highly motivated knowledge workers, capable of exponentially increasing productivity, streamlining processes, reducing costs, improving the customer experience, and ultimately, providing more value to their jobs.

It is not a utopia. Reality shows us that companies which opt for a manual or Taylorist model to improve performance have limitations. These dynamics are obsolete for this new era. Organizations that invest in and trust their workers, granting them autonomy and achieving appropriate mastery levels, will be closer to achieving the much-desired innovation and outcomes of excellence.

Many organizations' confusion begins when they seek the job satisfaction of their employees, establishing programs stemming from human resources departments. The logic is simple: the higher the motivation, the more productivity; therefore, actions are implemented to improve the work environment without paying attention to what is most important. However, the reality is that people are more motivated by their achievements and productivity from the first moment. There is little that programs can do to improve employee motivation if we still see them as manual workers without a voice. And we need to start improving their productivity by treating them as knowledge workers. Commitment and motivation will be the consequence of a job that offers them autonomy, mastery, and purpose.

# CHAPTER 6: LEADING A HIGH-PERFORMING TEAM

## A dysfunctional team in the stage of conflict

As the new General Manager and with just two days at my position, the situation was as follows: I had to deal with a problem of the highest priority. The stay of a Portuguese group, who booked practically the entire hotel at the end of the year, had been a disaster. From A to Z, everything went wrong. Reception made mistakes in assigning the rooms; VIP gifts given by group organizers were not well distributed; due to a system error and a lack of prevention from the technical services department, many room keys failed, and guests had returned to reception asking for assistance. Murphy said that if there is something that can go wrong, it will. And that's what was happening. The end of the year dinner also went downhill: the banquet oven broke down, and customers had to eat their lamb cold. On top of all this, the lack of coordination, communication, and support between departments made things even worse. The reaction to problems was always defensive, and the blame for mistakes was deflected to others.

I prioritized a visit to the tour operator that managed the reservation, accompanied by the sales manager. We both sat in front of the client and listened stoically to all the failures, one after another. We were embarrassed. Apologies would not be enough; we would have to offer a guarantee that this would not happen again. We also had to provide compensation. This intermediary was one of our best clients and the only one capable of filling a hotel in periods of low demand. With a good sense of timing, any of our competitors would be in a position to attack, poised to take this account from us. So, it was necessary to step up and take the lead.

In principle, we had to learn from our mistakes. **However, it is not possible to learn from our errors without a self-criticism process. This fundamental rule of thumb is easy to understand but challenging to apply as adults. This phenomenon is due to two real reasons. First, the ego. Secondly, our reluctance to expose our vulnerabilities to others. This inconvenience can be explained by the company culture. Many companies and some bosses tend to restrict the possibility of being honest with others.**

We returned to the hotel and met with the department heads. In short, errors happened that affected all teams. My intention was to produce a general debate that could make them think. We had to acknowledge mistakes, share them openly, and learn from them. These meetings are paramount to building knowledge and commitment. They seek to create a space of trust in which people feel comfortable recognizing problems. The premise of these dynamics understands that it is okay and safe to be vulnerable and expose self-criticism, as long as the intentions to improve are genuine.

I soon realized my naiveté about these lofty intentions: the group was not prepared for analyzing the problems with an open mind or self-criticism. I say 'group' because they couldn't really be called a team yet. They were a group of people who had worked together for a long time yet hadn't passed their conflict phase. They did not share values or goals, nor did they show social qualities; they could not put the common interest above the individual or their tunnel vision. They were not capable of seeing the bigger picture. They only looked after their department's objectives, without understanding that there are more important goals of common interest, such as customer experience and the business' bottom line.

What was intended to be a productive debate quickly turned into a conflict in defense of personal agendas and interests. Some blamed others, no one listened, and everyone fought to win the battle of arguments. It was like a political gathering, or worse, it resembled a debate in a reality show.

## Phases of a team: the balance between social and technical dimensions

This experience that I detail is frequent in many work teams. Bruce Tuckman, an expert in team dynamics and professor at Ohio University, defines it as a 'team in its storming phase' [1]. It is a dysfunctional phase in which people do not share common goals or values. They don't have clear rules and usually look after their own interests. Sometimes it is an unavoidable stage, but with the right leadership, it is always possible to get out of it. However, it is also possible that many teams get stuck in it, either because they do not have the right boss or because they don't have the right people. Yet most often is a mixture of both elements.

Many teams manage to advance to the next phase: norming or normalization. At this point the team rules are clear, they share objectives, and everyone has their responsibilities well defined. In this phase, we can start calling them a team. However, this team still has potential for improvement.

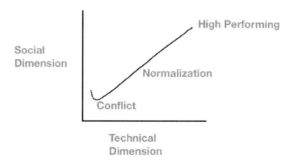

What is the last stage of development? Tuckman calls this stage *Performing*. But I would like to refer to this phase as 'High Performing.' The difference between good and mediocre teams is their ability to generate synergies that reverse mistakes or provide better solutions to problems. Good teams can solve a large part of their conflicts together and create a climate of positive pressure between them. Ed Catmull, president and CEO of Disney-Pixar sums it up very well saying that If you give a good idea to a mediocre team, they it will screw it up. If you give a mediocre idea to a brilliant team, they will either throw it out or come up with something better. [2]

This high performing team shares values, goals, and objectives. All team members show a higher degree of commitment and accountability, so people in this team keep the same level of effort. And yet, it is not only in the social

126

realm that this team is extraordinary. A high performing team is exceptionally prepared in the technical dimension as well.

Whole Foods Market is a multinational supermarket chain headquartered in Austin, Texas. Amazon purchased this organic grocer in 2017. Many teams at Whole Foods have higher-performing attributes.

## High Performing Teams in the stores

Whole Foods Market has more than 475 retail and non-retail locations in the US, Canada and UK.

The fundamental work unit of the company is the self-directed team. Such teams meet regularly to discuss issues, solve problems, and appreciate each other's contributions. Every employee belongs to the team.

Whole Food's structural organization is very decentralized. The basic operating unit is based on teams; each team - such as grocery, bakery, fruits and vegetables, meat and seafood, cashiers, prepared foods - works as an independent unit with much decision power, committed to business objectives, company values and the mission of the organization. Every team is also fundamental in company improvement and innovation.

Whole Foods recognizes the importance of smaller tribal groupings to maximize familiarity and trust. Trust is the glue that holds everything together throughout the company. They organize their stores -and company- into a variety of interlocking teams. Most teams have between six and ten team members, and the larger teams are subdivided further into a variety of sub-teams. The leaders of each team are also members of the Store Leadership Team, and the Store Team Leaders are members of the Regional Leadership Team. This interlocking team structure continues upward to the Executive Team at the highest level of the company.

Teams — and only teams — have the power to approve new hires for full-time jobs. Store leaders screen candidates and recommend them for a position on a specific team. But it takes a two-thirds vote of the group, after what is usually a 90-day probation period, for the candidate to become a full-time employee. This hiring referendum affects the behavior of everyone involved in the process: the job candidate, the team, and the store team leader. Store leaders take great care not to recommend people they don't think the team will approve.[4]

The team is the cornerstone of Whole Foods Market. In this way, the team meeting is where all values come to reality. Each team in all 475 stores meets on a continuous basis. Each store meets monthly as a team as well. They have the opportunity to swap stories, learn constantly by analyzing guest comments and job improvement opportunities, solve problems, and share information. Teams are central to how stores operate and improve — an essential ritual for promoting group accountability and reinforcing company values. Trust between team members and managers is key. At Whole Foods, that trust is optimized in this type of smaller team organizational structure. This is because each person is a vital and important member of his or her teams. The success of the team is dependent upon the invaluable contributions of everyone on the team. Trust is optimized when it flows between all levels of the organization.

The gain-sharing program is distributed among those teams that are over budget. Each team receives an allocation of costs as a percentage of its sales within the annual planning process. So, if they are above sales or below costs, they can run a surplus. A specified proportion of that surplus will be divided among team members and the company, and paid as variable compensation every four weeks. Another proportion will be allocated to a collective savings fund. This fund will compensate for those months in which the team does not meet its projections. For example, if in a specific month, they did not meet their budget because they were over on personnel expenses, they would be deducted from this savings fund. If the fund is at zero, it is discounted from future earnings. At the end of the fiscal year, those teams that have a positive fund will share it. 5

Teams compete against their own goals for sales, growth, and productivity; they compete against different teams in their store and against similar groups in other stores and regions.
This competition is a significant reason why performance information is so easily available within an open-book management philosophy. Since every team can measure other team's performances, there is a healthy competition among businesses comparing performance indicators such as sales, profits, and customer satisfaction. The primary vehicle for competition at Whole Foods is an elaborate peer-review system through which teams benchmark each other. But they also collaborate, sharing knowledge and best practices. John Mackey, the founder and Co-CEO of the company states: "it is natural for people to compete and collaborate."

## WORKING AREAS TO DEVELOP A HIGH PERFORMING TEAM

Once you have assumed what a high-performance team is and what its possibilities are, it is necessary to understand how it can reach this phase. As I said before, a team leader must consider different areas of work that involve two dimensions: the technical dimension and the social dimension. While there are priorities between these areas, managers need to work in both simultaneously.

Before explaining the five work areas, it is essential to clarify the appropriate team size. To be effective, any team should have a suitable number of people because when teams exceed their sizes, communication and coordination get more convoluted, and interactions between team members get more complex. Although it is not impossible to achieve good team dynamics with more people, it is more complicated. Jeff Bezos always talks about a "two-pizza team": it takes two family pizzas to feed a team [6]. We imagine that the pizzas are family-sized since the number of people will be between five and eight. The former Harvard professor and expert in team dynamics and leadership, Richard Hackman, says that four to six people are adequate numbers to form a team. [7]

What, then, is the ideal number?

Perhaps a team of five, six, or seven members is the most appropriate, but it is also true that leading a team of ten people is possible. I would say that from the eleventh person, cohesion and interaction become increasingly difficult. Therefore, it would not be a bad idea to subdivide a team of more than twelve or thirteen people, as some companies do.

## #1. Working area: Shared goals and objectives vs. tunnel vision

What is tunnel vision? It is the impossibility of seeing the bigger picture. Businesses typically encourage a kind tunnel vision when designing their goals on an individual or departmental basis. Such short-sighted vision can explained very well with the parable of the blind men and the elephant. In this Hindu parable, blind wise men were commissioned to understand and describe to the rest of the people how the elephant looked. No one had seen the size of the animal before, and because the blind men were the wisest people in town, they figured they would be the ones to pass on their knowledge to the rest. But the result was a disaster. The village acquired a skewed understanding of the animal and still did not know how an elephant looked. The one who touched its trunk described it as a kind of mighty serpent; to the one who caressed its ear, it was like a huge fan; another, like a firm tree, -when he felt its leg.
They were all telling the truth, but they were also wrong. Each of the blind men had a partial vision of the elephant; in their descriptions, they used similes that described the animal in a limited way. Each of these wise men was sure to be right and argued to defend their idea of the elephant.

Noel Tichy, consultant and professor at Michigan Ross University, was recognized as one of the most important management gurus 8. Tichy clarifies in a study that 80 percent of conflicts in groups are due to their unclear objectives and goals 9. This lack of clarity of direction is a complication due to companies' degree of fragmentation. The larger the size, the more likely that the vision becomes narrower.

There is a Harvard multimedia simulator - I usually use it in my MBA classes- reflecting the problem of individual objectives 10. The tool separates the class into different teams of five and encourages them to climb Mount Everest. Each member has a role, asymmetric goals and asymmetric information. For example, the leader has goals and rewards for getting the entire group to the top in the allotted time. Within the group, there are members such as the environmentalist or the photographer, who have opposite objectives. The top is not a priority for them; their goals are to stay in intermediate camps, and to take photos or clean up the garbage on the mountain. Will they be aware of this? Will they prioritize their individual goals, or will they sacrifice for the group? In this game, the most effective teams usually share input information and agree on priorities. These teams establish clear rules, are more transparent, and share their data with the rest.

I have a personal story about this contrast of objectives and lack of communication. It's a slightly surreal case study. I remember working for a family business, running two independent hotels. The owners had decided to separate the finance and administration departments from the hotel management. To do this, they hired another director. They thought they could better audit the business with this new structure. The problem was that both directors had different instructions and objectives. Hotel owners met with both directors separately and limited the communication channels. So, most of the time the right hand didn't know what the left hand was doing. The property had also set individual goals that encouraged tunnel vision. For example, the hotel management had objectives on revenue or customer satisfaction. The financial manager focused on costs. One was required to increase sales and the other to reduce expenses. The result could not have been more disheartening, and conflicts were continuous. The finance director reduced the budget for necessary supplies, like room amenities or photocopies. And we were all affected. Customers were also complaining.

Nevertheless, the person in charge of the finance department was proud of having done her job. The costs were lower than ever. Unfortunately, customers and other departments were also angrier than ever because they did not have the resources to do a quality job.

How can a company solve this tunnel vision? Should we forget about departmental or individual goals? No, but we have to complement them with other more global business goals. It is also advisable to align variable salaries with broader objectives as well. Two examples: JetBlue's metrics include: (1) net promoter score for customers (customer satisfaction), (2) net promoter score for crew members (employee satisfaction), (3) operating margin, (4) cost per available seat mile (CASM), and (5) free cash flow [11]. You can also set global objectives in a hotel such as business profit, customer experience, employee satisfaction, or fundamental quality and performance indicators in operations.

When the business's goals and purpose are above all else, there is less room for personal agendas or personal interests. Everyone knows what matters most. Therefore, sterile conflicts and unproductive selfishness have less space.

## Open Book Management (OBM)

In his book *The Great Game of Business*, Jack Stack, President and CEO of Springfield Remanufacturing Company (SRF) published a case study in which he explains the company's management process, known as Open Book Management. Jack Stack says that the problem for many companies is that people cannot see a bigger picture [12]. And what is that bigger picture that can best be quantified? The bottom line of the business. Many organizations have adopted an open book philosophy. All employees have to feel how their work can directly or indirectly impact the business's total profits.

Open Book Management also trains the most operational employees in essential financial matters: Bottom line employees need to understand and manage a departmental operating budget. How is this operating budget linked to the business as a whole? What are the company benefits? Are the benefits in cash and liquidity? Stack dismantles this fallacy, widely spread in many companies, doing significant management damage, which only affirms that information is power. Information is not power; it is a burden! The more widely and efficiently information is shared, the better the weight of leadership will be shared. [13]

In short, Open Book Management is a work system where financial results are shared with all employees in a transparent and continuous manner. The purpose of sharing this information, with a view to improving results, is simply to generate an owner mentality among employees, as well as knowledge, commitment, and motivation. Front-line employees must take joint responsibility for financial results. This system teaches its workers basic financial principles and then adjusts them to managing budgets and analyzing deviations. It engages them in critical responsibilities to harness the value they can bring.

Remember the team in the conflict phase earlier in this chapter? Well, we managed to evolve remarkably. However, the economic crisis came and affected us all. Revenues plummeted, and emergency measures had to be taken to reduce costs further. It is incredible to see the staff's response when you trust them, show yourself more transparent, and allow them to participate in the results. Above all, when managers share all the information regularly, they can understand how their ideas and actions can reduce costs or even increase revenues. One of the launched activities was sharing and explaining to all those interested in the hotel's budget and profit and loss account. We invited the most operational workers from different departments at the management meetings on the monthly results - chambermaids, receptionists, room waiters, cooks, and technical service. The room's capacity had a limit, and we rotated the invitations when we were more than 25 people. At these meetings, we projected the results, and everyone present reviewed line after line. We discussed economic deviations, and people were able to share different solutions. The best ideas arose from the interaction between several people, capable of analyzing problems with self-criticism and confidence. I still remember the incredible feeling of pride when I witnessed the team synergies and solidarity generated between department heads. These were the same people who months ago could not recognize problems or make the slightest reflection.

Open Book Management instills an entrepreneurial attitude in employees and rewards them for benefits. Southwest Airlines is an excellent example of this. This airline has always been known for sharing benefits with its employees. If the company wins, employees must win too. Southwest Airlines has been delivering profits for 45 years in a row. In 2018, Southwest distributed 544 million dollars among more than 40 thousand people who are part of what they call a family. [14]

## #2. Working area: Transparency, honesty, and vulnerability

Why do we usually hide our vulnerabilities? The answer is straightforward: because it is generally not safe to reveal them at work. The reality is that it is tough to be honest with our colleagues or bosses. I'm not talking about the work ethic. I speak of the possibility of being authentic and showing our strengths and our weaknesses, fears, and uncertainties in a genuine way.

Trust and security are by-products of being transparent and honest with each other. When bosses create an environment of safety in their teams, people can show their weaknesses without fear that they might turn against them. However, I am is not talking about creating a climate where employees encourage their faults. This is unrealistic because our human nature pulls toward mastery, recognition, and self-realization. The idea is to create an environment of psychological safety. People can be vulnerable to their colleagues and bosses to create a synergy. It is a kind of symbiosis in which everyone can correct weaknesses and promote company improvements.

How is it possible to do this? The first step has to be taken by the boss. You start by leading by example. It is the leader who must set the tone. Nonetheless, when he covers up his or her mistakes, uncertainties, or blind spots, a counterproductive message is sent to the rest of the team. People perceive that it is not safe to be honest.

On the other hand, it would be advisable to create a *golden rule* within the team that extends to the entire organization: "It is forbidden to criticize others if they are not present in the room." This is a way to avoid the national sport (very human) of criticizing our neighbors. Behind the back gossip and ridicule only contribute to creating a climate of insecurity, mistrust, and lack of integrity.

## Alan Mulally at Ford Motor Company

Alan Mulally was named CEO of Ford with a mission to rescue the historic company from bankruptcy. In 2006, Ford had a projected loss of $17 billion. This automotive giant had become an umbrella brand that housed many losing companies, such as Jaguar, Aston Martin and Land Rover. It was also an organization that operated in different parts of the world but in a way that was too divided, existing without generating synergies, economies of scale, or organizational knowledge [15].

Mulally knew that the world's most brilliant plan to put Ford on the profit track again wouldn't work without a cultural shift. That change would have to happen first among senior managers; all leaders worldwide met every week, at 7:00 in the morning, by videoconference, to review the plan and the management panel using a scorecard of 320 indicators. Everyone could see the plan through this dashboard. These indicators had red, yellow, and green lights. The yellow lights showed a potential problem; the red ones meant real problems and the green ones that everything was okay. Blue indicated a color change between gauges. In the first few meetings, the new CEO was surprised to see that the panel was all green. "How is this possible if this company is losing 17 billion dollars? Are you telling me that everything is fine?" He asked in exasperation. Nobody answered. Of course, there were problems, but the corporate culture that prevailed before Alan Mulally's arrival was distrust, secrecy, paranoia, and internal competition. So, covering up the problem was a natural defensive reaction to this dysfunctional work environment. The lack of security to expose them openly became a culture of little transparency and honesty. Nothing new under the sun; this is something that happens in many companies.

Little by little, his management team was getting the new leadership tone. A few weeks later, Mark Fields, leader of the American continent (Canada, USA, Central, and South America) decided to stop production at the Oakville plant, Canada, due to a technical problem, and 10,000 cars of the new Ford Edge model were stranded on the floor. They did not have a straightforward solution to the problem, so he marked a series of red indicators. Until then, nobody had dared to do it without a sure solution already in place. Despite this, Mark decided to expose his vulnerability and be honest with the rest of the team. At this moment, there was a great silence in the room. Everyone thought that would be the end of Mark. "Poor Mark. He is going to be fired". Alan Mulally, however, decided to applaud the action in front of the rest of those present and asks: "Mark, is there anything we can do to help you with the problem you are reporting?" Before he could respond, Benny Fowler, Global Quality Director, said, "Mark, I think I saw that same problem six months ago elsewhere." Production Director Joe Hendricks also chimed in: "Mark, you are also going to need several engineers because you will have to change the technical specifications on all those cars and make up for lost production. Let me send you the best people we have to help you at the Canadian plant as soon as possible." Derek Cusack, Global Head of Product Development, also intervened: "Mark, I saw that technical problem five years ago. We can also help". This succession of interventions lasted only a few minutes.

According to Alan, this was the turning point in Ford's change management. Mark Fields was still in his post, and the CEO of the company had reinforced his honesty stance. Now the message was clear: it was safe, to be honest. So in the following weeks, in a climate of transparency, honesty, and vulnerability, the scoreboard began to look like a rainbow of colors (blue, yellow, red, and green). That's when Alan thought, "My God, now we know why we lose 17 billion." The data was finally clear. But more importantly, a work climate had been created in which it was safe to reveal problems. In the future, everyone could help, share knowledge, resources, and progress on the plan. Despite the new scorecard's poor appearance, the CEO began to be more confident that now they could achieve the goals.

Harvard professor Amy Edmonson, and her colleagues found that nursing teams with the best leaders reported up to ten times more errors in the medical sector than groups with the worst bosses [16]. The first impression when seeing these results seemed contradictory. How could they make more mistakes if they had the best bosses? However, the answer was logical: these teams reported more errors because they could be more honest.

A high-performance team must establish a climate of transparency, honesty, and vulnerability to bring all problems to the surface. The path to excellence goes through continuous improvement.

## #3. Working area: Positive Peer Pressure

In the best teams, the pressure does not come from the bosses but from the teammates. It happens because the degree of individual responsibility is more significant. When a team reaches higher stages of development, it can create positive pressure that affects everyone. This impulse acts as an antidote to social apathy.

Everyone knows that when a boss is unable to address some people's performance problems within a team, the others can become infected. This problem gets worse when the group is more substantial; it's easier to slip away in a group of ten than when you're in a team of four.

When in a team of six, and we have one or two who undermine their commitment, the total team effort can be reduced to the level of those two people. From then on, that will be the new standard. Bosses typically fail to fix these situations because, in a way, it involves having to manage conversations that are not pleasant or deal with some conflict. However, it is also necessary to bear in mind that you -and only you- are responsible for setting the standard of work in your team. What you tolerate will set the standard.

Jocko Willink and Leif Babin, former Navy SEAL officers, tell in their book *Extreme Ownership* the four rules of all combat. SEALs are known as the most elite and probably the best Special Operations Forces in the world. It is also likely to be the hardest. They are made up of applicants from other select units of the Rangers, the Marines, and Delta Force. Even so, only around 40% of applicants pass the admission tests.
The SEAL's last combat rule speaks of decentralizing orders: leadership must be distributed among the entire team [17]. This means that each one is perfectly aware of their responsibilities. Failure to comply with obligations and doing a poor job can expose the lives of others.

For this reason, selecting the right people is essential. It's not just about choosing talents who display good personal attributes, such as passion, responsibility, or proactivity, but also those who have the necessary skills to make the team work. Motivation is a by-product of working with highly competent people who are committed to the project. Typically, the most responsible employees arrive motivated from home. Therefore, what good bosses have to do is keep commitment from falling apart.

Finally, a high-performance team is capable of being comfortable within a reasonable degree of stress. There is a sense of urgency to deliver on the results. The best bosses can maintain that sense of urgency, without resorting to condescendence. However, positive peer pressure needs to be linked to a climate of transparency, honesty, and vulnerability described above. My recommendation is that 360º evaluation reviews must also happen between colleagues, not just limited to evaluating the boss (upward feedback.)

Those organizations that have been able to increase their transparency, honesty, and vulnerability share the results of these evaluations openly. It is an exercise in constructive dialogue. Netflix began with a practice called "Start, Stop, Continue" among its executive staff. But after its success, the practice then moved to the rest of the organization [18]. In this exercise, one must ask out loud, one by one, the following questions:

*"What behavior would you like them to adopt again?"*
*"What would you like me to stop doing?"*
*"What should I keep doing?"*

I suspect that if I had practiced this exercise in one of my professional settings as a director, perhaps some of my collaborators might have concluded something more or less like this:

"You have to be able to listen even more, without interrupting; you have to stop being too close on top of issues that are not as high a priority; you have to keep showing your support and your closeness everyday."

# #4. Working area: Positive and negative conflict

Many bosses will agree that conflict management is the most cumbersome part to handle. That is why the ostrich technique -hiding the head in the sand and letting the conflicts go and thus hoping they solve themselves- is most often used within organizations. Avoid meddling so as not to escalate the conflict. Indeed, sometimes it is better not to get involved in some conflicts. And yet, you have to intervene in one way or another. Correcting someone or giving negative feedback is one way of dealing with conflict, as we will see in the next chapter.

In the first place, what we should be clear about is that there are two kinds of conflict: good conflicts and bad conflicts. We will call them positive and negative conflicts. Every team leader has to be able to promote the positive and reduce the negative.

## Positive conflict: Disagree and Commit

A good team is capable of introducing divergences in the conversation. That is why one of the responsibilities of a boss is to instruct people to debate in groups; how to defend ideas and to listen, and when to withdraw to support the adopted decision. The motto would be: *Diverge but Converge*. A phrase that summarizes this idea very well and enhances creativity in teams says: "Argue as if you were right but listen as if you were wrong." [19]. When problems are analyzed, or decisions are made in teams, it is more productive to confront opinions, as long as people do it for the good of the company and never to feed their ego. Our ego tends to swell when we are agreed with or when we are right on any matter. It is a phenomenon that increases our psychological status: we have the feeling of being more intelligent. But a good boss has to be the first not to fall into that ego trap if what he or she wants to teach others that the most important thing is the quality of the decision and not who makes the decision. Our ego, ultimately, must be put at the service of the team.

It is necessary to teach people to debate; it is also essential to impose rules in a dialogue about ideas. Indeed, it is good to remember these rules before starting the meeting or interrupting someone if they break the guidelines. For example, a necessary policy should be the *2 minutes rule* applied in Bridgewater: "You have two minutes to present your case, without being interrupted." [20]. Another rule that I consider necessary is prohibiting the mobile or laptop (unless strictly necessary) in a meeting. Why? The reason lies in the fact that a person reading emails or attending to other matters on their screen will be unable to process the conversations that arise at that moment. Multitasking is impossible when there are two simultaneous cognitive assignments. When we answer emails or read anything else, our mental capacity is equivalent to that of an 8-year-old child. As a Harvard study explains, multitasking is as if we have smoked cannabis, and we then pretend to uncover what is happening around us [21]. At the same time and no less importantly, we should ban laptops and smartphones out of respect for our colleagues, who should be heard and listened to.

And yet, what do we do with those who love to listen to themselves? Some people take a long time to present their case or can go off on a tangent, diverting the focus of the matter. There is another rule for this. In the days of Gordon Bethune at Continental Airlines, managers used to use the code word "Banana" in meetings 22. If someone used more time than they should or deviated from the matter, it was always possible to correct them by saying "Banana." In this way, he or she was humorously reminded to return to earth.

There are other rules for debating with the right attitude that are essential. For example, we always need a policy that reminds people that criticism can never be destructive. Often, personal disputes between employees can contaminate positive interactions. A boss has to be very aware of this. The moment you perceive that the criticism is dishonest and does not add value to the idea, you must stop it. In the dialogues, you have to be inquisitive but always with the right tone and honesty. *"How do you figure you're correct?"* or *"Please help me understand your reasoning"*. *"I don't quite understand the logic you are putting forward. Could you help me by expanding your explanations? "*. *"What objective data reinforces your opinion?"* These are the right questions to reinforce the constructive and critical tone of a debate.

The boss always sets the tone, so the possibility of fostering positive conflict has to start there. If you cannot accept that people must discuss your ideas with candidness, little more can be done. History is full of significant accidents or disasters because no one could tell the boss that he was wrong.

Some arguing with the boss is crucial. Specific professional industries, such as aviation or health, were the first to realize this. The blind bowing of co-pilots to commanders, or nurses to surgeons, has led to fatal accidents. So, to correct these communication and decision-making deficiencies, the aviation industry has long launched training courses and protocols called Crew Resources Management (CRM). These practices have been exported to other sectors such as healthcare to empower subordinates and avoid mishaps and unfortunate events. [23]

One of Amazon's fourteen leadership principles says, *Leaders are almost always right*. They are right because they can change their opinion once the data or the facts prove otherwise. They can also change their minds when more logical reasoning arises, without their ego preventing it. Usually, it is the most insecure or emotionally immature leader who has problems with this disposition.

## Negative conflict: how open your feelings

Negative conflicts can appear for many reasons, and the reality is that not even the best team is free of it. First of all, we are humans with feelings and perceptions. The question is, how are we able to deal with it? Even the best marriages or friends have problems. The difference is in how they can meta-communicate about their disputes and differences. That is, how easy it is to express feelings and, at the same time, listen to the other's point of view.

However, a more advanced team should not have as many harmful conflicts as in organizations that have been training their employees for years. When teams share a clear vision, goals, values, commitments, and rules, their disagreements are often significantly reduced.

Every team leader has to be able to manage a negative conflict. To do this, you have to ask yourself: "Is this a conflict that I should be involved in?" If we are overly proactive in resolving conflicts, we will likely not get people accustomed to resolving disputes on their own. Sometimes we might also escalate disagreements when it would have been best if people had settled them between themselves. But this cannot be confused with the *ostrich technique*. The ostrich technique denies the resolution of the conflict. It proposes to bury the head in the sand, do nothing, and wait for the conflict between the parties to resolve itself.

You always have to get involved in the conflict. However, there are two ways of getting involved: passive and active resolution of conflicts. By passive, it is understood not to interfere and wait for people to resolve their problems independently, keeping yourself informed of the dispute's progress. If, after a while, the conflict remains entrenched, it will be time to intervene. Then, it would be your time to be proactive. Southwest Airlines, again, has an excellent method for resolving disputes. The leaders of this airline, when they have to intervene in a conflict in which both parties are apparently right (as is typically the case in most situations), they call the parties involved to a meeting called a "Come to Jesus." It is so-called because the same session demands that both parties come with an open mind. They must be able to open their hearts and listen; state their points of view and feelings and try to understand the other's way of seeing things. The leaders present in the meetings have the role of moderators or arbitrators [24].

In my teams, we did not use this name, but the intention was always the same as in Southwest Airlines. Our way of resolving conflicts aimed to strengthen the relations between the opposing employees after these meetings. When we

146

succeeded, there was a shot of motivation and pride for having managed to resolve the conflict was very high.

## #5. Working area: Open-minded heterogeneous vs. Close-minded homogeneous team

Contrary to what many believe, an overly cohesive team can pose a problem. Too *cohesive* is understood as a group of people closed off to the outside and with little attitude for criticism. There is a name for this circumstance: 'Groupthink.' This a term coined by Irving Janis in 1972 [25]. A groupthink situation happens when there is direct or indirect pressure to agree with the group's opinion. Usually, the group has an illusion of joint invulnerability, which makes them act without self-criticism and critical reflection. When decisions are made, there is a collective rationalization of the group's findings. The central point is that, under this scenario, if a person detects an error and realizes that the decision to be made is absurd, they will end up omitting its discovery for fear of retaliation from the team.

One form of Groupthink is the *Not Invented Here Syndrome*. This is a form of invulnerability that manifests itself with the tendency to gaze at the navel. "No one is going to teach us to do things" or "we are the ones who know the most." The problem with these premises is that the answers can often come from outside. Humility and open-mindedness are essential. In one of the best TED talks ever given about teams, Margaret Heffernan demonstrates an excellent example of humility and open-mindedness. Arup, a reputable engineering company, was commissioned to build the equestrian center for the Olympic Games in Beijing, but they faced a challenge: How to better manage the waste of the

2,500 thoroughbred horses that they would have to house? This entailed proposals for logistics and technical solutions that had not worked before. Instead of spending months analyzing this problem and talking to veterinarians, horse groomers, and other specialists, they decided to go abroad to find the solution. In this way, they found the person who had designed the Jockey Club of New York. In less than a day, they already had the solution. [26]

Inducing positive conflict, being open-minded, and showing humility is one way to combat Groupthink or the *not-invented here* syndrome. But it is also important not to fall into the "Like Me" trap, which is the unconscious tendency that many managers practice when selecting or promoting people, letting them influence decisions just because their personality traits are similar and homogeneous. Perhaps the candidates' attributes are authentic to their personality, or the candidate acquired them trying to mimic the group's boss. The truth is that a team needs a certain degree of heterogeneity.

How heterogeneous should this group be? If we bring together people with personalities as far apart from each other as Jupiter and Mars, it may become complex to put them to work together. Still, the reality is that many divergent personal traits are very useful to have within the same team. This factor will give you more wealth. Suppose I am a very analytical and linear person. In that case, I should not surround myself only with people like me because we will always be losing ourselves in the details without going any further and finding new dimensions. It would be beneficial for me to have more visionary, creative people capable of seeing a bigger picture.

Introverted and extroverted personalities must come together on the same team. The synergy that arises from there can be highly positive.

Studies show that promoting diversity enhances creativity. What kind of diversity? IDEO refers to this form of a variety of profiles in a team as *Cross-Pollination*. That is to say, differences in culture, knowledge, area of expertise, and/or generational differences. A cross-pollinated team has a heterogeneity of professional profiles - departments, studies, and areas of specialization. [27]

As I said before, heterogeneity is also vital in personality traits. We need to complement the weaknesses and strengths of our inherited talents. Maybe we have too many big picture thinkers, and we lack analytical down-to-earth personalities. Teams must know these differences to improve their relations and communications. Therefore, we must do everything possible to adapt to others. For example, highly introverted people resent being interrupted while talking; their thoughts usually mature a lot in the head, unlike extroverts, who like to think aloud. In this way, extroverts should control their impulses, listening more, instead of interrupting the interlocutor. On the other hand, the introvert could start by opening the debate. Thus, important information and points discussed in the meeting can be provided beforehand. The introvert likes to be prepared in advance, so he or she can deepen into the arguments.

## Exceptional processes for exceptional teams

Leading high-performance teams is a task that managers need to conduct in stages, without rush but with a lot of dynamism, perseverance, and passion. As in any everyday

149

circumstance, the first task is to define what you want to do and for what purpose.

Therefore, this process begins by defining and embracing what an exceptional team represents. An organization may have groups housed in different interaction spectrum areas: conflict - normalization - performance. As explained in this chapter, an outstanding team ranks in the latter.

Groups in phases of conflict are unable to create synergies or increase value together. Therefore, if the group work is flawed from the start, there will be no way to lead efficiently.

Once companies have understood their value, it is time to build those high-performance teams. At this stage, effective leadership will be critical. Ultimately, bosses have to assume a series of philosophies and considerations that allow them to navigate the path successfully:

• Set shared goals and avoid tunnel vision to unite talents, make them converge, and create value together.

• Promote transparency and honesty: provide a safe territory for workers to express themselves, make mistakes, and propose improvements. The omission of ideas due to submission or fear is one of the most damaging vices that companies suffer. Reversing this scenario is critical to exceptional team management.

• Generate positive pressure and attend to isolated contingencies that damage the team. Exceptional teams have the motivation to work under specific doses of stress; they stimulate each other to boost their productivity and value. However, there will always be members of the group who create difficulties. The leader's responsibility is to detect these conditions and manage them quickly. The objective is to prevent the harmful elements from infecting the entire team.

• Align the team towards positive conflicts. Disputes that arise between groups should translate into opportunities for improvement and growth. This is achieved through conscious leadership that provides healthy and constructive discussion and reflection between the parties.

• Promote the configuration of heterogeneous teams. The richness is in diversity. Homogeneous teams tend to shut down by nature. Therefore, organizations must build plural teams that can complement each other to multiply value.

These can be viewed as guides to a more humane and efficient compass that will help bosses build exceptional teams that allow them to reach their goals and complete the objective.

# CHAPTER 7: THE BOSS WHO DEVELOPS PEOPLE

## THE QUALITY OF CONVERSATIONS IN PEOPLE'S DEVELOPMENT

### Is it coaching enough?

Just as children learn from their parents and their role models through observation, we too learn from our bosses. We look at what they prioritize or what their style is when collaborating with their associates. We take their actions and advice as valid. We gain professional knowledge from their insights, acknowledgments, suggestions, corrections and even reprimands. But what if we have mediocre bosses? Or, even worse, what can we get from a bad or terrible boss? What defects do we acquire from them?

Throughout my professional career, I have had many bosses. I have worked with very competent and trained bosses in the most technical areas of work. I learned from them how important it was to meet budgets or maintain discipline in controlling costs. I have also had more creative and commercial bosses, from whom I learned to be more proactive, boosting income. Others have been bad bosses, and from them I assimilated little. I've even had terrible bosses. These last bosses were insecure, unprepared, and emotionally unstable people who used fear and manipulation to achieve their ends. From these bosses I ran as fast as I could. But the truth is that even having intelligent, decisive, and visionary bosses, I feel that I never had that extraordinary boss from which I learned the human part of the job, not only the technical dimension, but understanding the *human* as the area of emotional intelligence necessary to bring out the best in the people you work with.

I wish I had a multiplier boss who enhances people's talent, brings out their best energy and makes them better. A chief coach.

**All in all, even though companies and markets are full of coaching training, boss coaches are in short supply**. Today, organizations often ask their bosses to be good coaches. But it would be interesting to understand what they actually mean by that. Maybe they hope that some coaching techniques courses will act as a magic formula and, from one day to the next, they will train their bosses in this discipline and bring out the best in them. Coaching attributes could be seen this way as a form of *Snake Oil Liniment* that cures everything, back in its day. Same happened to Leadership. The recipe for every problem was leadership, so it began to be used for everything and lost part of its concreteness.

**There are currently intensive Master programs and certified courses in coaching. Still, paradoxically, the best coaches aren't aware that they are indeed the best, even without paying attention to the techniques. This is because their natural style allows them to exercise their primary function in their jobs: to bring out the best in people.**

When in my seminars I ask my audience what they remember about their best boss, the stated attributes are usually very similar in almost all cases:

"She was my best boss because she brought out the best in me."
"He was patient but demanding at the same time."
"He was on hand in attending to my problems, helping me solve them."
"Somehow, she inspired me to improve myself constantly."
"His trust and recognition were fuel to continue my effort."
"She saw potential in me and gave me more responsibilities."

While training in coaching could help you develop these competencies and achieve these goals, the truth is that exceptional bosses already have the insight they need without having to go through the classroom.

A good coach helps develop self-awareness. Therefore, more than a teacher, he is a guide capable of activating people to find answers and solutions for themselves through useful and pertinent questions. This inductive process allows people to identify their opportunities and make a firm commitment to improvement. However, Sir John H. Douglas Whitmore, who has been a pioneer in sports and executive coaching, states in his book *Coaching for Performance* that a good coach does not have to be a specialist in the professional area of his coachee. Because in the end, what matters is that in knowing how to ask the right questions, your "patient" can generate self-awareness and find the answers for himself [1]. On these lines, there is a quote from the writer Herman Hesse that could shed light on what the role of a coach is: Only within yourself exists the other reality you long for. I can give you nothing that does not already exist within yourself. I can only make visible to you your own universe.

A boss needs to have these skills, but you must know that it is not enough. A good leader cannot always be asking questions since there will be times when he or she will have to indicate and firmly establish how things must be done. At the same time, you will face challenges in which you will have to make honest comments, and these must be evoked so that they do not leave doubts, gaps or confusion. That is, you must develop communicative skills of clarity and assertiveness. For this reason, coaching is not enough if it limits us to ask questions. The goal of developing people and getting the best out of them means caring about the person and being more candid, transparent, and straightforward. Bosses must be teachers, advisers and guides alike.

In the same way, we tend to perceive coaching as a structured and formal process when, in reality, conversations between boss and employee tend to be more spontaneous and casual. Dialogue is a valuable opportunity to build relationships with our employees. For example, in five minutes of chat, inside or outside the office, we can reinforce the commitment to the company's objectives and values. We can also acknowledge good work, correct dysfunctional behaviors, and listen to our employees.

## Performance appraisal systems exclude managers from their responsibility to provide continuous feedback

A standard procedure in companies undermines meaningful one-on-one conversations between boss and employee: the annual performance review (or biennial). This method, which is executed in most organizations with the intention of improving people's productivity, causes the opposite effect since it conditions the interaction between the parties. This annual performance assessment often restricts the boss and the employee to speak about performance only once a year.

On this occasion, the boss must indicate the subordinates' successes and failures, but experience suggests the situation will likely not go well. The person evaluated perceives unfairness in the manager's opinions. If her boss has identified her achievements and mistakes in advance, she must communicate them in time to enhance or correct her performance. Especially regarding the weak points.

It is an unpleasant time for bosses and subordinates.

David Rock, Josh David, and Beth Jones indicate that many companies have noticed that the traditional evaluation system locks employees. It prevents them from growing [2]. Organizations like Microsoft, Accenture, Gap, Deloitte, Goldman Sachs, Lilly, Adobe, Netflix, NASA, Dell, among many others, have modified their traditional performance systems or, more directly, have eliminated them. This procedure, which evaluates employee productivity is often perceived as unfair, and people are unable to internalize their opportunities for improvement.

Any rating lower than four or five activates people's suspicions and puts them in a defensive mode. If our boss tells us, smiling, that we have met expectations and places us at a three, our brains will begin to compare us with other colleagues, thus perceiving a threat:

— "A three? But why a three and not a four? You have given Ricardo a four and Julia a five. I don't deserve less".

So even if the boss does a tremendous pedagogical exercise to explain the reasons for a three, even arguing it as objectively as possible, the employee will not accept the explanation or the result. All this could worsen if the results are linked to the annual bonus since people's self-criticism capacity would be blocked entirely.

**But the worst thing about this system is that it inhibits a boss from giving continuous feedback, both good and bad**. In this way, performance feedback is seen by managers as a tedious moment, like having to deal with the tax declaration once a year. Thus, they do not see giving regular feedback as a function within their obligations.

**At a minimum, I recommend that the boss and employee sit down to talk once a week. Many organizations have begun to implement similar dynamics.** For example, Gap Inc. changed its evaluation system in its corporate offices and required its managers to meet their employees regularly [3]. They also trained them on how to give feedback. Within the learning process, they advise managers to start the meetings by asking and listening first. Three questions from the managers in these sessions include:

- "What is working?"
- "Where are you having problems?"
- "What do you think you would do differently?"

The traditional performance meeting could continue to be held once a year, but it would never bring surprises again because the boss would already have had many previous encounters with his subordinates.

## Recognizing good work: a principle of generosity

If we want to promote the best in people, we must learn to recognize work and be generous. This must be the first intention of a good boss. When a manager points out that we have done an excellent job and details why, our brain secretes dopamine. According to the latest neuroscience studies, this neurotransmitter reinforces people's learning and motivation. It is the gasoline necessary to maintain the effort. Dopamine is associated with reward and keeps us motivated in the task. A study from the Wharton School in Pennsylvania has tested this theory in a laboratory. If a worker performs a job that makes sense and is recognized for it, productivity can increase by up to 50%. Before starting to carry out the work, people doing the test received a previous talk from the head of the institution in which they thanked them for their work and explained the impact they would have on other people. Similarly, and according to Harvard Medical School, the mere act of thanking can be one of the best ways to feel better.[4]

Gallup asks employees in its 360º evaluation - a questionnaire that I have referred to in previous chapters - if they have received recognition for a job well done in the last seven days. According to the research, after seven days, dopamine levels are depleted [5]. Therefore, it is recommended to give more positive feedback to people to raise their dopamine levels again.

In my opinion, however, this reasoning could be a bit unnatural or forced. Giving positive feedback should not be subject to a weekly time rule, because this could lead to many bosses using it superficially. Offering recognition is necessary, but it should never be trivial because there is something worse than not giving praise, and that is giving it in a shallow and manipulated way.

Unfortunately, a popular myth has been implanted in the heads of many managers and directors, which paralyzes them from being generous in this area. The myth advises not to recognize a job well done because this quality is already within the employee's obligations. This idea is associated, in turn, with the conception that is continuously recognizing work as counterproductive since it invites people to relax or, worse still, to nurture potential delusions of grandeur that makes them believe they are essential.

All this is a bit absurd and contradicts the most elementary of psychological laws. Generosity and assertiveness are not mutually exclusive. A boss must be generous in his recognition, and at the same time, he must be quick and direct in giving negative feedback. While good bosses accentuate the positives over the negatives, they must maintain their objectivity and insight.

## Miss Sloane's leadership doesn't make people better

We admire the determination and intelligence of our bosses. If you have to choose between having a very skilled boss but lacking in the caring dimension, and another boss who cares a lot yet doesn't know how to do the job and is completely incompetent, we prefer the former. Although competency and caring are not in contradiction, we should ask ourselves if the competent boss who complies with the numbers either diminishes or makes others better.

I call 'Miss Sloane leadership' the one that Jessica Chastain represents in the movie *Miss Sloane*. Elizabeth Sloan is a star executive and a very confident woman at a firm that defends powerful lobbies. When Miss Sloane walks into the meeting room and speaks, everyone is silent and stares open-mouthed. Everyone admires her intelligence and determination. If she asks you a question, you better have the answer ready. Be clear and direct. Don't ramble and, of course, don't say, "I don't know." Miss Sloane is the only one who sees beyond the rest. When her collaborators are analyzing a problem, she is already onto the next challenge.

Miss Sloan personifies the myth of heroic leadership, like Mr. Wolf in the movie *Pulp Fiction*, who is capable of solving any problem.

This leadership style that is projected in many films and media has been implanted in the collective consciousness. The problem with this heroic leadership is that it does a disservice to management, to the extent that it dwarfs the rest of its employees. Also, it is not realistic. Such heroic management micromanages people; it prioritizes meeting budgets over people's growth and the boss is unable to listen to others, concentrating his or her leadership style on imposing orders. In short, this type of boss subtracts knowledge and skills from collaborators instead of empowering them.

This leadership style can be useful in crises or when teams are stuck in a conflict phase. It can also be helpful in the short term. Nevertheless, such a management style can impair performance in the medium and long terms because it does not promote improvements in people, teams, or the company. This heroic boss pretends to have all the answers to problems and makes decisions without consulting the rest of the group. He does not extract more intelligence from his team because he does not challenge them to discover for themselves solutions to complex problems.

Miss Sloan's leadership happens in the first person singular. Often in my conversations with managers and executives, I also hear achievements in the first person. It is as if the unconscious myth of the hero leader had affected them, and it was all about trying to sell themselves better:

"I have changed this and that."
"Since I arrived, I have prioritized these issues."
"I have implemented these ideas ...".

Everyone wants to look like Miss Sloane.

It is also common in the hotel sector to see the figure of the director or department head as a micromanager or hero leader. It is common to hear phrases like:

"You have to be aware of everything so that there are no failures."
"The director has to know everything, including how the bed has to be made..." 6

In this way, the manager's figure is reduced to giving orders to others and saying how they have to do their work, correcting deviations and promoting new ideas and ways of working without considering the participation of the rest of their team.

## The conscious boss who multiplies talent

It is a myth that we only use only 10% of the brain. However, not so when it comes to assessing the 'percentage' or synergies of knowledge in most teams and organizations. We would win on the bet that 100% of the team's intelligence is not met in most cases. This is because many systems, conflicts, interests, beliefs, and bosses are not capable of multiplying the knowledge of people and groups.

161

A conscious boss is an agent capable of multiplying the knowledge and capabilities of the people he leads. It makes them smarter and more productive. In her book *Multipliers: How the Best Leaders Make Everyone Smarter*, Liz Wiseman states that the most influential leaders bring out the best in people, to the extent that they extract and extend their intelligence. [7]

Multiplying leaders see knowledge and skills as continually developing.

A company is made up of people. Therefore, their competitiveness will depend on the managers' ability to improve the talents and teams they lead. Best answers to problems or ideas to improve work must be generated by all. The more we involve our employees in the organization's cognitive system, the better the results can be. But for this to happen, a boss should be able to develop people and teams.

A manager requires skills in planning, change management, coordination, control, and results. However, companies should ask: Are the people who work there growing so that it impacts the growth of the organization itself?

## LEARN TO BE DIRECT WITHOUT FAILING TO BE OPTIMISTIC IN THE PROCESS

### The lack of honesty in the job

Let's do a hypothetical exercise. Let's imagine that we are entrusted with replicating the famous NPS (Net Promoter Score) tool. This tool, which will be explained a little more in later chapters, measures customer loyalty. The creators of this resource, Fred Reichheld and Rob Markey, emphasize the importance of asking the right question to users. For example, a good question for companies to ask is: "How likely are you to recommend the product or service to a family member or friend?" Like in the NPS, if we only asked one question, what should this single question be that measures the boss's quality?

In 2011, James L. Heskett proposed a similar exercise on Harvard's Working Knowledge platform, a space where academia and business share opinions and knowledge [8]. An interesting conclusion was that the most crucial management question should focus on trust. The level of trust we have in our bosses is key because it is the glue that holds everything and everyone together. But reality shows that there can be no trust if we do not have integrity and honesty. The word integrity comes from the Latin *integritas*, which also means wholeness. It is precisely the wholeness that often fails in people because they feel incapable of being themselves, with their defects and virtues. In short, they cannot be authentic.

Robert Kegan, a Harvard professor and Doctor of Psychology, has devoted his professional career to research, education, and consulting. His field of knowledge is the development of people and organizations. For him and many companies, such as Next Jump, Bridgewater and Decameron, professional and personal growth must go hand in hand. Besides, personal growth and business benefits must be put in the same equation [9]. Therefore, those companies that seek to separate professional development from staff should consider whether they are effective in their endeavors. Kegan reminds us that in most organizations, people put effort and energy into doing a second job for which they shouldn't be paid [10]. This second job, on the other hand, is very human, and consists of hiding weaknesses from managers and from others. Investing time to manage others' impressions, selling yourself better, getting into the political game, hiding uncertainties and doubt, is an utter waste of time and energy. In short, covering up our incompetence and limitations is a significant roadblock to any company's competitiveness. It is a stumbling block that prevents progress.

This lack of honesty is accentuated when companies try to implant an image of false professionalism, which affects collaboration between people, the intelligence of the organization, creativity, and problem analyses. These predispositions act as a stopper in people's adaptation and growth since they prevent them from feeling comfortable accepting that they have areas to improve. This scenario creates an environment of trust where people (including bosses) can feel safe to assume their vulnerabilities and work accordingly. A good boss has to foster an environment of honesty in which criticism does not feel like a personal attack or a job threat but as a real opportunity to continue advancing to the next level.

Let's see it in a more illustrative way. The following is a real case, but with fictitious names.

Elena is the main character of this story. She is very good at interpreting data and at numerical analysis. Also, she displays good technical knowledge and is very keen on troubleshooting. However, Elena is also known for her bad temper in dealing with her collaborators. She tends to get defensive and escalates the conflict if someone reminds her that she is not doing a good job. She is curt and unfriendly with many colleagues. However, she shows herself friendly and available with her bosses or those people in her inner circle.

Elena has signed up for several internal job offers, as her wish is to continue moving up within the company. But after showing her candidacy and going through one or more interviews, they always reject her profile. What Elena does not know is that she is already sentenced from the beginning. It is common knowledge that she has a severe relationship problem. No one will dare to see her in another position where collaboration and interdependence are more critical.

Elena can be defined as a zombie within the organization; she wanders without being aware of others' perceptions or feelings. She is also a walking dead in terms of career development. Everyone knows her well, which may be why they have resigned themselves to accepting her as she is. But what is clear is that no one would be willing to put her in positions of greater responsibility since her temperament would end up making things even more difficult.

The problem is that no one has had an honest conversation with her either, starting with her new boss. Elena has been with the company for more than six years, and neither her old nor her new boss had been able to clearly explain her problem. Neither did her colleagues, nor the heads of other areas of the company, such as Human Resources. Other workers in her situation may have already interpreted the signals, but Elena is not a person with great emotional intelligence. The vision she has of herself is that of a great professional, very competent, and with a great capacity for sacrifice at work. She spends many hours on it and sees her current situation within her company as very unfair.

Cases like Elena's are pervasive in organizations. Many people like Elena are unable to improve because no one takes on the responsibility of talking honestly with her. We would agree that one of the most challenging tasks for a boss

165

is to give negative feedback to collaborators, primarily when it is known that the receiver will not take it well. This is the main reason we sweeten our comments; we put a kind of verbal jam on our words to mitigate criticism. Other times, we tend to avoid these sensitive conversations because we don't want to hurt people's feelings or simply because we want to avoid conflict. So, therefore most bosses tend to adopt what Kim Scott defines as 'ruinous empathy', a position that consists of the famous "I am not going to be straight and tell her the truth because she is going to get defensive." The conversation could happen like this:

- Boss: I must acknowledge your excellent work with the management and results reports. You are always able to offer an excellent explanation of the financial data.
- Elena: Thank you. I strive to see patterns within data, and the truth is that I spend hours on Excel charts.
- Boss: Perfect. That's another thing that you have that we highly value: your ability to dedicate time to work. We all appreciate your effort.
- Elena: I'm glad you see it that way too. The truth is, I am very committed to my work.
- Boss: Maybe I should add, but only as an improvement, that you can be a bit more friendly with your colleagues. Sometimes we see you too focused on work and with little patience for others. But, well, nothing you can't improve. I'm sure that with the bit you put on, you will gain a lot.
- Elena: Thanks for the advice. You are partly right. I'm sure I could be a little warmer. The truth is that with some, it is not easy, but I will try.

And there Elena leaves happy to be recognized and satisfied to have received a good evaluation. It is also possible that her boss believes that after her words, Elena will be self-critical and improve in her relationships with others.

I like to call this illusion of having fixed things "The Gordon Ramsay Effect." The name comes from the famous television show in which the renowned chef must improve restaurant and hotel businesses. At the end of the show, and Gordon has given his recommendations, the audience might get the wrong impression that the character of a particular person has improved and perhaps that it will last. Many bosses have the same feeling after a conversation, but the reality is that a personality change does not happen overnight. In some cases, it does not happen at all.

## To be candid and caring

Kim Scott, a Google executive and CEO coach in Silicon Valley, wrote a great book about people's candidness. There is a general lack of honesty that prevents us from being honest and direct when correcting something in our collaborators or peers. The question is the following: Can we give criticism without sweeteners while being caring about the person? In her book *Radical Candor*, Scott shows the two crucial areas that every boss or colleague must pay attention to in order to face unpleasant -but necessary- conversations.

Every good boss must focus on performance and challenge people to grow. This implies that you not only have to acknowledge good work, but you have to correct people when necessary. A good boss must apply the appropriate corrections without neglecting the feelings and motivations of the person. In other words, great managers must take care of performance and the persona's human side equally. This is called Radical Honesty (Radical Candor) [11]. It is not about imposing our criteria to make the person inferior, nor about forgetting empathy in showing our collaborators what they have to improve. Difficult conversations will be easier to deal with if the employee perceives that our intentions are honest and optimistic. We give negative feedback for one purpose: we honestly believe that the persona can improve.

Other bosses are too direct and have no problem being assertive and straight with their employees' flaws. They can be defined as tough bosses. But Kim Scott warns that this is not the worst thing that can happen to a company. What she describes as Obnoxious Aggression allows people to react and wake up from their lethargy, at least.

As mentioned previously, Ruinous Empathy or Manipulative Insincerity are the worst things that could happen to an organization: neither of these two styles is direct. Hence, people don't quite see their problems.

See Elena's case with her boss: not wanting to hurt her feelings and avoid conflict, her boss avoided giving direct feedback (Ruinous Empathy). However, even more damaging is Manipulative Insincerity: feedback is emitted flawed with the issuer's interests, and any sincere concern for the employee is put aside.

Caring about the person

| Ruinous Empathy | Radical Candor |
|---|---|
| | Challenge the person |
| Manipulative Insincerity | Obnoxious Aggression |

Most bosses and companies fall into the Ruinous Empathy or Manipulative Insincerity quadrants because they want to avoid conflict and don't want to hurt people's feelings. Some famous techniques for giving feedback, such as the Sandwich Technique 12, in which the issuer begins with recognition or positive feedback, then insert negative feedback and ends, again, with positive feedback, can quickly turn into Ruinous Empathy or, worse, Insincere Manipulation. This is because many employees are only interested in the slices of bread and discard the sandwich's contents; that is, negative feedback. On the one hand, people tend to hear only what they want to hear; it is a difficult filter to remove. On the other hand, if the procedure demands positive feedback, it may force or even invent it. And thus, it implies falling into the territory of Insincere Manipulation.

It is not easy to be direct and attend to empathy simultaneously; the line between Radical Candor and Obnoxious Aggression is fragile. There are very clear and tough bosses when it comes to correcting people, and they forget to attend to the human part. They often articulate statements like: "I don't have time for sentimentality" or "behave like a professional" and usually have a mentality of zero tolerance for mediocrity. Although this management style can get short-term results, and people can respond accordingly to higher demands, I don't think it is entirely realistic.

Steve Jobs is credited with the phrase that says: "If you want to make everyone happy, don't be a leader. Sell ice cream." We can agree that there will always be unpopular decisions to make, but if we rely on these kinds of ideas, we will discard people's feelings. Even executives like Steve Jobs, Jeff Bezos, Michael Dell or Bill Gates, known for their zero

169

tolerance for mediocrity and an overly aggressive style, had to correct their temperament when giving feedback. Jeff Bezos is reported to have worked with a coach [13], and Steve Jobs tempered his character in his last professional stage [14]. Bill Gates today is a philanthropist who has little to do with Microsoft's aggressive Gates. Michael Dell also strove to improve his temperament - together with CEO Kevin Rollins - [15]. Ultimately, the point is that not all people accepted their ways of operating, and many brilliant collaborators didn't accept their aggressive manners. In the end, these negative episodes made talented people leave the company.

I've also had several autocratic bosses during my career who have never been shy about being direct. The problem was not only in the way they handled feedback but also in the content. The style was undoubtedly intimidating. Rather than arousing my self-criticism or motivation to improve, they produced the opposite: feelings of anxiety and fear that put me in a defensive mode and sapped my confidence. Furthermore, these bosses were also essentially wrong because while criticism was necessary, they were never able to recognize a job well done. They abused negative feedback to the detriment of positive feedback.

Let's establish the premise: A boss who only focuses on negative feedback is missing the mark. Such an approach demoralizes subordinates and creates feelings of injustice that will block their ability to reflect. These bosses, as we have seen before, are also dopamine killers.

## The Transcendent Leader: Optimism and Faith in People Matter

Abraham Maslow wrote the following: "The good boss or the good leader in most situations must have as a psychological prerequisite the ability to take pleasure in the growth and self-actualization of the people." [16]. The psychological prerequisite that Maslow mentions, which is also defined as an ability, is a part of the character linked to generosity. This is also a state of emotional maturity for which there are no shortcuts. It is challenging to teach, and in some cases, it is impossible to acquire. Most effective coaches positively infect with their optimism. They honestly believe in their collaborators' potential and often provoke positive reactions that allow them to meet their expectations in people.

The psychological ability to take pleasure in others' growth can be seen in the following situation: imagine that one of the members of your team, whom you admire, fails to progress in your company, either because it is a small company and there are not many opportunities or because other people do not detect the same potential you see in him or her. So, without much future ahead, this person decides to accept a job offer in another company, and your paths separate.

The question is: would you be deeply happy for him or her, knowing that your work will now be more difficult and that your company has lost a great talent? Only people who show that psychological prerequisite of being happy and proud of their employees' professional growth can answer *yes* to this question.

On the other side of the spectrum, there are insecure, emotionally immature bosses who will do everything possible to cover up your talent. They may be able to appropriate your ideas or reduce your prominence to the extent that they hide you from other managers. They see in you a threat or, selfishly, they can see your promotion only as a problem. If you leave, they will have to work more because you solved many issues. They will also have to train a new person for doing your job. This will make them roll up their sleeves and work more. Now they must get out of their comfort zone and get involved.

I always say that any company that cares about developing its employees' potential should warn these bosses that the talent does not belong to them. Talent must be available to the organization. On the other hand, it would be convenient to recognize and analyze quality indicators to measure in executives and managers, such as the number of people who have left their department and promoted to another area. More people, more recognition.

## The nature of the coach matters more than the technique

The technical part of coaching is often given too much importance. As I said before, coaching seems to be in fashion and, therefore, companies are training their managers in this discipline. They expect their bosses to be good coaches.

**The problem is that the most important thing about coaching is not its technique but the nature of the coach. If a boss is perceived as dishonest and mistrustful, there is no path forward.** Most likely, no one will internalize what the boss says. In most cases, people will show dissatisfaction with boss criticism in two ways: by giving up or being defensive. Regardless of how accurate the boss is in his or her feedback, people are not going to display self-awareness. It's elementary: if people perceive their boss's intentions as insincere, there will be no questions, comments, or observations that will make them change their approach.

A boss's credibility is built through the history of actions that he has made with his collaborators on a day-to-day basis. It is the same emotional bank account that Stephen R. Covey talked about in his famous book *The Seven Habits of Highly Effective People* 17. The personal bank account metaphor is nothing more than the positive actions you have taken on, day to day, reinforcing your credibility. Therefore, you must ask yourself the following question: How positive do you think your bank account is?

Awakening self-criticism or generating self-awareness in people is not easy. While there are more open-minded people who recognize that they may have a problem, the truth is that there are others who are rather close-minded. And with them, it may not be worth continuing. **On the other hand, it must also be made clear that inducing self-awareness in people happens only by influencing others. And like trust, influence goes in two directions. Therefore, you must reflect if, in some way, you too are letting yourself be influenced by your collaborators. Are you also open to self-criticism when feedback comes from your direct collaborators? Are you open-minded enough to reflect on what they are saying?**

Let's go back to our case with Elena. Now the new boss is more honest and transparent. She is also more empathetic and sincere in her intentions. The following might be a *radically honest* conversation the new boss would have with Elena:

- Boss: Hello, Elena. I would like us to have an honest conversation that no one has had with you so far. Can I be

173

frank with you? Will you be able to listen with an open mind to my feedback -which you may not like, but is intended only to improve you and make you succeed in this company?

- Elena (getting serious at this moment): Sure.

- Boss: Good. In this conversation, I am not going to go into assessing what is good about you. I think you already know what your strengths are: you are very good with numbers, you know how to do your job, you work hard and, without any doubt, you show that you are committed to the company goals... However, these positive light rays are obscured by a dark cloud that covers everything else. Everyone sees that dark cloud, and that prevents them from perceiving the positive in you.

Elena becomes more serious, but now she is getting a little pale as well. She is anticipating emotional pain.

- Boss: You have a fatal flaw in interpersonal relationships. The truth is that I should have had this conversation with you before. But I needed to confirm for myself your predecessors opinions. So, I have to be self-critical as well, on my part and the part of the company because I am sure that no one has been direct enough with you about this fatal flaw of yours.

You have a severe problem with interpersonal relationships that is affecting everything that you do. Your collaboration abilities and your relationships with others are usually very curt. You are often defensive when someone suggests an improvement to you. For example, a week ago, I had to warn you about your overbearing behavior in responding to Enrique's email.

- Elena: I don't see it that way. Enrique is always delaying our work from the purchasing department, and I thought it pertinent to remind him. My work is also affected by these delays. (Elena is moving from a passive attitude to a more defensive one).

- Boss: Enrique may have to improve some things as well. The problem is that your way of saying things amplifies the conflict. People don't reflect on what you are saying, rather how you are saying it. In any case, I do not want you to be left alone with this incident but to be able to reflect more objectively and generally on your availability, open-mindedness, flexibility and reactions to your colleagues.

- Elena (Now crying. Her irritability has turned to a feeling of frustration and anger): It is not fair that my work is judged on this! I don't see it this way!

- Boss (bringing her a box of Kleenex tissues from the drawer): I understand your feelings of frustration. You may not see it right now, but surely you will, after a moment of deeper reflection. You have to do *something,* because otherwise, you will not be as effective as you want. My intention with you, being so clear, has only one purpose: that you succeed in this company and get the best out of yourself. I understand that now your feelings may prevent you from clearly seeing this weakness. It will only be possible to overcome this phase if you recognize the problem. When you see that there is an issue, then you can improve your relationships with others and be more effective at work.

Regardless of the results after this conversation, Elena's boss is that transcendent leader I am referring to. He is a sincere and direct leader, but he shows empathy when correcting his collaborators. He doesn't get carried away by the other person's emotions, but rather understands her feelings. Above all, he is a leader who injects optimism and confidence despite being the bearer of negative news.

Whoever has such a boss indeed has a treasure. I never had that treasure.

## MEDITATION IN THE FACE OF CRITICISM

## Pain + reflection = progress

This conversation would continue to unfold that day as well as in the following days. An improvement plan will also follow, agreed between Elena and her boss.

Elena lacks emotional intelligence. First, she cannot be self-aware about her impacts on other people. Second, she cannot manage her emotions well. Nor can she empathize with others or see the effect that her interactions generate on her colleagues. Likewise, she fails to address her social capital or networking. She does not recognize the importance of the relationships with others in her work.

Ray Dalio explains in his management principles at Bridgewater that it is inevitable to go through the "pain phase" when receiving negative feedback. The author refers to this emotional pain as "touching the nerve." Psychologists call it "the hitting button" [18]. It is a stage in which feelings arise because the amygdala is entering the scene, expressing a wounded ego. Our amygdala has a critical role in the brain, as it allows us to react to threats. This component of our limbic system has contributed to our evolution and survival as a species. The problem is that in a work environment, our amygdala can send us wrong messages of danger. But nowadays, there is no longer a saber-toothed tiger at the door. We must be aware of this and not let our amygdala take control unless the danger is real and threatens our physical integrity.

The pain Ray Dalio refers to corresponds to feelings of agitation, frustration, and irritability, when someone tells us that we are not that good at something or that we have a problem. Neuroscience studies show that rejecting criticism from others is more humane than we once thought. In reality, criticism poses a full-blown threat to our psychological status. David Rock talks about the feeling of exclusion or psychological pain that is generated when receiving negative feedback from others. The alert instinct is activated through the amounts of cortisol that our brain is producing from the moment our boss approaches us with a serious face and says: "Can I comment on something?" 19. The reality is that people do not want to be unskilled or wrong. For this reason, our amygdala, personified as our ego, will do everything possible to activate defense mechanisms that protect us.

That is why it is essential to create environments of psychological safety to face these very human reactions. **People will not be open to criticism unless they perceive that it is safe to do so. For this reason, bosses must be the first to show that it is safe to be vulnerable. They can achieve this if they start by setting an example: admitting their mistakes to others, accepting that they also have weaknesses to work on, acknowledging their indecision in some event and even confessing aloud possible ignorance of specific complex problems.**

It is known at Bridgewater that you can only advance to the next level if your vulnerabilities are addressed. What happens is that these vulnerabilities, which we all have, are usually protected unconsciously. Ray Dalio indicates that pain also sends us a message.

"Why do I have this feeling of irritability?"
"Why was my ego threatened by this person's comment?"

If we meditate on it, the pain disappears.

I will cover the topics of Mindfulness and Meditation in Chapter 9. Presently I'd like to put forward that we can practice mediation in many ways. Basically, it consists of sitting and observing, from the position of spectator, without judging; you must see yourself in the situation and contemplate the emerging feeling. It is a personal moment of reflection.

**During a meditation practice, our brain's most evolved structure enters the picture. I am referring to our prefrontal cortex. This part of the cerebral cortex can observe spectator feelings and body reactions as neutral without being carried away. In a meditative exercise, we can recreate the conversation and the emotions we experienced while our boss told us that we had a problem. Our pain can now be the focus of our attention.**

In Elena's case, our protagonist could have begun to adopt the routine of meditating 10 or 20 minutes a day. Get home, sit down to meditate and contemplate the scene. This exercise will allow you to examine what is happening in your body: the accelerated heart rate, the pressure in the head and stomach, among other processes. All these biological and physiological reactions in your body can be seen and felt from a higher position, like an impartial linesman in a tennis match. The objective is to recreate a moment and observe it from a fixed vantage point, without being carried away by feelings.

**You don't have to be a meditation expert to see results. You only need apply yourself to detect the immediate effects in reducing stress, frustration, and irritability.**

We cannot ignore the possibility that, despite everything, Elena might not end up recognizing her problem. This impossibility is a way of getting stuck: your amygdala has taken control of your life, and your feelings of irritability, stress and restlessness have transformed into resentment and dissatisfaction. It seems that there are people who feel that trillions of stars and galaxies in the universe have conspired to mark a fate of injustice and suffering on them. Therefore, perhaps here we would have an impenetrable bottleneck. The following questions may arise from this scenario:

• How big is this problem?
• How is it affecting the rest of the team?
• What might it entail?
• Do this person's strengths outweigh their weaknesses?

Depending on the answers, we would have to act in one way or another. Making a decision becomes essential.

# Part II: Enhance the power in yourself

# CHAPTER 8: THE LEADER'S INTERNAL OPERATING SYSTEM

## WHAT IS INSIDE AFFECTS WHAT IS OUTSIDE

### Los Rodeos

The next story I'm going to tell is not a pleasant one. It is about the worst plane crash that has ever happened in the history of aviation. Still, it is a working example to illustrate how hard skills, such as technical knowledge, experience, or judgment, can be affected by our internal operating system.

Los Rodeos, Tenerife, March 27, 1977. Two Boeing 747s are about to collide and cause a devastating air catastrophe: 583 people will die that tragic day. Those planes shouldn't have been there, but they were diverted because of a terrorist attack which occurred at Las Palmas airport.

A host of circumstances, problems, mistakes, wrong decisions, and bad luck will coincide in a few hours. But among the series of unfortunate events, there was one that the investigation highlighted above all: Captain Jacob Veldhuyzen Van Zanten should not have taken off without the final authorization of the control tower.

That day, with a fog that reduced visibility to less than 700 meters, KLM Flight 4805 would run over Pan Am America

Flight 1736, which, disoriented, was trying to leave the airport's only runway, following instructions from the control tower.

This is what happened on the KLM plane:

-Captain Jacob Veldhuyzen: OK. We have 700 meters visibility here now..." (pushing the accelerator lever)
-1st Officer Klaas Meurs: "Wait a minute. We don't have ATC clearance"
-Captain Jacob: "I know that" (slows down, showing his frustration). Go ahead, ask!"

After a few seconds, the capital begins takeoff again without authorization from the control tower. This time, affirming with assertiveness: "We're going." But this time no one disputes his decision. In a few seconds, it would hit the Pan Am plane in the middle of the runway.

- What happened that day?
- How can this negligence from one of the most renowned KLM pilots be explained?
- How is it possible that the rest of the crew allowed the captain to break such an obvious rule?

Jacob Veldhuyzen Van Zanten was one of KLM's most experienced pilots, with more than 11,000 flight hours. Instructor and trainer of young pilots, he had been chosen by the airline to participate in international forums on safety. Van Zanten was foremost in his field and a celebrity within the company. Moments after the accident, unaware that their captain was involved in the incident, he was contacted to be part of the investigation team.

The Dutch civil authorities did not acknowledge the investigation's conclusion, which placed most of the responsibility for the catastrophe on Van Zanten. The Dutch claimed that part of the fault had been the radio communication system, the Spanish controllers, and the airport. [1]

But the reality was that Jacob Van Zanten was frustrated that day. He wanted to take off at all costs and make up lost flight hours; he also wanted to avoid the crew and passengers having to spend the night in Tenerife. The captain's plans were focused on leaving as soon as possible to Las Palmas, and from there, return to Amsterdam that same day. This also explains his decision to refuel an extra 55 tons of fuel in Los Rodeos. Van Zanten was in a rush to take off and recover his original flight plan.

As the fog receded again, the captain's anxiety increased even more. It is a familiar feeling. Although in another context, we have all experienced a moment of similar frustration and stress. **In such an anxious situation, our amygdala is activated, taking control. This small almond-shaped structure located in our brain's hippocampus can hijack our neocortex when this happens. Suddenly, the amygdala has deactivated vital cognitive resources such as attention span and judgement.** It is the 'fight or flight' that makes it impossible for us to make the correct decisions.

However, the facts demanded prudence and more attention, not only to the external context but also internally. Perhaps Captain Van Zanten could have reflected diligently, generating self-awareness, and say to himself: "Wait ... what am I feeling? Why this anxiety?" "Why am I in this rush to take off?" "I have fog in front of me, preventing visibility, and this airport has a dangerous history of accidents."

183

In other words, the internal operating system has to send alarm signals and activate adequate resources in an uncertain and complex scenario. The situation demanded more attention, temperance, a dose of prudence, and patience.

It is also very likely that Van Zanten knew the history of Los Rodeos. This airport was notorious for its safety issues; it had seen an accident in 1972 and was perceived as an unsafe airport. German pilots considered it a "nightmare" 2. The experienced pilot could have been humbler, reflecting more internally. Probably, in a moment of lucidity and calm, when the first officer reminded him that they did not have authorization from the control tower, he could have paused and realized:

- "But... what am I doing!? I am contravening the norms that I usually teach to others". "Why am I so frustrated? Could this anxiety lead me to make a fatal decision?

The preparation and technical knowledge of the captain were not the problems. Something went wrong, and it wasn't his expertise as a pilot.

What went wrong? His internal operating system failed. Van Zanten could not generate self-awareness in action; sit back and breathe, waiting a few seconds before making his decision. Marc Brackett, a psychologist at Yale University, calls this the meta-moment 3. **It refers to the moment of stepping back and taking a deep breath in the face of a negative emotional state. By doing this, we activate our parasympathetic nervous system, reducing the cortisol that our body produces, which induces stress levels. This simple action could have changed the course of events.**

Victor Frankl, a famous neurologist and psychologist, father of logotherapy and existential analysis, is credited with the phrase: "Between stimulus and response, there is a space. In that space lies our freedom and our power to choose our response. In our response lies our growth and our happiness." Although it is not clear that Frankl was indeed the author of the quote, it is interesting to mention it because it warns of our automatic responses. **That space in which 'freedom' and 'power' lies is called self-awareness. And it is vital to improving our quality of thinking, judging, and deciding.**

Jacob Van Zanten could have been able to visualize his emotions and label them. This process allows us to understand our feelings and react better to the situation. Studies prove that only the simple act of translating emotions into words contributes to calming our amygdala [4]. So, Van Zanten might have been able to label and observe his internal processes while maintaining an internal dialogue: "Wait ... what I'm feeling is anxiety". "It's interesting to see how it's affecting my body."

Ellen J. Langer, a psychologist and professor at Harvard has long studied the illusion of control and decision making. Langer was one of the first psychologists to focus her research on treating full consciousness or mindfulness. It's the opposite state, a lack of awareness or lack of attention in our daily processes, called mindlessness. This lack of awareness makes us closely follow the rules and routines, like automatons, without paying attention or discussing them. [5]

Inattention was also fatal on Air Florida Flight 90. In 1982, an Air Florida plane taking off from the Washington DC airport crashed into the Potomac River bridge. The accident investigation concluded that the pilots forgot to activate the aircraft's anti-ice system, despite the external conditions of snow and ice, and with a temperature of -4º on the tarmac. The inattention that Ellen Langer refers to as mindlessness happened during the checklist procedure before leaving. This was the conversation recorded moments before takeoff [6]:

-Captain Larry Wheaton: "Pilot heat?"
-First Officer Roger Pettit: "On.
-Captain: "Engine anti-ice?"
-First officer: "Off."

The same checklist that they would have repeated hundreds of times, this time required a different answer: the plane's anti-ice system would have to have been activated. Investigations into the accident also concluded that Captain Wheaton was in a hurry to get out after being delayed by 45 minutes. Just like at Los Rodeos.

**The point is that this same case study could be repeated in different contexts, with various actors, and still have a similar outcome, an outcome less dramatic but as regrettable from a business point of view. It could be the top executive in a multinational who makes the fatal decision to buy another company. Maybe a successful entrepreneur unable to see the threat of a new competitor. Or the founder of a company that does not know how his behavior affects his organization's culture.**

## The character of the leader

Our character is made up of our belief system, values, motivations, and personality traits. It is the code with which our internal operating system is written.

This chapter will focus on the leader's inner operating system. In their book *Developing Leadership Character*, Mary Crossan, Gerald Seijts, and Jeffrey Gandz, professors at the Ivey Business School in Toronto, write that character is the fundamental principle for decision-making and the essential functioning of a leader. Our internal operating system affects everything that surrounds us: what we prioritize, our values, and how we interpret the world. Our character will also determine how we manage our conflicts and cope with our frustrations and setbacks. It also defines the goals we pursue and the way we interact with other people. 7

The leader's inner operating system is vital for determining his or her effectiveness in life and work. It is also be paramount to developing the right culture and values within a company. Nelson Mandela explained that one of the most challenging things to achieve was not changing society but transforming people individually. Gandhi also said that people should be the change they want to see in their peers and in the world.

Because this is the issue: we can never bring out the best in others if we cannot bring out the best in ourselves. In previous chapters, I described a conscious high-performance organizational culture. I also shared the vision of a knowledge service worker. For this to be possible, a boss has to be a good team leader and a people coach. **However, as we have seen, exceptional coaches, rather than simple technique, have the credibility. And the credibility of any person is not achieved without emotional intelligence, and especially the ability to generate self-awareness. In other words, understand your own emotions, motivations, and values, and at the same time, generate awareness of others.**

People with inner power are more aware. They are prepared to operate in a more uncertain and complex environment. They are leaders who are aware of their limitations, but without being unaware of their strengths. In fact, they make good use of each of them. In reality they are people who make better use of their emotions. Their power emanates from a more evolved personal internal operating system, which makes them work more efficiently.

## KEY COMPETENCIES OF THE CONSCIOUS LEADER

Have you ever felt powerful?

Leading is a way of using power: not only the ability to influence others, but also yourself. The latter is the most difficult, and also what we work on the least, both personally and professionally.

Social power is the capacity to control others' states and behaviors. Personal power the ability to control our own states and behaviors, says Amy Cuddy, a Harvard professor, in her best-selling book *The Power of Presence*. "Personal power is characterized by freedom from the dominance of others. It is infinite, as opposed to zero-sum — it's about access to and control of limitless inner resources, such as our skills and abilities, our deeply held values, our true personalities, our boldest selves". [8]

**We all have an inner power to develop. Most of the time, it is there hidden, asleep, and forgotten. However, this power can significantly influence us in such a way that it can affect our vision of things, our value system, decisions, motivations, and behaviors. This inner power will determine**

**our success as individuals, not only at work but also in personal relationships and life.**

Leading yourself is a way to use that inner power. However, this facet is often neglected. Our professional development typically focuses more on acquiring knowledge, adding experience, and applying our technical skills to the job. Among what we would define as a successful career, there are times when we are offered more responsibility, money, and power; we have the opportunity to lead a team or an organization. Or start a company. However, this career path does not guarantee personal development.

Like so many other managers, I have found myself in this situation. At one point in my working life, my motivation was to advance positions and get promotions. This also means gaining more knowledge and experience. Some of us invest a lot of money and effort into executive professional education. We achieve new professional skills, more excellent strategic vision, and knowledge in different areas of the company. However, degrees and experience are not a guarantee of personal improvement. What's more, we may even suffer a roadblock. For example, corporate degrees or professional academic certificates can give us the illusion that we are very good at what we do.

Remember the entropy I mentioned in chapter 2? Entropy can show up in many ways. For example, it could be disguised as complacency in the form of professional superiority. An inflated ego clouds our ability to evaluate ourselves objectively. In this way, we can deceive ourselves, believing ourselves better than we are, and our judgment can be disturbed when making decisions. Gary Vaynerchuck, a famous entrepreneur and one of the most acclaimed authors at the moment, notices many entrepreneurs' error when it comes to misinterpreting the market. In some way, they think they are invulnerable because they have done it before. They believe that their intuition is superior and that their business ideas are destined to succeed... Until the market surprises them and puts them in their place. [9]

Neither business schools nor the corporate world delves into personal growth. This has also produced a limited view of professional competencies. **When we strive to improve and advance in our work facet, we are inclined to work on everything that makes us more expert and knowledgeable. But when it comes to working on other inner areas, such as our character or our emotional intelligence, we don't put as much effort into it. Perhaps we can anticipate its importance, but we do not give it the same affection that we would give to the more technical or creative facet. And here lies a big mistake, because we try to be more effective without realizing that we are operating with an outdated operating system.**

The so-called 'hard-skills competencies' required of a manager, such as solving problems, good judgment to make decisions, strategic vision, and analytical skills in interpreting information, are essential but not enough.

Warren Bennis is the author who has probably done the most for leadership. Professor Bennis was among the first to show us that leading others is also a personal challenge. He wrote: "Leadership is character. It is not just a superficial question of style but has to do with who we are as human beings and with the forces that have shaped us. The process of becoming a leader is much the same as the process of becoming an integrated human being." [10]

What are the essential internal areas that a conscious leader must work on? There are two:

1. Self-awareness
2. Knowledge and management of emotions

## AREA #1: SELF-AWARENESS

Warren Bennis warned that the leader should not lie to himself, and himself above all. "What is true for leaders is, for better or for worse, true for each of us." And he continues, "We are our own raw material. Only when we know what we're made of and what we want to make of it can we begin our lives—and we must do this despite an unwitting conspiracy of people and events that move against us." 11

But how realistic is this statement?

**Although Bennis described a critical path in our professional trajectory as exceptional bosses, the reality seems more complicated. The leader does lie to himself. Indeed, he or she tends to do so continuously and unconsciously. We all deceive ourselves to a greater or lesser extent. It is the most human thing we have.**

Most of us have blind spots. Our ignorance, for example, prevents us from recognizing and naming our emotions. Not only do we fail to vocalize what we often feel, but we are also unable to understand what exactly we are feeling.

But we also have blind spots; we can see ourselves in a way that is not consistent with other people's opinions. Again, we can fall into the delusion of competency and think of ourselves as more competent than we are. It is a self-awareness gap shown by managers and directors. Most

191

bosses rank above average when they are asked to evaluate themselves, hence self-awareness is a widespread inability, one which eventually affects a better use of our internal operating system. The same way the iOS of our iPhone or iPad continually updates, providing better features, self-awareness allows us the update to a more improved internal operating system.

Professors David Dunning and Justin Krueger showed in their studies that people often might be more incompetent than we think [12]. A lack of intellectual humility can be confusing, and it is known as the Dunning-Krueger effect. **This cognitive bias causes people with less preparation or knowledge to believe that they are more prepared or intelligent. In this way, they incorrectly measure their skill and ability against experts.** The ignorant one thinks he is smarter. But as we deepen our knowledge, the opposite happens. With more knowledge, little by little, we become aware of our ignorance, eventually even being able to underestimate ourselves. Humility invades us and can lead us to a sort of 'intellectual despair.' In the book *Apology for Socrates*, Plato talks about his teacher. The philosopher Socrates, convinced that he could not be the wisest, decided to investigate among the guilds of wisdom. He spoke with politicians, poets, artisans and speakers. He claimed that everyone believed they knew more than they did. Socrates said: "I am wiser than this man, for neither of us appears to know anything great and good; but he fancies he knows something, although he knows nothing; whereas I, as I do not know anything, I do not fancy that I do. In this trifling particular, then, I appear to be wiser than he, because I do not fancy I know what I do not know." [13]

In colloquial terms, this illusion of an expert can be referred to as 'The Brother-in-Law effect': a reference to the many brothers-in-law's tendency to give an opinion on any matter, wanting to appear to be smarter than others. However, the Dunning-Krueger bias can also affect people who are supposed to be experienced in a field of knowledge. Many entrepreneurs and managers suffer from this cognitive bias. A lack of professional humility could play tricks on them. Conscious leaders like Ray Dalio have always been clear about this cognitive dysfunction and have created guiding principles in their company to avoid it. In this way, some corporate values at Bridgewater Associates are governed by self-conscious postulates such as:

• "Truth at all cost." Ego and hierarchies can be an obstacle to the truth.
• "It is even important to know what you don't know." We all have blind spots, and our job is to discover them with others' help and through our reflection.
• "Be assertive and open-minded." To get to the truth, you have to be transparent with yourself and with others.

Tasha Eurich speaks of self-awareness as the meta-leadership capacity of the 21st century. In her book *Insight*, Eurich introduces us to self-awareness from a broader perspective 14. It is the ability to get to know ourselves better and see how others see us. Eurich cautions that the fact that we are good at generating self-awareness does not guarantee that we will also see how other people perceive us. I can know my internal processes very well but be utterly ignorant of how others perceive me.

Self-aware people know their values and the principles that guide their decisions. They are clear about what they like to do most and what motivates them. They are self-conscious of their inner processes understanding better their emotions, but they also know the impact their emotions and behaviors have on others.

They are conscious leaders. The opposite of a mindful leader is a bad boss or a mediocre boss. Any manager can have a brilliant academic profile, be highly intelligent, and have extensive work experience. Still, they will never increase their effectiveness if they cannot update their internal operating system. Perhaps this leader shows a big ego that does not allow him to change his mind or listen to others. Maybe she is an insecure person, unable to make essential and unpopular decisions because she urgently needs to please everyone. It is also possible that he is an executive incapable of bringing out the best in others because he is not sincere or authentic with his collaborators, hence no one trusts him. It is also likely that anxiety and temperament are affecting the performance of employees. Therefore, the internal operating system is diminishing their technical competencies, such as the ability to manage information, analyze context, develop an accurate strategic vision, and make critical decisions.

But the willingness to generate self-awareness is also related to organizational culture. In this book's opening chapters, I examined the importance of working on the company culture. There, I said that the corporate culture is linked to its leaders' character, starting with the founder of the company. The fact is that even the most brilliant entrepreneurial project can collapse over time if the founder and his closest management team are not capable of generating self-awareness. Suppose they are not apt to examining their beliefs, values, and behaviors properly and thoroughly.

## Uber: how a leader's lack of values can affect a company's culture

This second anecdote that I am going to relate might at first sound repetitive, but rather shows something new. It is a story of a visionary businessman who nonetheless was unable to unleash other people's potential and improve his organization. It is the story of an executive who only attends to technical skills, without paying attention to character. A leader who does not reflect on his values and instead displays dysfunctional behaviors that infect his organization

**As happens with patients who are unaware of their condition, companies also tend to ignore their asymptomatic ailments until the symptoms materialize. At the time, Uber was seen as an example of innovation, talent and job satisfaction. But inside, the environment was beginning to suffocate some.**

The founder of Uber always wanted to create an organization governed by leadership principles similar to those of Amazon. Values that promote innovation, talent, meritocracy, proactivity, and employee autonomy. But are these leadership guiding principles enough for creating a great organization? The problem often arises when businesses focus only on 'hard' values and competencies, only looking at performance. They are certainly necessary, but they need to be balanced with 'soft' values and competencies, such as respect, tolerance, humility, and honesty. Similarly, when companies treat financial results as an end in and of themselves, they often overlook toxic behaviors, especially when an offender delivers results.

Such was the case with Uber, a company that was becoming an ill organization, where toxic and unethical behaviors were encouraged.

In Uber, furthermore, cases of sexual harassment were happening to several women. Susan Fowler was one of them. This computer engineer had reported the harassment of her boss to Human Resources. She had even provided evidence from screenshots! In these captures, you could read her boss's sexual advances. However, when Susan reported the abuse, human resources passed the buck. Even though the evidence was so obvious, they were unwilling to take action. This attitude was that the harasser was a manager with outstanding evaluations and obtained excellent results in his work.

Wondering if it was just happening to her, Fowler decided to talk to other workers. In her research, she discovered other cases, women who had suffered the same type of harassment from the same person or other men who worked in the company. Tired of reporting to Human Resources and having them do nothing and seeing how her bosses threatened to retaliate for persisting in her accusations, she decided to accept another job offer. But first, she decided to publish her story on her Blog: the article was titled: *"Reflecting On One Very, Very Strange Year At Uber.* [15]

The New York Times noticed and recognized the relevance of the post. What could have been a publication of little significance became a story of vast magnitude. There were many other allegations, like Susan's, from employees about the company's work climate.

The board of directors, alarmed by the reported events, decided to hire a law firm's services to investigate all these accusations. This law firm initiated an internal audit, arranged interviews with active employees and others who had left their jobs, looking under rugs, and problems began to come to light. Unacceptable behaviors such as cocaine consumption at company parties, vandalism, sexism, unethical cases with suppliers and customers, toxic people who were untouchable, internal wars over colleagues and bosses' work, projects having stopped due to fights between departments, etc. This entire process ended with the forced resignation of the CEO and founder of the company, along with other executives.[16]

What does all this have to do with Travis Kalanick's personal values?

As I've mentioned often in this book, the leader sets the tone. When one investigates Kalanick's statements or behavior, one may detect a worrying lack of values. **The common thing is that those entrepreneurs who founded their companies widely spread their character throughout that company. But the opposite can also happen. Their lack of moral values creates a void where behaviors are allowed that wouldn't happen elsewhere. Often this process is unconscious. Therefore, we should ask ourselves if the character we reflect helps make the company better or if inappropriate behaviors are poisoning the organizational culture.** In this case, Travis's business brilliance was overshadowed by the playboy demeanor he often displayed. He used to brag about picking up and sleeping with girls because he was famous [17]. He even encouraged male staff to pick up women at corporate parties.

In an email addressed to 400 employees, pretending to make a joke of it, he notified them of the hours they could have sexual relations, based on two rules. The email said:
Subject: *"URGENT, URGENT. READ THIS IMMEDIATELY !!!! You better read it or I'll kick your ass."*
Message: *[...] I hope you have a fucking experience. This is a celebration! We all deserve it. [...] Do not have sex with*

*another employee UNLESS a) you have asked that person for the privilege and they have responded with an emphatic 'YES! I will have sex with you' AND b) the two (or more) of you do not work in the same chain of command. Yes, that means that Travis will be celibate on this trip. #CEOlife #FML."* [18]

Travis, like millions of people on the planet, had not matured mentally despite being an adult. His character faults had clouded his intelligence, strategic vision, and technical ability. His internal operating system was dysfunctional, not being able to generate self-awareness. He needed to be aware of his actions and behaviors and how they were affecting others. He also had to be mindful of how they impacted the business. Travis was simply unaware of how his dysfunctional internal operating system affected his company's work environment, employee motivation and team collaboration. Just as a virus can affect a computer's operating system, Travis's work was affecting his company's culture.

## AREA #2: UNDERSTANDING AND MANAGING EMOTIONS

How many times have we heard about emotional intelligence (EQ), yet still know so little about our emotions? After so many studies and conclusions confirming the importance of emotions in the working environment, how is it possible that many bosses are so ignorant of their feelings?

For example, it is curious to see how this emotional ignorance can affect a company's most influential people. The president or CEO may be allowed to express negative emotions, such as anger or frustration regularly, but the lower one in the hierarchy could well lose his job if behaving in the same way. And yet it is the emotions of those higher up that have the most impact. Why? Because they spread more quickly to the rest. Psychologists speak of emotional contagion [19]. Fear, anger, anxiety, negative stress, envy... all of these can destroy a team. If the boss - or anyone else - frequently expresses these emotions, the team will suffer. In some ways, all of this also affects work.

The good news is that the contagion of moods can also be spread more productively. Exceptional bosses bring out the best in us by encouraging these more positive moods. Their ability to influence us, align us towards common goals, inspire us, or draw more energy from the team, does not happen by chance. "Great leaders move us. They ignite our passion and inspire the best in us. When we try to explain why they are so effective, we speak of strategy, vision, and powerful ideas. But the reality is much more primal: Great leadership works through the emotions." Says Daniel Goleman. "No matter what leaders set out to do—whether it's creating strategy or mobilizing teams to action—their success depends on how they do it. Even if they get everything else just right, if leaders fail in this primal task of driving emotions in the right direction, nothing they do will work as well as it could or should." [20]

By this, I do not mean that we have to suppress emotions like anger and anxiety and see things in a rose color all the time. Emotions such as anger or surprise can be productive at specific times. For example, the occasional anger of a manager can redirect priorities or wake people from their lethargy. Good bosses can also induce a sense of 'urgency' or positive stress to draw more energy from people at work. The surprise of a manager can also redirect priorities. However, these emotional tactics are no longer significant when the manager *only* uses these tools. A boss's emotional ignorance manifests itself when they raise their voice frequently, displaying frustration. Or when they are communicating non-verbal expressions of anger or a cutting demeanor, or when they use derogatory responses when addressing their collaborators.

When bosses aren't aware of their negative emotions, they incorporate them into their management style by default. We could call these bosses *emotional consciousness dimwits*. Other times they are *emotionally unconscious dimwits*, ignorant of their moods and how they affect others. And yet they are dimwits in both cases because they are unaware of how their emotions affect work. In my professional career, I have had the misfortune to come across more of the former. But the common thing is that many bosses are unaware of their emotions. It is as if they live in a parallel work universe.

Making matters worse, they also often suffer from the Dunning-Krueger effect that I referred to earlier. If you ask them what they think their employees think of them, they may evaluate themselves positively. **For this reason, organizations are urged to implement 360º feedback systems, any feedback tool that allows people to evaluate their bosses.**

Emotions, therefore, influence everything we do. They are there to make us smarter and more effective. We cannot exclude them from our lives. Although some managers may see them as an impediment to being more rational, practical, and effective, the truth is that science has already proven that they are there for a reason. We can try to suppress them, but they will turn against us.

Emotions should not be suppressed but rather recognized and understood. And ultimately, we must handle them. In the next chapter, I will explain how to do this. But now, it is enough to understand that emotions are natural and that they can help us be more effective.

How?

1. By offering us more information.
2. By improving our judgment in decision making.
3. By enhancing our learning and creativity.

## Emotions can bring pearls of knowledge about ourselves

If we reflect on them, our emotions can provide us with pearls of information. My feelings of anger, surprise or satisfaction can give me useful information about my mental processes.

What subliminal information can this anxiety that I am feeling offer me? What message can my specific anger provide? These feelings contain valuable information about the environment and us. But first, we must stop and reflect on them. For example, my sense of fear may be caused by an excessive fear of failure or rejection. The fact is that this feeling can offer me a very important pearl of knowledge about myself.

Similarly, anger or irritation are almost always related to feelings of injustice. Remember Elena in the previous chapter? It is possible that she first experienced surprise, but later, it is very likely that she felt inner rage or anger; her first intuitive reaction was to think that her boss and the company were being unfair to her. Elena perceived that she was not fairly valued in her work.

The first thing to ask of a good boss is to be able to understand these spontaneous feelings. But this does not imply that you have to accept them as correct. Nor would Elena have to stop at her first reflection: her sense of injustice. If she keeps digging even more deeply, she may be able to generate self-awareness and self-criticism.

Negative feelings can also guide our actions more productively. My nerves and anxiety about working on a report, or public presentation, can mobilize me to prepare myself better. Not all negative emotions are bad, *per se*. My pessimistic mood may make me more inclined to detect errors in my report. I have overlooked failures because I was in a more optimistic and happy frame of mind when I wrote them.

Similarly, the feeling of rejection that I feel towards my boss or towards a colleague can provide me with valuable information. My first reaction may be that he's a jerk. But if I continue to dig deeper, my feeling of aversion may reveal that I tend to lose patience because he often speaks to me in a condescending tone. Now, the information tells me something new about me and can mobilize me to do something.

## Improving our decision making

You may think that you make decisions on a rational plane, but the reality is that most of the decisions we make happen more on an intuitive and unconscious plane. Business schools and some executives have delved into a rational tree decision making, evaluating the possibilities, alternatives, doing a risk test, calculating possibilities ... etc. But, as Daniel Kahneman's work has shown, many statistical processes are fraught with cognitive biases. And our emotions have a lot to do with incurring these biases.

Kahneman was the first non-economist awarded with the Nobel Prize in Economics in 2002, specifically for having integrated insights from psychological research into economic science, especially concerning human judgment and decision-making during uncertainty. His psychological studies opened a new discipline in economics analyzing fundamental insights from cognitive psychology. In his book, *Think Fast and Slow* 21, he warns us that most of our decisions happen in an automatic and unconscious area. (Remember the plane accidents at the beginning of the chapter?)

Kahneman presents two systems of thought: one intuitive (System 1) and the other logical-analytical (System 2). We usually operate on System 1. This way of thinking is spontaneous, driven by instinct and prior learning. It does not mean that we work on automatic pilot all the time, but we mostly think in an unconscious way which we do not control. This makes us save energy, since thinking or making decisions operating in System 2 requires more effort.

System 1 thinking carries many cognitive biases. For example, we have cognitive confirmation biases. That is, the tendency to investigate or interpret information that confirms our preconceptions. These types of cognitive biases, such as the halo effect, tend to occur in job interviews. But it is also certain that you will read your favorite political or sports press because it confirms your existing opinions. We also have group biases that can condition our decisions. In short, we have many emotionally charged cognitive dysfunctions.

System 1 is fast and saves us from having to use a lot of energy making the effort. We save energy when we operate in this system. We work under this thinking by default, thinking which is also emotionally conditioned. Hence many brands and marketing gurus often profit from common unconscious feelings. Our habits and customs constrain this intuitive system. And, according to Kahneman, it is challenging to control and modify. 22

Making matters worse, Kahneman cautions that groups can be biased even more since they don't lay the proper foundations to analyze problems and make decisions. (In Chapter 6, I proposed efforts in several areas to avoid some of these biases.)

System 2 is more infrequent, logical, calculating, and conscious. This way of thinking is more inclined towards reasoning, but we might be lazier in using it. It is intended and deliberate but slower and requires more effort. System 2 requires following proper rules and can help us escape cognitive biases and emotions in the decision-making process. But we must follow their postulates.

For example, Kahneman explains that most business leaders make their decisions under the intuitive system. Even being aware of their mistakes, they still do not really learn from them, given that they do not keep a track record of their decisions, a historical record of decisions and the consequences. 23. Again, Ray Dalio shows us how to escape from this cognitive trap. At Bridgewater, employees and staff are gifted students and faithful disciples of System 2. Not only do they systematize their investment decisions without being fooled by the traps or cognitive biases of System 1, but they are also capable of keeping historical records of all the decisions they make, in addition to history, markets, and different countries. [24]

Does this mean that we should banish emotions and always prioritize in System 2? This would not be realistic or healthy for proper functioning. First, without emotions, we would not be able to make straightforward decisions such as preparing for dinner, what tie to choose in the morning, or what brand of milk to buy at the grocery store. Emotions are there for improving ourselves as human beings, however it is also prudent to know how they can impair our thinking.

## Improve our learning

How long can a student's attention last in a class? Studies indicate an average of about 10 minutes. After 10 minutes, it is typical for our attention to wane. This rule should also apply to a large number of corporate presentations.

Emotions capture our attention and reinforce our learning. Good teachers know that the best way to prepare a class is by using originality, adopting novel ideas or concepts, following an appropriate structure. John Medina, a famous molecular biologist, warns that our brains do not pay attention to things presented in a boring way [25]. Hence when we share our ideas or information, it is preferable to do so with a mix of rigor, novelty, and emotion.

Our memory is also affected by our ability to pay attention. Our focus capacity increases when the content is of interest. However, as good communication coaches know, to connect better with our audiences and communicate our ideas better, we need to present them in a way that stimulates feelings and captures audience attention.

Aristotle warned a long time ago that good rhetoric should combine logic (logos) with emotions (pathos.) But how does one do this? One example is through the use of stories. Storytelling is necessary to present ideas more effectively. An emotionally charged story can awaken hormonal responses in our brain that enhance attention, such as dopamine, oxytocin, and serotonin [26]. It is also a way to strengthen memory. On this hypothesis, the consulting firm Price Waterhouse Coopers (PwC) advises that the best way to inspire employees of a company's purpose is by telling stories. And the best people to communicate those (emotionally charged) stories are the leaders of the company. [27]

On the other hand, negative emotions that increase our cortisol levels can impair our ability to retain information better. An employee who is stressed continuously, or an organization with high levels of negative stress (distress), can destroy learning. Besides, the generation of ideas can suffer since creativity is enhanced with more positive moods and in less stressful environments. [28]

If we agree that emotions matter in order for workers and employees to be more effective, we must now understand how to treat them. We already know that they should not be suppressed, nor should they be an emotional volcano continually exploding, unstable, with random peaks and troughs. We have to be able to visualize our emotions, understand them, label them and manage them. To do that, we need to adopt a proper mindset. Emotions have to be observed, understood and labeled, yet without judgment. And we must remember not to let ourselves be carried away by them.

## The RULER system and the Mood Meter

Marc Brackett brings us an approach based on social and emotional evidence composed of five steps following the acronym: RULER. [29]

We take for granted our emotional intelligence when we might be more emotionally ignorant than we think. Indeed, emotionally intelligent people exist, but, as a rule, we are not very aware of our emotions (at the very least, in a granular way). Brackett often asks the same question in his seminars. The question is one that should be easy, although with limited answers. The problem is: "What are you feeling right now?"
The usual thing is to hear incomplete statements such as "Good," "Okay," "I'm not sure," "At ease." In the same way, if we ask: "What have you felt since you got up until you went to bed?" You might indeed also have trouble labeling and describing your multiple emotions that arose during the day.

People must work with the following objectives:

(1) **Recognize** your emotions. The opposite is to suppress them. If I feel fear, disgust, irritability, or nervousness, I need to allow myself to feel it. This means that I shouldn't judge it, allowing a neutral and impartial mindset.
(2) Afterwards, I have to be able to **understand** what I feel. Reflect on the emotion in a neutral mindset. Again, without judging the feeling.
(3) Know how to **label** your emotions. It means that I have to name the emotion. To this end, using a menu of emotions is very useful. One tool that can help us in this purpose is the *mood meter*. This matrix of emotions, presented in the following table, labels different emotions and groups them into two categories: energy expense and pleasantness. For example, more enjoyable and energetic emotions are

represented in the yellow box. This box contains feelings such as surprised, proud, cheerful, inspired, energized, joyful … etc. The opposite quadrant is blue -less energy and less pleasant- and brings another group of emotions: apathetic, discouraged, dull, bored, tired, lonely, sullen, depressed, and even desperate.

(4) We must also allow ourselves to *express* our emotions. But be careful, because here we must bear in mind that this process involves multiple people. That is why we should ask ourselves: how do our emotions affect others?

(5) Finally, emotional intelligence involves *regulating* our emotions. The opposite of this is to get carried away by emotions and express them uncontrollably through our behavior.

This is not to say that the conscious leader is an emotional automaton, incapable of expressing emotions. Quite the opposite. He is a good boss who knows how to communicate and use emotions more productively. However, understanding and verbalizing emotions do not imply that we have to be looking within ourselves all the time. But there are specific emotional moments that are worth attending to. Nor does it mean that we have to ruminate on emotion; overly examining the sentiment, letting ourselves get carried away by it, and going over it again and again. **Understanding and naming an emotion is a process that can take less than a second. The trick is to be aware of the feeling without being swept away by it.**

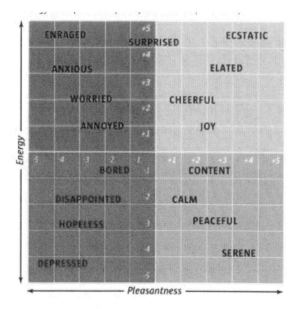

In short, a conscious leader is a person capable of generating self-awareness and self-evaluation more objectively. He is a more intelligent person on the plane of emotions.

How can we improve our self-awareness? How do we better understand our emotions? Are there any tools or methods that can help us develop our internal operating system?

All of this will occupy the next chapter.

# CHAPTER 9: HOW TO ENHANCE THE POWER IN YOURSELF

## EUDAIMONIA

Quite a while ago Stephen R. Covey published *The Seven Habits of Highly Effective People*. Time Magazine has ranked it among the 25 most influential business books ever written, selling more than 25 million copies in 38 languages. The last part of the book talks about habit Nº7: 'Sharpen the saw'. Covey noted that highly effective people spend more time cultivating their physical, emotional/social, spiritual, and mental/intellectual fitness. The spiritual dimension is at our core, our center, the commitment to our value system. It is a very private area of supreme importance [1]. He also talks about meditation but does so in a superficial way.

In this chapter, I would like to delve into where Covey did not go. I will also merge three of the four areas of personal development covered in the seventh habit: the emotional, spiritual, and mental spaces. These dimensions of inner growth correspond to the leader's internal operating system discussed in the previous chapter. Here, we will see what the most effective method is.

Although physical exercise and nutrition have been adopted more into our lifestyles, the same is not the case with the mind's cultivation. Today, societies seem to be more aware of leading a healthy lifestyle. People practice more sports and eat better. But what about mental exercise? Take, for example, the management of stress, irritability, worry, and anxiety that we can all suffer at any time. Judging from multiple statistics, things are not looking good.

In Spain, 71 percent of workers acknowledge suffering from work stress. This poll, conducted by the *360º Well-being Survey* in 2019, surveyed 13,200 people in 23 countries. It displayed a higher stress average globally, standing at 84 percent [2]. Gallup also draws worrying conclusions about stress and feelings of anger in another 2018 study. In the US, and even though the economy grew that year, 55 percent of Americans reported experiencing stress, even up to the day before the survey [3]. Up to 45 percent of respondents acknowledged feeling regularly worried. And 22 percent confessed to feeling angry frequently.

In any case, these results fall short after the COVID era. For example, in a recent study, a group of psychologists and scientists from the Complutense University have investigated public perception after the pandemic. Of the 2,070 Spaniards participated in this survey, 22.1 percent (one in five Spaniards) have high symptoms of depression. 16.6 percent with anxiety. And 19.7 percent post-traumatic stress [4]. Another study in the UK from the University of Sheffield offers similar data.

Confinement has also posed a risk to our physical and mental health [5]. So, this pandemic highlights that we are more concerned than ever about our health, jobs, and economy. That is why, also more than ever, we should focus our priorities and dedicate more time to our minds. Only in this way will we be able to find more effective solutions to the problems within our power to change. That is, expand our circle of influence. And accept with an equanimous attitude what is not in our ability to change.

Cultivating the mind includes our emotional condition and our spiritual dimension. I want to clarify that the spiritual dimension to which I refer is not following the holy scriptures or being faithful devotees of a religion, rather to the spirit's growth. **It is about our inner growth or *eudaimonia*.** This concept was coined by Aristotle and proposes a path to virtue or the improvement of character. It is a path of personal growth, a commitment to developing ourselves internally.

The word *eudaimonia* is made up of two terms: Eu = good and daimon = spirit. The consensus on this concept reflects a search for personal excellence, the best within ourselves. It is a purpose that can give meaning to our life. A significant challenge that never ends.

**However, on the path of *eudaimonia*, the goal is not as important as the process. What matters most is effort.** Carol Dweck, a psychologist at Stanford University, names the right attitude to face this path of inner growth. Dweck speaks from a growth mindset to the belief of people who value the effort. People with this mindset think that talents, personalities, and abilities can be improved with work 6. It is an attitude that motivates them to try harder. Individuals with this disposition do not worry about looking smarter or more competent because there is always room for improvement. "Why should I scourge myself for my vulnerabilities if I can evolve?" "I'm not ready yet, but I will be." There is also an inner trust in these thoughts. The opposite, according to Carol Dweck, is a fixed mindset. This ingrained mentality in some children and adults is the inclination to think that certain qualities are inherent and

212

fixed. If you can't make progress to a point, why strive? A fixed mindset is also more affected by the ego; it seeks to *appear* competent instead of really being so. For this reason, people with a fixed mindset do not feel so comfortable in the face of challenges because they can induce errors and put the image of a capable and prepared person at risk.

The growing mind and *eudaimonia* are supported by scientific advances in neuroscience on the *neuroplasticity* of our brains. Contrary to what scientists thought not so long ago, adults can grow mentally and evolve in their personalities. Research leaves no room for doubt: brain neuroplasticity is a reality. The brain's ability to adapt and change due to experience and behavior changes is called 'neuroplasticity.'

Mistakenly, neuroscientists once thought that, at a certain age, the brain did not regenerate cells or reestablish new neural connections. But recent technological advances in the field of neuroscience have allowed us to see its interior better. New technology and research have illuminating results: in reality, we can generate new neurons, and we are capable of generating new neural connections capable of modifying our personalities. For this, it is necessary that just as we dedicate time to physical exercise, we also do it with our mind.

So how to do it?

Through attention, full consciousness, and compassion. All this, applied in a millenary methodology that today is widely implanted in the West: meditation and mindfulness.

## MEDITATION AND MINDFULNESS

Imagine these two situations. They could well correspond to two different days in your life:

## Day A:

You start the morning very tired. You didn't sleep well because you have a cold. You also stayed up late watching your favorite Netflix series. You didn't eat very healthy last night - maybe a frozen pizza. Plus, you ended up with two French toasts that you had in the fridge. You don't wake up feeling healthy or comfortable with yourself, as you have neglected your diet. This feeling of personal dissatisfaction is still aggravated because you have been procrastinating physical exercise and meditation practice for several days. You look out the window and see a terrible day: wind, cold, rain. You are not very excited, but you feel even worse because your husband has brought up some issue (again) that you thought had been settled. You argue. You look at your calendar and remember that a hard day is coming: many meetings and appointments. One of those meetings is with your boss, and just thinking about it generates you some anxiety. Driving to work, you notice a slight stutter and sound, "Bang!". Suddenly, the sound becomes more apparent and more evident: "Pac, pac, pac, pac ......" Now you cannot control the car and have to slow down: you have a flat tire. Now your anxiety has increased. And you say to yourself: "I can't believe it. Please, not today!"

## Day B:

You don't have a cold, and you've slept like a baby. You wake up alone without the alarm clock ringing because you went to bed early the night before. You feel good and healthy. You have been doing meditation and physical exercise the previous afternoon. You prioritized it before spending idle

214

hours on the internet, between news and social networks. You are in a good mood. You look at the window and see a fantastic sunny day. You have had a good breakfast with your partner, and you are charged with positive energy. Also, you see that your planning for the day has hardly any meetings: you will be able to focus on the presentation for next week. You only have an appointment with your boss planned. You feel optimistic and confident, just thinking about it. Driving to work, you suddenly notice something hit your car: "Crash!" You're OK, just a little confused and scared. Another vehicle has collided with you from behind. You pull over to the side of the road - still frightened. Maybe the other driver is too. The person who hit you asks for forgiveness and acknowledges his guilt. You swap documentation to manage insurance, but all with a calm feeling. You feel patient and equanimous. "These are things that happen ..." you say to yourself.

These [slightly adapted] examples brought to us by Dr. Ronald Siegler, clinical assistant professor of psychology at Harvard Medical School, illustrate two very different responses. [7] From a psychological point of view, Day A presents us with what could be classified as a 'moderate challenge': a flat tire on a rainy, windy and cold day. However, our mental capacity to cope at that time is more limited. You may feel overwhelmed by this.

Day B, objectively, presents a more severe challenge. You have had an accident. You've been hit from behind. And although you don't have any physical injuries, your car has been seriously damaged. We must add to it the shock that you have experienced at the moment of being hit. Now however, your ability to deal with this situation is more remarkable [8]. You find yourself calmer, more patient—more equanimous.

Dr. Siegler says that most of us tend to feel better by reducing our exposure to unpleasant experiences. It might seem obvious, but it presents an escape strategy. Instead of facing problems head-on with adequate resources, what many people do is the opposite. They avoid them. Many psychiatric interventions are also designed to reduce the intensity of pain caused by these types of experiences.

The practice of mindfulness, instead, will help us deal with negative experiences differently. Through mindfulness, we can acquire more mental resources to face difficult experiences. Above all, they are the moments that we cannot control because they do not depend entirely on us. Mindfulness proposes dealing with the problem or negative emotion head-on, and from a neutral position of observer, without getting carried away by the situation, pain, or emotion.

In the previous chapter, I wrote that we all have the inner power to develop. This inner power will determine our success as people at work, our social relationships and in life. Mindfulness and meditation can unleash that power in us. Science corroborates it.

## What are mindfulness and meditation?

Although mindfulness and meditation overlap each other, they have their nuances.

Mindfulness consists of focusing attention on the present moment without making value judgments. It is an intentional state of mind. More specifically, Dr. Jon Kabat-Zinn defines it as the awareness that appears when paying conscious attention in the present moment, without judging. It is the consciousness that unfolds the experience, moment by moment 9. This state of mind can be practiced daily, at any time. Maybe when sipping a cup of coffee, walking down the street, listening to someone else while you talk, brushing your teeth, writing a report, etc. The opposite of a state of mindfulness is a distracted mind or mindlessness. Mindlessness is usually the state of mind that occupies us much of our day, distracting us from the present moment. It is our mind that wanders all the time. It happens when you are making value judgments - about yourself, another person, or something. Or when you are thinking about your vacation or remembering how comfortable you were on the weekend. A state of mindlessness also occurs when you're doing a mental checklist of the things you have to do during the day while listening to the radio and driving. Or when you are brooding over worry during your walk on the beach. A state of mindlessness leads us to run with the automatic pilot most of the time.

An ancient story tells us of a monk who asks his teacher about the meaning of Zen and mindfulness, and he responds:
-Master, what is the true essence of Zen?
-And the teacher replies: When I'm hungry, I eat. When I'm thirsty, I drink. When I'm sleepy, I sleep. When I walk, I contemplate. That is Zen.

Meditation is more profound than mindfulness. It is a practice that cultivates the state of mindfulness, among others. It can be defined as an ancient technique or a method that helps us focus our attention and develop our spirit. In essence, meditation has a more spiritual and psychological component, since it is a practice that can help us to transcend ego and suffering through our conscious awakening. We can practice meditation sitting, walking, or

217

lying down, although sitting is the most common form in its practice.

"Mindfulness," says the Spanish Lama Tashi Lhamo, "is meditation, and it is found in both Buddhism and Hinduism. The first meditation technique is learned, which is called 'hamata' in Sanskrit or 'shiné' in Tibetan, after which one goes to more advanced practices. It has been extracted from the spiritual context and has come to the West with a certain psychological language. It has become very accessible because it has been able to present itself well". [10]

## Mindfulness in action: detecting the *'corroncho monkey'*

The *corroncho monkey* is the metaphor for our infinite capacity to judge. In Latino countries such as Venezuela, 'corroncho' means rough, harsh, or hostile. Sullen, not very friendly. Our *corroncho monkey* mind automatically wanders all the time and judges. Our mind makes us judge other people, judge situations, and judge ourselves.

Shirzad Chamine defines it in his book *Positive Intelligence* as the master of saboteurs [11]. If some of our mental processes, one day, could have an essential role in our survival and evolution, today are less effective. Our predisposition to judge ourselves and others, or judge the context, is the reason for many of our disappointments, regrets, anger, guilt, shame, and anxiety.

The *corroncho monkey* could induce thoughts like the following:

"If I don't put pressure on you, you will become lazy and incompetent."
"If I don't present you with a bleak future, you won't try hard enough."
"If I am not hard on your failures, you will not learn."
"If I am not able to judge others, I will not be objective or see reality."
"If I am not hard on myself, I will not improve."
"If I am not critical of the situation, then I will be the guilty one."

All these value judgments are very human and are part of our repertoire of daily thoughts. Some of us judge more severely and others less so. But we all judge. Buddhism calls it the 'monkey mind'; a harsh monkey mind that whispers in our ear all the time. The saboteur monkey also warns us of how unfair others are to us, makes us feel like victims, reducing our capacity for self-criticism and self-awareness.

Some people live trapped by the *corroncho monkey*. "How unfair my boss is." "How ungrateful is my mother-in-law?!" "How unfair life is." And although life may seem to present some form of existential injustice, mindfulness offers us a different strategy. Shizard speaks of Positive Intelligence (PQ). The truth is, (and although the author does not define it in the same terms) it is nothing more than a form of mindfulness in action. It is a capacity that we can all develop to generate awareness of our negative thoughts without judging them when they happen—noticing the *corroncho monkey* when it enters the scene.

Shizard proposes to tag these sabotaging thoughts with a name and laugh at them when they appear. For example, when my boss or my neighbor doesn't stop to greet me with a friendly smile, refraining from saying: "How rude my neighbor is." Or worrying about my boss's serious face. The warning could appear, saying: "The *corroncho monkey* is already telling me that my neighbor is a jerk." or "the *corroncho monkey* just wants to worry me because my boss passed by without greeting me."

## To meditate: a practice towards attention

My intention in this chapter is to decontextualize meditation and mindfulness from any religious practice. I want to present it as a practice that focuses on mindfulness and compassion. Meditation and mindfulness are the best habits to pursue *eudaimonia*. Through both, we can better cultivate our minds and characters.

**William James, the father of modern psychology, warned that attention was the key to our development and potential.** The ability to focus attention on what we were doing, bringing it out of its rambling state, profoundly impacts people's character and behavior. James claimed that all the geniuses in history - mathematicians, scientists, philosophers - have excelled in their ability to focus their attention and prolong it voluntarily. 12

### How to meditate?

When we meditate, we can direct our attention to any object. That object can be anything like our breath, a candle, a noise, a pain, thoughts, or a part of the body. However, we must do so without judgment when we focus our attention on any of these 'objects.'

If you have not meditated before, I recommend that you try it for a few minutes. You can try it 5 or 10 minutes initially, sit cross-legged or in a chair, and close your eyes. A start of focusing on the breathing is the easiest.

As you breathe, try to focus your attention on the act of breathing. You can feel your diaphragm and stomach expand with each inhalation and contract with each exhalation of air. You cannot see your lungs, but you can feel them when they are in action. The chest grows more extensive when you breathe in air and gets smaller when you breathe out. You can also feel the air flowing from your nostrils. However, you will soon see that the exercise is not that easy; your thoughts will enter the scene. "How well I'm doing this." "I'm OK." "I'm uncomfortable," ... There are many thought-forms that can divert your attention from your breathing.

Meditating is not about putting the mind blank, as some may mistakenly think. It is an intimate moment in which we gather and sit - we can also be walking or lying down. It's all about focusing your attention on your breath. However, an untrained mind tends to scatter; thoughts resurface and, in a few seconds, distract us from the main task of focusing our attention on our breathing. This is normal since the mind has an independent flow, and its normal state consists of wandering. When this happens, we cannot despair. Realizing that we have diverted our attention from our object - the breath - we must return and focus our attention. And again, our thoughts will invade. Then back to the breath. To facilitate concentration on the breath, we can count for each inhalation or exhalation; counting can be done up to ten, then starting over. For every moment we've been distracted, we can start over. Another variant of this exercise could be counting to one hundred.

It is easier to stabilize our attention starting with the breath. Still, we can also focus our attention on another object like our body or the physical sensations in our body or thoughts. Maybe our leg itches or our knee hurts. Our attention will then focus on the feeling that the itch or pain produces. But without judging. Instead, we can investigate the itch or pain with a curious mind. We can feel it. See it within us. Although we should not think about pain; for example, judging how bad or uncomfortable it is. It is also possible that we have had a hard day at work, and thoughts of some conflict crowds our heads. My attention can then focus on my feelings of stress, anxiety, frustration, or anger. We will then dedicate our attention to our body without giving an opinion; we will stop and observe without judging the pressure that the anxiety is exerting on our chest. The sensation that we are feeling in our stomach. The heat and faster heart rate. The common thing is that the mind gets carried away by a problem. If this happens again, we should refocus our attention on our sensations or breathing. When we see our thoughts from an independent observer perspective without judging, we will soon know that they will disappear. They will dissolve like soap bubbles.

If you are too upset to sit down, you can always meditate while lying down. We can also meditate by walking slowly through the corridor or garden. In this form of meditation, you focus on your movement, your feet's pressure with the ground, your breathing, and your thoughts. Again, you should never judge.

Meditation may relax us. However, its purpose is not relaxation. Similarly, your breathing is likely to be very deep and pleasant. Or short and restless. This is neither better nor worse. You can be aware of both.

It is crucial to understand three things:

1. There is no bad meditation. Even if you feel that it has been a disaster and that you have done it completely wrong, just the fact of returning your attention, again and again - from a wandering mind - to the object to which we lend our awareness, would be improving certain qualities in you such as the ability to concentrate, self-control, stress management and reduction, as well as willpower. 13

2. Self-compassion is necessary. Don't be hard on yourself. Even if you are an unwavering person and like to do things with perfection, there will be many days when your meditation will be like that exasperating day playing golf or tennis. So, remember that previous point.

3. It is essential to be consistent in your practice. Your growing mindset will be crucial here. You may tell yourself many times that you don't have time. But 20 minutes a day can be easily taken. Some people prefer to do it in the morning when they get up. Or at night. Find the most suitable moment. You may even find yourself able to meditate longer. If so, you are in luck.

## What does science say?

In fact, the contemplative practices aimed at improving well-being are ancient. Even before the Buddha or Lao-Tzu. In the West, they were not adopted with greater acceptance until the last century. 14

Science in the West did not begin to study meditation until the 1970s. But it has been in the last decade when scientific studies have exploded. Academic articles published just in English exceed 6,800. And this data today falls short because it only runs up to 2016 15. It is important to clarify this point, as I would like to present meditation and mindfulness with scientific rigor.

Richard Davidson, a psychologist, and neuroscientist, professor at the University of Wisconsin-Madison, is one of the first scientists to study meditation from a neuroscience perspective. In the 70s and 80s it was a professional risk to dedicate one's self to this field of study. When Richard Davidson proposed to his Harvard professors to do his dissertation on the effects of meditation, they promptly tried to persuade him that his idea could be the end of a promising career [16]. However, Richard gradually incorporated meditation into his daily habits, and he also traveled with his wife to teacher-led retreats. For a long time, he hid his practices from his fellow scientists.

Time, persistence, improvement in neurotechnology, dedicated working peers and other researchers who joined this field of study have paid off. Today, the advances and evidence of the benefits of meditation and mindfulness are very conclusive. Richard Davidson shows the following discoveries in 5 areas:

1. Neuroplasticity. As I mentioned before, the brain changes in response to experience and training. Contrary to what science believed just two decades ago: it is possible to regenerate new neuronal cells. Meditation can help improve our personality, emotions, and memory by recomposing new neural patterns. In the same way that we go to the gym to exercise our muscles or run to feel better and control our weight, meditation should be seen as a routine to improve our minds. In the words of Daniel Goleman: "We should see meditation as a mental gym." [17]

2. Epigenetics. The study of how behaviors and environment can cause changes that affect the way our genes work (without altering the DNA, as in genetics). Epigenetics can be seen as a genetic thermostat. For example, we may have a genetic predisposition to develop diabetes. If this were the case, sugar might activate the genes that cause us to develop diabetes. Conversely, physical exercise and good nutrition would deactivate them. Meditation could also neutralize them. However, there have yet to be conclusive tests (studies were made on people with a long history in this practice; we are talking about yogis with more than 10,000 hours of meditation). But the results do prove an effect on the genes. [18]

3. Mind and body are the same. The body and the brain are in continuous two-way communication, and our mental and physical well-being are intertwined. We all know that eating well and exercising makes us healthier. But mental exercise also complements physical activity and vice versa. Meditation affects the body just as physical exercise affects the mind.

4. Compassion and empathy. As we will see, there is a practice in meditation that improves these qualities. As science shows, both qualities are innate in all of us, even in other species. Davidson confirms that the tests in children under 6 months are conclusive: we are born with an inherent capacity for kindness. What happens is that, at some point, our most compassionate empathy becomes selective. A meditation practice that focuses on compassion can restore these abilities to us.

5. Happiness. It's that simple: we are happier if we focus our attention on what we are doing now. But we don't live life in the present moment. Research says that we roughly spend 47 percent of our time in a mindless state of rambling. Our

mind is in a state of mindlessness instead of mindfulness [19]. How? For example, we continually recreate the past or the future. We daydream, make plans, or imagine scenarios where we succeed or worry—or recall better or worse moments. Our minds are everywhere but what where are (perhaps sex in an exception. Studies conclude that activities such as sex do indeed force a focus on the present). But our minds tend to wander; we make plans, ruminate on problems, make mental lists, etc. In short, we are in everything except the moment. We ignore what we do, especially if what we do involves a routine task such as eating, driving, washing dishes or jogging. A Harvard study of 2,250 people found that the people who reported feeling better were those who were paying attention to the present moment. This research was carried out through an application, asking individuals several times a day, two questions: (1) What were they doing at that time? And (2) how did they feel?

Results showed that people who were paying full attention to what they were doing at the moment, like cooking, running, brushing their teeth, driving, reading, listening to music, etc., reported better happiness rates. Their happiness rates were even better than those who were recreating a positive mental image or scenario, such as a trip or other type of plan [20]. These conclusions were already noticed by the fabulous writer Pablo d'Or, expressing it more poetically: "Whoever abandons the chimera of dreams enters into the of reality. "[21]

## MEDITATION FOR IMPROVING OUR EMOTIONAL INTELLIGENCE

In the previous chapter, we discussed the leader's character as a mixture of values, motivations, and personality traits. It was also written that the leader's internal operating system has to be updated through self-awareness. Good bosses are also more emotionally intelligent. All this comes together in our internal operating system. It determines our effectiveness in life and work for better or for worse.

Facts and data prove how our emotional intelligence can shape our success as individuals and professionals. And meditation can help us increase our emotional intelligence.

Our emotional skills are the ones that allow us to work better with others, bring out the best in people, or make better decisions. In the same way, emotional competencies, can allow us to focus on those things we can control; saving us energy to be more creative for finding better alternative solutions or mobilizing people toward goals that matter.

Mindfulness and meditation can enhance the following essential qualities in a leader:

1. Self-awareness
2. Managing emotions
3. Empathic concern: compassion
4. Equanimity

## #1. Leadership begins with self-awareness

Meditation and mindfulness are pure awareness. Both will enhance this inherent - but dormant - ability in us. In the previous chapter, we talked about this fundamental quality to update our internal operating system. Without self-awareness, we do not have the possibility of being objective with ourselves. Nor are we able to see how other people perceive us.

The ability to generate self-awareness is the substitute for being always in a mindlessness state or with the autopilot on. We operate without stopping to reflect on what we are doing or why we are doing it. Many of our reactions happen on the subconscious plane.

Anyone looking to improve their leadership skills needs to be able to work on their self-awareness. If we cannot recognize our own emotions, we will not have adequate resources to manage them. But we won't be able to see them in other people either. Studies show that if we improve our self-awareness, we also strengthen our ability to interfere with our emotional states and others. Empathy can be defined as "awareness in others." [22]

## #2. Our amygdala has us kidnapped

Do you remember the fatal accident at Los Rodeos? Captain Van Zanten was unable to make proper decisions because his amygdala had taken over. Remember Elena in the chapter on the boss who develops people? Her first reaction was defensive, closing herself to self-criticism: zero self-awareness.

Daniel Goleman talks about the kidnapping suffered by our amygdala [23]. This fundamental organ in our brain is in charge of managing emotions and memory -among other functions- and it is essential for optimal function. But it can also play tricks on us. **If the amygdala detects some danger - usually imagined - it will pull us and block other cognitive functions in the central lobe.** The 'danger' the amygdala detects might be a bad response from a co-worker, an unreceptive audience, negative feedback from our boss, an unrealistic deadline for our report, etc.

I remember the occasion of giving a class in which I was mentally blocked and went blank. I was a bit paralyzed by stage fright. This same sudden panic many artists have suffered before—for example, Pastora Soler. The Spanish singer once collapsed on the Fibes stage in Seville. After that, she decided to cancel all her concerts. But other artists like Scarlett Johansson or Adele have also suffered panic attacks at some point. [24]

Some tests to measure cortisol and stress levels in the laboratory reproduce the same sensation that I experienced that day. My audience's serious and unexpressive faces continued, even a few minutes after I started my class. At that point, my cortisol levels skyrocketed. My amygdala went into action, sensing a danger. In my case: an unreceptive audience. The same presentation that I had repeated so successfully on other occasions suddenly disappeared from my mind. It was difficult for me to associate ideas, focus attention or remember concepts. In turn, my nerves were increasing, experiencing what is known as a vicious mental spiral, a mental loop that induces the amygdala. The *corroncho monkey* reproduces an internal dialogue: "My God, I'm nervous", "The audience is going to notice my nerves", "I can't control them!", "I'm going to fail", " My God!"

My amygdala had detected a danger in the room and had taken over, increasing my cortisol levels. The question is: How can it be calmed down?

Meditation increases the power in our prefrontal lobe, capable of calming the activity of the amygdala [25]. For example, meditating on this scene without judging has helped me a lot personally. How did I do it? I sat down and watched the panic attack in my mind; I recreated the scene. But from an independent observer perspective. Again,

229

without judging. However, when the stress or anxiety appeared in practice, I focused my attention on how it felt in my stomach, increased heart rate and breathing.

And yet, the problem happens only in the moment. So how are we able to stop this negative emotional spiral the moment it appears? Mindfulness in action can attend to the sensations that we are experiencing at that moment, without judgment. In this way, you could observe with curiosity the feelings that are happening in the moment, without labeling or classifying them as 'nerves', 'anxiety' or 'danger'. You could also complement it, telling yourself that what you are going to say matters, focusing all your attention and energy on it. The latter is a form of cognitive tactic that can help us regulate emotion.

## #3. Why compassion matters in leadership

According to Tania Singer, a social psychologist and neuroscientist at the Max Planck Institute, we have to distinguish between empathy and compassion. We tend to think that they are the same since both are responses to the suffering of others. But they are two very different social emotions that occur in different brain circuits 26. Empathy can be classified into three different levels:

1. Cognitive Empathy. I can understand and know how other people feel. The least I expect from my boss is that he understands what I'm feeling, even if he doesn't feel it himself. Nevertheless, this empathy is more superficial. Psychopaths can mentally reproduce this type of empathy that happens on a purely cognitive level, yet it does not occur in the emotional areas of the brain.

2. Emotional empathy. I can observe other people's emotional feelings, and my neural systems will be activated as if I felt them too. This emotional empathy is the precursor to compassion. Still, it can also lead us to disconnect or become mentally ill if our work is exposed to a lot of suffering or anxiety. For example, workers in the healthcare sector can be overwhelmed and blocked. Or perhaps journalists and soldiers in war zones.

3. Empathic concern or compassion. I care about you, and my feelings are directed towards wishing you the best. Compassion motivates us to help others. It is the same feeling a mother has when her baby cries. She feels affection and a concern to take care of the baby. Compassion mobilizes us, prompts us to action. Its formula might be written as: empathy + action = compassion.

Why not limit yourself in emotional empathy? After all, it is that which is in me naturally. Because empathy has its weak points. As mentioned, it can lead us to disconnect. For example, when we see a beggar on the street, we are very likely to ignore him or her. But we can also experience what is known as *schadenfreude*. It is the feeling of satisfaction in seeing other people in a rival group suffer. Our mechanisms associated with reward are activated in this situation. We can see it in the pleasure we experience thinking about how badly the fans from another soccer team are feeling when they lose. *Schadenfreude* is also materialized in the feeling of 'joy' we experience when seeing the voters' faces of anxiety and disappointment of an opposing political party's loss. This feeling can also be aggravated if someone has mistreated us. For example, it is possible that we feel happy because the boss, who has inflicted bad treatment on employees, has been fired. Or because the city has fined that unbearable neighbor who behaves in an uncivil manner.

231

According to Tania, the best way to avoid such an empathic block is through compassion. This is achieved by transforming emotional empathy into compassion. Feelings of compassion happen in other areas of the brain.

How to do it?

Her studies conclude that meditation focused on compassion - a type of meditation that I will explain in a moment - can change the emotional empathic response towards a more compassionate one. In her research, a few months of daily meditation was sufficient. [27]

What leadership qualities can compassion bring us? I can think of a few:

• **Better coaching qualities.** A compassionate boss can improve the self-awareness of others who have blind spots. Why? Because compassion is contagious, and it's hard to fake. This could lead to the other person being more open and acknowledging another's problem. Now your boss's intentions are sincere and optimistic. Compassion is required to give useful feedback and generate self-awareness in others. It can help bosses to give feedback in the *radical candor* fashion I mentioned in Chapter 7. "What I'm about to tell you, you may not like, but I am doing it because I care about you. I want you to get better and be successful." On the other hand, these words might sound hollow in a leader who only shows cognitive empathy. A collaborator could be more open in front of a boss who infects compassion because she or he seems more credible.

• **Greater inclination to contribute to society.** In the following chapters, we will see what drives the social entrepreneur. This goes beyond the usual Corporate Social Responsibility practices of many companies. A social entrepreneur is a person who is moved by compassion to improve things and make money.

• **Better response to demanding customers**. But also more significant commitment and proactivity to solve the problems and needs of our customers. In short, as we will see in the next chapter, an exceptionally human service has these attributes. Compassionate meditation practices can become routine in any company. I am sure the results could be seen soon and would be more effective than any customer service training (supplementary in any case).

• **More authentic leadership**. New management paradigms demand authentic leaders, more upright and credible people who can inspire others with values. But being authentic also means showing our vulnerabilities to others and discovering blind spots in ourselves. However, this is not usually an option for many people. Meditating on compassion is also contemplating on ourselves, generating self-compassion. This does not mean taking the passive victim role. On the contrary, a growing mind has to allow itself deficiencies in the process of continual improvement.

• **Less stress.** Both mindfulness and compassion meditation decrease our stress levels. Earlier I said that meditating on compassion also means meditating on yourself. Kindness starts within. Self-compassion will help us not be so hard on ourselves, notably reducing the stress levels we usually induce.

• **Better conflict management**. Many conflicts happen because we judge other people in a biased way. We tend to put intentions and motives in others that do not correspond

233

to reality. In this way we escalate the conflict. A compassionate mind is a mind that sees the better in other people. Meditating on compassion helps us to be more flexible when it comes to solving problems with others. This should not be confused with being cowardly. On the contrary, a compassionate mind is courageous because it faces conflict head-on with humility and firmness in a more collaborative and open-minded way. For example, a situation in which we were upset with a co-worker could happen like this: "Your delay in giving me your part of the report caused me to leave very late today" - this is an objective and direct assessment. "I've been frustrated by this" - emotions are acknowledged. "I propose to you for next time you deliver it to me the day before. And to do this, I can offer to help you or let you know that previous day"- this second part is compassionate and open-minded.

• **Better social capital in the company**. If companies meditate on compassion in a generalized way, they would see increased collaboration and closeness among their collaborators. Personal interests, envy and conflicts can be significantly reduced.

• **Better ability to listen to others.** Just as mindfulness meditation helps us improve concentration, compassion meditation better prepares us to understand others' points of view. In his book *On Dialogue*, the famous physicist David Bohm brings us the key to understanding. He says that in a dialogue, a battle of ideas is not won; it is constituted as a way of "thinking together," collectively. People do not have to give up their principles but be able to "suspend" them momentarily to explore other points of view. Without prejudices 28. This principle, known as the 'Bohm Dialogue,' can be improved by meditating on compassion.

234

## How to meditate on compassion

Meditating on compassion begins by focusing your attention on your breath. After a few minutes focused on breathing or on other sensations in the body, we focus on someone who produces a lot of love and compassion. This exercise can also be reproduced by seeing ourselves at childhood, awakening self-compassion.

When we meditate on compassion, it is easiest to think of the people closest to us. For each inhalation, we can imagine that we absorb all the worries and their problems. We hope they are well and healthy. For each exhalation, we extend our love to them in the form of well-being, health, and happiness. We wish them well. Little by little, we will expand the circle of influence. Next, we can continue with those people we know but are not so close to. We will extract all their problems and worries for each inhalation, and for each exhalation we will wish them the best. We will expand the circle, continuing with all the people of our city, country, and planet. Even with those people who might dislike us most.

Another version of this exercise proposed to us by Bruce Alan Wallace, a scientist and Buddhist, in his book *The Attention Revolution* [29]. In this practice, we would again begin by focusing attention on the breath. Once we believe that we are more focused on the present moment, we will ask ourselves three questions. The first is: What would I like to receive from the world to be happier, fill myself with purpose and meaning in life? They can be tangible things like food, clothing, a home, or healthcare. But there are also intangibles such as: the harmony in your environment, the company and affection of others, or wise advice from other people to guide us along the way. Bring to your mind those things that might look after your basic needs. Allow your

235

wishes to arise. Think about other people close to you and how you would like them to have these things too. But you will also expand the circle to cover all the people on the planet.

The next question you might ask is: What kind of person do I want to be and become? What qualities would I like to have? This question incorporates inevitable change, both physical and mental. Imagine how the person you are seeing is you, with those qualities. And little by little, you become that person as you breathe.

The last question raises an offer. What would I like to offer the world? What mark do I want to leave in this world? Invite your vision to appear in detail. But don't judge. Don't get carried away by your ego. Imagine that your dream comes true and benefits those closest to you as well as the whole world.

## #4. Equanimity

Stephen Covey spoke of the need to expand our circle of influence versus concern: "In bad weather, a happy face." [30]. They are equanimous. Equanimity is the ability to accept "what is" without resistance. An equanimous person is a person who is characterized by being stable, balanced, and emotionally constant. They are not carried away by emotions. However, this should not be confused with a cold-hearted person who does not feel, since emotions make us more human and complete.

In these times of Covid-19, many people have been affected. But the most balanced people, instead of lamenting or brooding over their bad fates, have accepted what is not in their power to control. This does not mean that they have

236

passively resigned themselves. On the contrary, in their more equanimous position, they have been able to think more lucidly and seek better solutions. Their energy, then, has been focused on what is possible: what is it that we can change? Equanimity, in this way, is a form of emotional control. Instead of focusing on the more negative emotions, it reserves attention and energy for those things we can control: our circle of influence. This way, our circle of influence expands, reducing unproductive worry.

Mindfulness meditation enhances this quality in us. Again, it has a component of self-compassion. Instead of eliminating parts of our personality that we are not comfortable with or trying to suppress our fear, worry, or stress from our head, we accept what is and what comes without applying mental avoidance techniques. The fair person does not judge. No regrets. It does not prophesy.

Mindfulness helps you see and accept things as they are, as well as to move and work on the things that are within your power to change.

## MINDFULNESS IN THE COMPANY

These difficult times of the pandemic require even more clarity of mind from authentic leaders with the ability to grow in the face of difficulties. People who are comfortable in the face of uncertainty and challenges. Indeed, this COVID era is very challenging. It is significant challenge for everyone, but meditation and mindfulness can help improve leadership and business. While it is true that some organizations have launched corporate mindfulness programs, most of them have been limited to stress management. But meditation and mindfulness can do more for the people and culture of many companies. Companies such as LinkedIn, Google, or Salesforce -and many others- have begun to implement it among their work practices, including spaces where people can meditate for a few minutes. Or even organizing meditation retreats on weekends [31]. Executives like Marc Benioff have incorporated this practice into the organizational culture. For example, in executive meetings, Marc urges his team to meditate for a few minutes before starting [32]. In this way, they adopt the right mindset to listen more carefully, build on others' ideas, and to be more open-minded.

I want to conclude this chapter by noting that meditation and mindfulness can help us develop the Level-5 qualities that Jim Collins discovered in exceptional top executives [33]. Unlike the more charismatic, selfish, or heroic leaders, these CEOs were more modest people. Their modesty, however, did not detract from their determination to do the right thing when necessary. Even if their decisions were unpopular and painful, albeit always for the company's good, the motivation to achieve results did not happen to enlarge their ego. Their ambition was channeled into the organization, not into them. They had achieved the correct homeostasis between personal humility and professional will.

This balance is nothing more than the result of feeling powerful.

# Part III: Enhance the value among all stakeholders

# CHAPTER 10: PROVIDING AN EXCEPTIONALLY HUMAN SERVICE

## MEDIOCRITY IN SERVICE

How important are customers in your company?

Most would agree that today this is a truism, a statement that is so obviously true that it is almost not worth saying. For example, United Airlines executives and employees may agree that the customer is imperative in their company. However, when this airline dragged passenger David Dao Duy Ahn away due to overbooking issues, no one in this organization seemed to reconsider the case. Not even its CEO, Óscar Muñoz, showed signs of having questioned the approach; the first statement he issued, in which he defended his staff from the recorded actions which circulated around the world, generated even greater outrage on social networks [1]. Even the CEO's apology to the passenger was vague, confusing, and insufficient [2]. We can all agree that there are more subtle ways to resolve these types of contingencies.

The reality is that unfortunate situation like David Dao's is more common than we might think. Perhaps they may be less dramatic; we are not often beaten up and dragged out of tourist class, thankfully. However, many of us have suffered feelings of dissatisfaction, frustration or anger when buying a product that was not what we expected or when we find ourselves victims of poor service.

In 2017, the consulting company Accenture carried out a multi-sector study to determine consumers' expectations and experiences. To do this, it surveyed more than 24,000 consumers in thirty-three countries 3. The research identified the three factors that most annoy customers:

1. Having to contact many people to resolve an issue.
2. Dealing with unfriendly and rude employees.
3. That the company fails to deliver what it has promised.

Staying with someone who doesn't appreciate us is not loyalty but stupidity. Accenture's research confirms what seems obvious and common sense: People tend to abandon brands when they get lousy interactions. The study recommends that companies invest in their customer experience, even though the return on investment may not be as clear cut. After all, bad experiences not only negatively impact revenue but also brand image.

However, the research highlights the complexity of creating and maintaining personalized user experiences. There is a gap between changes in customer expectations and the ability of companies to adapt. People continuously raise the bar for demands; what was valuable proposition yesterday is an ordinary product today.

## The human factor in service continues to be a fundamental pillar in customer experience

The problem is that when we talk about experiences, we tend to neglect the human factor. In the race to deliver more value to customers, the common strategy often prioritizes technology, product development, price, location, convenience, or quality. Though these variables are fundamental, an essential thing is left aside: the service. Failures in service do not necessarily mean a bad service. Instead, there is an inability to offer more value through the people who provide it.

At best, most customers receive an average or mediocre service. The word 'mediocre' comes from the Latin *medio*, which means common/ordinary, and *ocris*, which means mountain. The analogy of the mountain is appropriate because, as we will see in a moment, companies are content with the regular results they obtain at their base. The value service proposition is mostly circumscribed in the middle of the mountain.

I shall note that a superior service does not necessarily imply having to raise prices. Nor should it be positioned in premium or luxury market segments. Low prices, low costs, and exceptional service are supported. JetBlue, Southwest Airlines, Mercadona, Starbucks, Quicktrip, IKEA, Decathlon, Costco, Amazon are clear examples of this.

## Bureaucratization in service

Mediocre service is a bureaucratized service. It focuses on procedures, standards, and policies rather than customers. It is worth asking yourself: what value does it bring us to have to listen to canned scripts from employees who want to sell us a service? What value does a waiter add who takes our order without looking at us and serves us the dishes in the

242

same old way? What superior value does a hotel receptionist offer, beyond registering us in the system, giving us the key and directing us how to get to our room?

Many years have passed since I graduated in Hotel and Restaurant Management. Too many. However, I still remember my first few months of work. At that time, I was driven by an inherent passion for solving problems and even anticipating customer needs. Indeed, I had a talent for it, but this initial passion gradually faded. Why? The reason is that the companies where I worked did not prioritize their customer service strategies. They all shared a blind obsession with maximizing financial benefits.

For this reason, what mattered most was complying with organizational procedures, rules, and policies to make more money. These organizations weren't thinking about the user experience; there was no real strategy. This prevented us from offering a better service: we had to follow rigid scripts like automatons. We could not take the initiative to solve problems or take the lead. Other times we did not have the necessary resources. In some cases, company policies were totally at odds with people's wishes.

The bad thing about these vices is that they end up being contagious. Even being able to do so, employees can avoid offering exceptional service. Employees prioritize following the instructions imposed by the management. In this scenario, corporate systems become an end in and of themselves: they start from the objective of doing work more efficiently to maximize profits in the short term. Customer service is taken for granted. Under this paradigm, it is difficult for employees to see customers as anything more than an irrelevant, unimportant routine.

## Robotization, Artificial Intelligence (AI), and the automation of activities that do not add value to the customer

Will automation end the bureaucratization of the service? Could this change bring new opportunities? A study by the consulting firm McKinsey predicts that 800 million jobs could be lost by 2030. However, the research clarifies that technology will not only be a destructive force and an element of change and evolution. Many employment and functions will have to be redefined, new professions and job functions will change. Workers will be forced to adapt. [4]

In a speech in Chicago, former President of the United States of America Barack Obama warned: "The next wave of economic displacement will not come from abroad. It will be born out of the relentless pace of automation that will make many good middle-class jobs obsolete." [5]. In an article for the MIT Technology Review, David Rotman explains Trump's rhetoric of making America great again with the recovery of jobs which were eliminated, in the former American president's opinion, by globalization and the relocation of factories abroad.   He does not consider a more evident reality: the loss of these jobs is mainly due to automation.

Still and all, artificial intelligence, Big Data, automation, and robotics will not be able to replace 100 percent of most jobs. Indeed, many jobs will disappear which will become fully automated, especially those that demand manual or physical tasks, but many others will change. Likewise, automation will provide an opportunity to improve those service processes that add little value to the customer. For example, Auchan supermarkets are already incorporating a product scanning system through their mobile app. People only have to

244

present a barcode on the machine at the exit; the payment is generated automatically (though these payment processes are more designed for quick purchases). Little by little, they will become more common and replace the people who work at the checkouts. [6]

Amazon Go is already a reality in many cities. It will become more and more usual to buy in stores without staff. Hotels are also incorporating Check-in and Check-out processes that prevent customers from going through reception to collect the key or leave their credit card. This technology will transform the hotel receptionist's work, who will have to concentrate on providing higher-value activities. For example, online sales giant Alibaba is opening hotels where not all human labor will be eliminated, although technology will exponentially reduce the number of people working there. [7]

Despite this trend, if hotels today can incorporate robots, the truth is that they are far from replacing people. Hotels that have integrated robotic applications of some kind assume it more as an advertising element than as a value proposition to renew their service. Furthermore, it has been shown that customers are not willing to pay more for these technological solutions. [8]

Even the most automated restaurant in the world hasn't completely replaced people. The Spyce restaurant, located in the city of Boston, was created by a team of MIT graduates, in collaboration with Michelin Star Chef Daniel Boulder. In Spyce, they have automated almost everything, not only the orders but also the kitchen preparation. There are no cooks, only robots. Despite this, the founders of this initiative recognize that the human touch remains a primary factor for success. Spyce managers' opinion is that a restaurant will always be evaluated for its service, hospitality, and food, not only for technology and innovation. Creators view automation as a tool that helps them improve service, but not replace it entirely. 9

**Analysis of automation and the threat it poses to many service jobs should focus on activities. Those mechanical and lower value functions are the most susceptible to change. However, automation cannot substitute for compelling human value propositions such as empathy, creative problem solving, anticipating needs, or simply a genuine smile. In short, technology can solve simple manual activities so that people can focus on the factors that add value for the customer. Namely: an exceptionally human service.**

## Function vs. purpose

It is impossible to differentiate a company through service and provide more value to customers, at least consistently, if it is not codified first within the company culture. In previous chapters, we have seen companies' cases where all the staff is aligned towards this purpose and goal.

Famous American restaurateur and businessman Danny Meyer defines extraordinary service levels as hospitality. Many companies' service is a 'monologue' because companies set processes and procedures without listening to customers 10. Service is just a measure of whether a product is delivered on time. Hospitality instead is a 'dialogue'. Hospitality is how you make the customers feel when they are receiving good service. It is an experience. Many businesses only give space to the monologue because they limit the people who serve customers. This phenomenon is what I define as bureaucratic service Meyer refers to it as service which focuses mostly on the technical part of the work: the standard, the policies, norms, the representation, technology, the context, etc. Though these dimensions are crucial for providing higher levels of service, they aren't enough. Why? Because they lack soul.

Companies must distinguish between the function and purpose of service. Ritz-Carlton is a company that has always considered the difference between them. Employees in these hotels have to pursue the purpose, fulfilling the function. For example, the goal of a person working at the front desk is to register the customer in the system, give them a room, provide him with information, etc. (This part corresponds to the function.) However, Ritz-Carlton employees know that this is only a primary part of the job. The purpose of the job is not only to follow a standard or to fulfill the technical role of a check-in process; it is also about creating an exceptional welcome experience. [11]

**Indeed, the technical part of the job is needed to achieve superior service. Still, that responsibility only covers the bottom of the pyramid. Anyone can solve the technical aspects of the function. Instead, not everyone can fulfill the purpose.**

The reality is that unfortunate situations like David Dao's is more common than we might think.

Note: someone can always be trained to perform the duties. The real challenge is covering the human qualities necessary to fulfill the purpose.

## AN EXCEPTIONALLY HUMAN SERVICE MUST BE MEASURED: THE SERVICE PYRAMID

It is not the first time - nor will it be the last - that a service pyramid has been presented to generate a reference framework on service levels. There is nothing new here. However, rather than innovate, the approach presented here seeks simplicity. A pyramid should be as intuitive and practical as possible since it works as a frame of reference for executives and employees in any company.

### Companies usually measure the lower levels of the pyramid

It is common for companies to seek to meet their customers' satisfaction. The problem is that they are not aware that their usual measurement systems restrict the level of service. Often, quality management systems implement limited levels of service to the base of the pyramid.

Why? Because many methodologies only seek to satisfy customers. However, nowadays, customer satisfaction is not enough. A satisfied customer says, "everything is fine, my expectations are met, but that's it." Customer satisfaction is at the bottom of the pyramid. Jack Welch, the former President of General Electric, has been titled the greatest CEO of the last century. He defines customer satisfaction as the minimum a company must accomplish. It is the key to be taken seriously in the party of minimally decent people. [12]

Customer Satisfaction is the first step to go further in service. It involves the daily operations in a company that ensures clients receive their appropriate products on the agreed day; it is the processes and procedures that guarantee that dishes

248

in a restaurant arrive without delay and the food is tasty; it is the standard applied to make sure the rooms of a hotel are properly clean; it is the discipline involved that makes sure a flight arrives on time; the systems that reduce queues in a store, etc..

**It only responds to the fulfillment of expectations. And yet, in order to provide more value and differentiate our brand from competitors, we must exceed expectations. Fulfilling expectations and customer satisfaction aren't enough because they are both commodity variables. A commodity service proposal that it does not provide any differentiation or extra value in the people's eyes.**

Richard, the character played by Leonardo DiCaprio in the movie *The Beach* puts it bluntly: "I just feel like everyone tries to do something different, but you always wind up doing the same damn thing."

## Net Promoter Score

Before explaining the three levels of service of a conscientious company, it is first necessary to understand a tool that measures customer opinion. It is known as the Net Promoter Score (NPS).

NPS is a management tool that predicts customer loyalty based on the degree of recommendation they are willing to give. In his article *The One Number You Need to Grow*, published in the Harvard Business Review in 2002, Frederick F. Reichheld proposed to change the usual methodology in measuring customer value. He brought a new measurement to focus on a single question:

*"How likely is it that you would recommend this company to a friend or colleague?"*

In this way, companies would classify their responses of customers from 0 to 10. User responses from 0 to 6 are grouped into the customer category of 'Detractors'. People who rated a company between 7 and 8 points would be defined as 'Passives'. And the users who granted a 9 or 10 would be classified as "Promoters." Only the latter count as engaged customers. Passive customers do not add nor subtract. And detractors subtract. Reichheld advised only taking into account those customers who were "excited" about our services and products. 13

Why not include a rating of 7 or 8? After all, these are good numbers for many companies. Reichheld argues that if all the variables are taken into account, an effect called "grade of inflation" would occur, thereby affecting many evaluations. In other words, if organizations value the options of 'passive' clients positively - they would settle for mediocrity. And this is inadmissible if companies seek excellence and higher standards.

## Two adequate levels and one dysfunctional lower level

My simplified service pyramid proposal incorporates a measurement tool that consists of two suitable levels:

At the bottom there are satisfied customers. They are equivalent to the neutral users of the NPS (scores 7 and 8). This level meets customer expectations; it is the base camp. Jack Welch defined it as the 'decent' level. Users rationally value the service and product they receive. Their expectations are met concerning the price they have paid. Satisfied people are neutral. They don't add, but they don't subtract either. Companies should not be happy at this level because it installs them in the field of commodities. They fail to set themselves apart themselves by the service and the product they offer in their customers' eyes; they do not add more value than the competition.

At the top there are enthusiastic customers. (Scores between 9 and 10). They would highly recommend the brand. John H. Flemming and Jim Asplund of Gallup indicate that highly engaged consumers are at this level. These users are rationally satisfied with the product and service they receive, but they are also emotionally engaged. Engaged customers see their most rational expectations met and find the service above average. Somehow it exceeds their expectations. This category of customers sees additional service components such as more caring and genuine attention from employees, more generous return policies, a better solution to their problems and greater personalization of service.

Finally, there exists an unacceptable level, below the pyramid's base, which we will call dysfunctional. This level corresponds to the 'detractors' in the NPS model. (Scores between 0 and 6). Somehow, they acknowledge that their expectations are not being met. An evaluation of 0 or 6 denotes a dysfunctional service. At worst, the customers have received lower-quality service, not meeting their expectations. At best, they mean that they have received a different service than they expected. Either way, this category is below acceptable satisfaction levels. It usually corresponds to several factors, such as a bad product or service, prices above the value they offer, etc. In general, people's opinions regarding this range are clear and rational.

## THE FOUR COMPONENTS OF EXCEPTIONALLY HUMAN SERVICE

### #1 A shared vision and goal: exceptional service that generates enthusiastic customers

How can you achieve these levels of service that generate more excited customers? Why are organizations like Zappos, Ritz-Carlton, Southwest Airlines, Costco, Trader Joe´s and Nordstrom offering superior levels? What do they have in common?

These companies have conveyed their vision of service to all of their employees; they don't take it for granted and work every day to make it a reality. Actions follow their words. They have aligned their organizational culture with a vision of providing superior service, and all the systems and processes follow such vision. Employees in these companies have one common goal: to generate enthusiastic customers. To do this, they have selected the right people to serve customers and provided them with the necessary resources. Similarly, these organizations have propped up their systems and processes to bring more value to their clients. Everyone is aligned and shares the same vision.

### Shared Vision

Peter Senge, Director of Systems Thinking and Organizational Learning at the MIT Sloan School of Management explains in his book *The Fifth Discipline* why some organizations are smarter than others. Intelligent companies are open to learning, they are trained to react to adversity and they continually improve. These companies are always discovering new opportunities to keep moving forward. Senge mentions this idea of a shared vision as one the five disciplines: "A shared vision is not an idea. It is not even as important a concept as freedom; it is a force in people's hearts, a force of awesome powers. It may be inspired by an idea, but if it is so compelling that it gets the endorsement of more than one person, it ceases to be an abstraction and becomes a palpable element. People begin to see it as if it exists. Few human forces are as powerful as a shared vision." [14]

The entire organization must share the vision of an exceptionally human service because it will become real only in this way. Also, as Senge warns, it has to be palpable. By 'palpable', we mean the ability to see and understand what the company means by exceptional service without being swayed by marketing slogans, artifice, or great words. From the top executive to the company's front-line operator, everyone needs to be on the same page.

**The vision of exceptionally humane service inspires employees to provide value in every interaction of service. Every moment of service is unique and provides an opportunity to generate a positive impact to customers. Either by attending to a client's request, offering information, solving a problem, or anticipating a need they may have.**

Meeting the goal of generating more engaged customers can certainly be more effective than any traditional marketing investment. Tony Hsieh, CEO and founder of Zappos, recalls that the most effective marketing action happens when an employee has positively impacted their interaction with the user. "Our business philosophy is to offer happiness to our employees and customers. People may not remember exactly what you did or said, but they will always remember how you made them feel." [15]

That is why Zappos invests a large part of its marketing budget in its personnel and the employee's interaction with the client.

Between 1981 and 1993, Jan Carlzon, CEO at Scandinavian Airlines System (SAS), was the ultimate driver of cultural change and service. His proposals were able to reverse a profound crisis that the company had suffered. The levels of internal motivation and customer satisfaction were in the gutter. In his book *Moments of Truth*, Carlzon points out the importance of maintaining a 15-second interaction with the user. "No matter where you are and what service role you are fulfilling, those moments of interaction can make a difference with the customer." [16]

These phenomena are defined as 'moments of truth'. They are instances that can improve the experience and generate a very positive impact on the customer. Therefore, all the people who provide a service have to focus on those moments of opportunity. They are situations that are above the functions and are capable of defining the service purpose.

### Shared Service Goal: To Generate Engaged Customers

All service employees must be aligned with this goal. In turn, this goal has to become a shared vision within the company.

The service's objectives should focus on increasing the number of Promoter clients (9 and 10). The goal should not just be that they become promoters, but that they stay; for this, research must be constant. You always have to analyze what users want and assess whether you are providing them with a consistent solution. Likewise, deviations from Detractor clients (0 to 6) must be corrected immediately. Companies must find the reasons behind such low ratings.

**Employees should also ask themselves everyday: How can my job help make this goal come true? This questioning helps to give a purpose and meaning to work. It will not matter where the person is in the company. The ability to generate a positive impact on service is transversal: value can be added directly to the client or through collaboration with other people in the company and different departments. This is what is known as internal service.**

## #2 Motivated and committed employees

A prominent rule companies need to remember is employee motivation and customer experiences are linked to each other.

Companies talk of passion and urge their employees to serve their customers well. But employee motivation does not appear spontaneously. The word 'motivation' derives from the Latin term *motivus* or 'motus', which means 'cause of movement.'

Employee motivation is the energy required to deliver exceptionally humane service. However, this energy is variable: the stimulus of people responds to particular conditions. Therefore, a diversity of factors can define whether a worker is more or less collaborative, responsible, proactive, whether or not he remains focused, enthusiastic. These conditions are the ones that largely determine the quality of the service to be provided.

**An exceptionally humane service needs to be realistic, and companies must understand that people's motivation is indispensable. The same reason companies cannot take for granted loyalty or customer engagement; employee engagement won't happen alone.** To generate enthusiastic customers, we must have fully motivated and engaged workers. John Mackey, founder, and co-CEO of Whole Foods Market simplifies it this way: "[...] all are linked interdependently. Management's responsibility is to hire the right people, train them well and ensure that those team members flourish and are happy while they are at work. The team member's job is to satisfy and delight customers. If we have happy customers, we will have a successful business

256

and happy investors. [...] You end up with a virtuous circle." 17. Like Zappos, Whole Foods understands that the best marketing investment begins with investing in your customer service employees.

Maybe the motivational nirvana indeed does not exist. It is not realistic to believe that organizations will have 100 percent of entirely enthusiastic and engaged employees, especially those with thousands of workers. However, David Sirota and Douglas A. Klein explain in their book *The Enthusiastic Employee* that keeping engagement and motivation levels very high is a realistic goal. The authors define this goal as the ability to generate "excited employees." To achieve this goal, companies have to address the main factors that affect motivation. These are classified in three areas: (1) Equity and fair treatment - reasonable wages and job security, adequate work environment, conscientious bosses (2) The achievement of employees and being fulfilled at work (3) The camaraderie and teamwork (the social capital) of the company. 18

Employee motivation and customer experience are two communicating vessels. This apparent maxim seems not so clear for many executives and companies.

The function of measuring employee motivation is often delegated to Human Resources and user experience to Marketing. In their book *Human Sigma*, John H. Fleming and Jim Asplund detail that service companies miss the mark when trying to separate the two measurements 19. Here we might have the beginnings of the problem. Employee motivation and customer experience should be the responsibility of the entire organization. Marketing and Human Resources departments can lead both metrics, but they have to count on everyone's commitment to improving them.

Likewise, it is critical to be transparent when measuring employee motivation. Employee's motivation and engagement must be measured at two levels: micro and macro. It is possible to attend to both in the same questionnaire. Still, it is necessary to distinguish between the questions that will measure the climate or organizational systems (macro) and a direct boss (micro). For example, these two questions do not serve the same purpose:

- "From 1 to 5, evaluate how committed you think the company is to its values."
- "From 1 to 5, evaluate how clear the roles and responsibilities among the members of your team are."

The first question affects executives (and direct bosses) and the second on the immediate boss's responsibility. In turn, it must be taken into account that the results are to be quantitative *and* qualitative. A qualitative answer implies that the employee has space (and is encouraged) to argue his answer.

Any employee evaluation survey should be carried out at least every six months. Waiting a year to do so is too long, especially if corrective measures must be taken. It is also essential to do excellent communication exercises to explain the reasons for these measurements. Likewise, public survey results must be communicated openly. Reporting with transparency, the actions that must be maintained or corrected are relevant to improving motivation.

## #3 Adequate resources

Beware of the mantra "Do more with less." Although this is a good and necessary idea in some contexts, it can turn against us when one is not realistic with the required resources. Then it becomes "Do less with less."

The third strategic area for achieving superior service is providing adequate resources. This does not mean that we necessarily have to invest more. Still, we must provide the resources needed to do a good job serving the client. It is not as evident as it might seem since, in many companies, a lack of minimal resources often discourages employees from doing a good job.

### *I shall tell you a story of a lack of resources...*

I have long worked as a director for a family vacation hotel company. At that time, the hotel group owner prioritized one goal: to maximize the economic benefits at the end of the season. For this, he had implemented a micro-management system in which only he could authorize personnel's hiring. This provision created a bottleneck in communication with the president. Furthermore, the company implemented policies to save personnel costs. If "x" was the minimum number of employees needed to guarantee a standard hotel's operation, the president demanded quality results to be achieved with that small number of workers.

As the high season approached, the hotel's occupancy increased, and the need for more reinforcements became evident. Rooms, bars, and restaurants were filled with customers, and the hotel wasn't staffed enough to provide adequate service. As the director, I implored the president to hire more staff, but my petition was always denied.

The hotel staff did the best they could. However, the lack of resources to do a decent job created widespread frustration. Worrying situations began to occur: unattended food buffets, uncleaned tables, lines of customers waiting at the restaurant door. I couldn't do anything other than help the waiters and attend to the entrance of the restaurant. It is not normal to see a hotel director pick up dirty dishes, clean tables, or accommodate clients. However, I couldn't bear to watch the waiters go the extra mile without doing something. Nor could I see customers waiting at the entrance of the restaurant without being served. The image was pitiful.

Tired of all that, through an act of courage and many risks, I decided to meet with the director of the tour operator group that brought us the most business and whom I knew personally. I made her an atypical and confidential request:

- I have an unusual favor to ask of you.
- Tell me, how can I help you?
- I was hoping you could write a letter, as the tour operator's director, to my hotel group's president. You would tell him that you have noticed an alarming lack of staff after many complaints and a personal inspection of the facilities. Therefore, you would demand this problem to be fixed immediately.

After that letter, I was authorized to bring in more staff.

This story is not uncommon in other employees or executives who cannot do quality work because they don't have appropriate resources. No matter what level of responsibility a person is in, the lack of resources to do an exceptional job creates frustration that undermines their motivation and commitment to the company. In his book *Getting The Service*

260

*Right*, Jeff Toiser asserts that companies' faulty systems and lack of resources can lead employees to mental states of 'learned helplessness.' [20]

This psychological state conditions workers to adopt a passive behavior because a lack of resources produces impotence and inability to improve things. "Why should I care or worry about doing a great job, going the extra mile, if executives don't care?"

Employees who perceive that companies deny them the necessary resources to carry out their work develop negative feelings. They can easily disconnect from their responsibility to serve the customer well or solve their problems. Why would they if the organization only cares about numbers instead of workers and customers? In this of lack of resources story, at least employees saw a concerned director, trying to do everything in his power to get help.

We must all be aware that resources are often limited. Still, bosses need to understand that the lack of minimal resources to do a good job is unacceptable. People expect bosses to be brave and use all their effort and credibility to maintain service quality.

"Work is personal," says Teresa Amabile, a Harvard doctor, and professor, in her book *The Progress Principle* [21]. The need to feel effective motivates us to undertake challenges and persist in the face of difficulties. But some setbacks, like a lack of resources, can ruin everything. People expect their companies to be consistent with what they profess; executive calls for quality and customer satisfaction cannot contradict a lack of resources.

### *Standardization and Empowerment*

Standardizing work processes is necessary. Companies have to ensure that customer expectations are met. In turn, employees need to perform operational tasks without having to constantly reinvent the wheel. Therefore, quality management and continuous improvement must start from an operational base.

However, standardization cannot limit exceptionally humane service. A standardized script should not condition the initiatives of the workers. Levels of autonomy must be established that allows collaborators to make relevant decisions about customer service. Not even the best standard can foresee all the service situations that a company may face. It would be absurd. Organizations that make these mistakes end up stranded in bureaucracy and inefficiency.

The capacity for self-management, participation, and autonomy of the employees build the idea of 'empowerment at work.' An exceptionally humane service has to strike a balance between standardization and empowerment. Service employees have to master operating systems, but they must also rise above the ordinances. There will always be routines to follow to ensure service functionality. But to serve a lofty purpose and create moments of opportunity in service, you need to empower employees.

**In-service empowerment encourages people to be more proactive. It motivates employees to positively surprise users by either anticipating or solving a service problem. However, the idea of empowerment must be aligned with sufficient resources such as information, training, and decision-making power.**

Empowering workers allows you to seize opportunities. Gallup points out that customer problems can be an alternative for strengthening relationships and improving the set of experiences 22. Solving a customer issue is a 'Moment of Truth.' To take advantage of these instances, the author indicates six steps that must be followed:

1. Recognize the problem: If the customer says they have a problem, they have a problem. Let's not treat the user like a capricious child.

2. Authentic and genuine apology. An apology is the least a customer expects. To do this, the person on the other side must develop empathy. Apologizing does not mean you have to accept blame. It is possible that the customer has misinterpreted information, that he or she is confused. However, the causes should not override your ability to understand the frustration.

3. Become aware of the problem and take responsibility. Once the customer has complained, now the ball is in your court. Does the complaint have an easy solution?

4. This step overlaps with the previous one. Here you will try to fix the problem in the first attempt. Do you possess the necessary resources to try to fix the problem on your own? Can you give a solution on the spot? Customers hate when they don't have alternatives or immediate answers to their demands. Why? Because like all people, uncertainty causes us anxiety. So, no matter how slight the concern, it would be convenient to offer them certainty and assurance that we are working on their problem.

5. It is also possible that the problem is more significant. Do we have to adjust it to our bosses? If so, the employee must

continually monitor and keep the customer informed. The dynamic cannot work in reverse, or the users have to ask for news of their case.

6. Solve the problem. The solutions provided should position the customer in a higher level of satisfaction than they were before the inconvenience. Suppose the problem resolution has been made correctly. In that case, the user will recognize the company's integrity and reinforce their commitment to the brand.

### *Standards and policies must be aligned for promoting outstanding service*

I remember my first working experience as a hotel receptionist. I had spent time outside of Spain, doing my studies and internships between Switzerland and Asia, where I was taught that customers were the most important thing. A company's policies and norms should be aligned to offer more value to the client through outstanding service. That should be the priority.

However, back then the hotel industry was not as competitive as it is today. These were times of high demand and low supply. The customer was not seen as a scarce commodity on which to prioritize any strategy. On the contrary, I could see that the user was often seen as a hindrance in those days. In this hotel where I worked, only policies and rules mattered. We had to follow standards like those of the mute oxen I mentioned in Chapter 5. Managers repressed any initiative that didn't follow hotel policies. The problem was that policies and norms weren't designed to provide more value to customers but rather to maximize hotel profits. They were designed from the inside out: the clients had to adapt to our standards.

264

"Why didn't clients understand our policies?" "Are they dumb?" I started to wonder. "If users stick to our 'well-designed' policies and processes, there would be no conflict," management would often reply. I began to see the client as 'capricious' and 'unpredictable'. Therefore, the solution was to make them see reason, condescendingly explaining our rules. This is the acculturation process that I talked about in previous chapters; only this is a case of negative acculturation. The 'vices' or 'bad practices' are also being acquired.

Similar stories with different characters and other contexts keep repeating themselves. Company rules and policies are an extension of managers' beliefs and priorities: they shape the organizational culture. The rules are designed by ignoring the fact that first it is the users who we must "fall in love with." Because without their "love," there is no money. "There is only one boss:the customer. And he can fire everybody in the company from the chairman on down, simply by spending his money somewhere else.," says Sam Walton, founder of Walmart. [23]

The organization's policies, norms and procedures must be considered resources for our employees to do a great job serving customers. They should not be an impediment, as is the case in many places.

Is the customer always right? Of course not, but the user is the boss. Indeed, rules and policies can protect companies from certain abuses by unethical users; however, the general view cannot start by considering the customer as the usual suspect. In the end, only a small minority commit illicit or dishonest acts.

Employees must be trained to apply their judgment, depending on the context. Specific rules should be flexible. In any case, management must put rules and procedures in quarantine if customers do not value them.

## #4 The right employees

Not all people are suitable for serving customers with passion, thus providing an exceptionally human service. Therefore, it is crucial to hire the right people.

Some jobs seem like anyone can do them. Supposedly, some jobs do not require qualification and are positioned as job opportunities for many young people who have not completed university degrees or even high school. An article in the newspaper El Confidencial entitled *The Lost Generation* warns of how the hospitality industry has replaced construction as the great employer of teenagers without studies. The recovery of employment highlighted a failure of schools. [24]

There is a problem that young people sometimes do not finish their high school studies. It is also true that many do not complete a higher education, university, or professional training. The category of "junk jobs" created by many companies not only responds to wages and working conditions, but to the career path they offer. However, the worst consequences of this phenomenon are suffered by the organizations themselves. Any company that limits job descriptions to functional tasks, such as bringing dishes to a table or taking orders from customers or cleaning a room, are also limiting their levels of service and limiting people's development.

As we have explained, motivation alone is not enough. You cannot encourage those who do not have a vocation to work with clients: 'passion' must be hired. Although it is always possible to train people, certain employees' inherent attitudes cannot be easily developed.

These personal qualities are the minimum that we must attend to in a selection process. Most of these factors make up what is known as Big Five personality traits. It is easier to train a technique than to develop character traits; the latter is determined, to no small extent, from a high degree of emotional intelligence, social stability, and personal confidence. It is part of a person's character.

### Agreeable personality and empathy

We can all be nice in any given moment, but only those who have a personality inclined to be agreeable can consistently maintain close and authentic treatment of others. The agreeableness personality trait causes people to be more cooperative, sympathetic, friendly, patient, polite, and understanding. This quality is usually inherited from parents, or developed through education and in the environment in which one lives.

On the other end of the spectrum, and opposite of kindness, lies the 'defiant', 'sullen' or 'detached' personality. A personality towards a lack of agreeableness. These people tend to be unpleasant in their daily interactions. They even manage to feel better when they show themselves this way to others.

People who are agreeable to others show higher empathy levels, therefore they can better deal with difficult or unpleasant clients. Their levels of patience and

267

understanding enable them to handle complaints and service issues better. The last thing you would expect from these types of employees is a response like: "Will you please calm down" or "I will not tolerate your tone of voice."

It should be noted that this type of response arouses the client's nervousness and activates defense moods like anger or even rage.

### Be aware and control your emotions

Emotional intelligence is not just about empathy. An emotionally intelligent person generates self-awareness; someone who can identify emotions as they happen, capable of recognizing of how one's own emotions affect others.

Although being self-aware is not enough on its own, people must be able to control their negative emotions. Danny Meyer, CEO of Union Square Hospitality Group, explains that service employees should be aware of their internal weather report. "We all have bad days. You are not a bad person when you have a bad day; however, hospitality is teamwork. Therefore, you must be aware of how your 'personal' weather report is impacting other people. "[25]

### Emotionally stable = positive

The opposite of emotional stability is neuroticism. A person more inclined towards this side of the personality spectrum tends to see more negative than positive. He is a hyper-vigilant individual who is continuously concerned about something. These are people who have a more sensitive amygdala: they perceive more dangers - real or imagined - and are on perennial alert [26]. For this reason, these people tend to suffer more stress and anxiety.

268

The ideal is to have workers who are outside a neurotic personality.

Efforts must be focused on adding more emotionally stable people who focus on positive factors; they can detect opportunities where others only see problems; to remain resilient in the face of adversity; showing more tolerance to stress. This disposition does not imply that these types of workers see life in through rose-colored glasses. They are not naive. They are realistic-optimistic people.

In service, these personality traits matter a lot. Serving ungrateful, dry, or difficult customers is no easy task. It would be best to have adequate internal energy that allows you to manage stress and manage self-control.

### *Proactive + Core Self Evaluation (CSE)*

Finally, it is advantageous to hire people who show confidence in their abilities; let them be humble and assertive. This security can be provided through training or by creating a business environment of psychological protection.

Confident, knowledgeable, and proactive people can generate more moments of opportunity with customers because they tend to be more creative and resourceful at solving problems or anticipating customer needs. They are also more competent at making decisions or managing service contingencies.

These four strategic service areas are equally important. They must work simultaneously. Companies that address these variables will be able to achieve higher levels of service and generate enthusiastic customers.

In the final chapter of this book, we will study sustainable purpose: corporate social and environmental responsibility. This purpose focuses on sustainability, a factor that not only enhances an organization's brand image, but can also create exceptional, coherent offers of products and services.

# CHAPTER 11: THE SOCIAL COMPANY

## BEYOND CORPORATE SOCIAL RESPONSIBILITY

Why should ethics and business be contradictory?

Edward Freeman, a professor at the Darden School of Economics, known for being the father of the theory of interest groups (stakeholders), suggests this crossroads:
"We have an idea of the business world in which ethics and business are disconnected. We think that business only involves competition and profit, but I think this is a mistake when it comes to an understanding of the true nature of a company. "[1]

The point is, we remain stuck in the business paradigm that prioritizes short-term profits. Most companies' main goal is to make more money at the end of the quarter or year; that is, to keep shareholders happy. This goal inevitably implies having to sacrifice interest in customers, employees, suppliers, and local communities.

You only need to read the newspaper or go through a library to see the countless unethical companies' efforts to make more money. For example, what would motivate Epson to tamper with its printers? Their teams reported the cartridges as empty when, in fact, they had 20 percent and 40 percent ink. Why did Volkswagen falsify the polluting emissions of its diesel vehicles, altering the calculation software? Why should

271

a company delay paying its suppliers, taking unfair advantage of its dominant position? What is the reason that many organizations hide the truth from their employees?

Some more questions:

Why should consumers have to go to official bodies to defend their rights against a companies' arbitrariness?

Why would a hotel chain pay local authorities to build a hotel in a protected area? 2

The likely reasons for these actions rest on an erroneous premise: if the shareholders are to be satisfied, there is no choice but to accept certain collateral damage. To increase their profits, companies make some sacrifices with the agents involved. "The business of business is business," defended Milton Friedman, father of economic neoliberalism.

Through this contradiction between ethics and business, the idea of Corporate Social Responsibility has arisen. CSR demands the deontological, ethical, and moral obligation of companies within their different interest groups. Although their intentions and actions may be right, the reality indicates that CSR fails to integrate itself into organizations' DNA; it is not given relevance in corporate decision making. At best, the CSR approach is not ambitious; at worst, it is merely ornamental.

Sustainability, well understood, is not Corporate Social Responsibility, explains John Elkington, a researcher who coined the concept of 'sustainability' and the idea of the 'triple bottom line.' 3 In his book *Cannibals with Forks* 4, Elkington anticipated 20 years ago that companies' success would depend on their capacities to manage three fundamental areas: profits, the environment, and social justice. However, experience indicates that the profit maximization paradigm continues to be the priority of organizations; it is the disposition that breaks the triple bottom line balance.

## Skepticism and ignorance of opportunities

Part of the inability to keep this triple bottom line is due to widespread skepticism. For this reason, the priority to reduce environmental impacts is tepid; sometimes, companies limit themselves to complying with current legislation; in others, they start projects to mitigate the ecological effects only when the savings are immediate.

**Often, companies also promote their CSR projects as sustainable milestones. Actions to reduce energy and water consumption, recycle waste or reduce plastic consumption are communicated as a panacea. But customers are becoming more demanding of the sustainable role of companies. The trend is bullish, and consumers expect companies to do much more than simple cosmetic actions to protect the environment.**

Social actions tend to be vague and fuzzy, as well. Often, they are limited to a philanthropic drive or sporadic collaboration with an NGO. Other times, they follow a well-intentioned stream of solidarity. For example, hotels that lend their facilities to set up hospitals to treat patients infected with coronavirus, or organize collections of clothing and non-perishable food to mitigate the effects of a natural catastrophe in some countries in the world, among others. In any case, the idea is to present itself as a brand that cares about the community, customers, and employees.

Concerning this phenomenon, a recent Gates Foundation report by Leaders' Quest found that most respondents - 50 experts and C-level executives from 30 companies - said that it is necessary to drive change. However, they were also cautious when asked to define *how* to do it 5. Respondents' data could be summarized as a 'yes, but no' approach. Many managers' prudence is justified in their fear of pestering shareholders: they do not want to be ahead of what investors demand.

What are investors asking for? They expect companies to minimize their costs in the short term, compared to focusing on long-term investments. Or they are more inclined to favor innovations that lead to improving profits more directly, compared to other types of social and environmental initiatives with a more tentative return in the short term. Many prefer to play defense, limited to corporate risk management in the face of ambitious strategies that could impact people and the planet. Ultimately, the importance of putting shareholder value first reinforces the dilemma for many CEOs.

Skepticism from executives is also joined by skepticism from customers and employees.

Employee skepticism is not in the results of social or environmental initiatives but in the authenticity of the organization's purpose to which they belong. Therefore, their motivation and commitment are often limited, either because the companies they work for do not seek a higher purpose or because they are not credible enough when they sing their praises. In both cases, organizations miss a golden opportunity to inspire their employees and attract more talent. According to several studies, a fundamental factor to attract and retain talent in companies is linked to the

274

employer's purpose. Not surprisingly, companies of different sizes and sectors have begun to realize the importance of creating an organizational culture guided by more inclusive values with employees, customers, and the community in general, as well as with nature.

A global study carried out by LinkedIn and the social platform Imperative has yielded exciting results on this subject. After conducting 26,000 surveys of LinkedIn members in 40 countries and 16 languages, the results reiterate the importance of purpose in companies. [6] Research questions focused on the motivation and attitudes of people when looking for a job. What moves them?

- "Is money that matters most to you?"
- "Is it the titles and position in the company?"
- "Are you motivated by the purpose of the company?"

The results indicate that 37 percent of those surveyed are mainly motivated by the purpose of a company when choosing a job. Another 38 percent of people place this factor at the same level of importance as the money or the position he or she will occupy within the company. The study also confirms that purpose is highly valued by baby boomers (48 percent), above Gen X and millennials (38 percent). These results break the myth that only millennials care and ask companies to be more responsible in their environmental and social goals.

Customers also show a high degree of skepticism. Like employees, they distrust the authenticity of the purpose of many businesses. Numerous studies show that consumers buy not just quality, functionality, price, and convenience, but also value.

According to an Accenture study, which covered more than 30,000 consumers in 35 countries, 62 percent of people ask companies to advocate for sustainability, transparency, and fairer labor practices with their workers. Approximately 5 billion people, between generation Y and Z, are and will be even more sensitive to the purpose of business. This study defines them as the "generation of purpose." [7]

In this sense, Deloitte has published work that seeks to guide executives on global marketing trends in 2020. Of a total of seven trends, two stand out:

(1) The purpose of the companies
(2) The human experience

The purpose that consumers demand is authentic and people-centered. Just as clients demand a more humane treatment, they also require that this disposition of companies be aligned with the facets of their general operations and that they focus on making a better world. [8]

This widespread skepticism makes the CSR approach of many organizations the subject of constant criticism. Public opinion does not recognize the altruism of companies' sustainability actions; they consider that their initiatives only seek to wash their image, incurring what is usually defined as 'greenwashing,' in the case of ecological and social actions.

## THE SUSTAINABLE COMPANY WITH A HIGHER PURPOSE

### The conscious enterprise: the best remedy is to combat widespread skepticism

The business must be part of the solution and not part of the problem. Together with state, civil society and non-governmental organizations, they must lead many of the world's challenges.

**Beyond CSR, you can find organizations very committed to their social and natural capital. These companies have a reason for existing beyond profits. For them, the purpose is compatible with the business bottom line. Indeed, profits are a by-product of the purpose and the company culture.**

**A new paradigm of capitalism has been developing for years; it is a more conscious system. In this new trend, companies prioritize their purpose and seek to connect assertively with their stakeholders, starting with employees and customers.**

Why?

Because there is no other way. "The capitalism we know is dead," says Marc Benioff, co-CEO of Salesforce. He continues: "[...] we need a new model of more just, egalitarian, and sustainable capitalism, a capitalism that includes all stakeholders, and not just shareholders" [9]. Salesforce is a company committed to its social and environmental actions. Marc Benioff has implemented his 1-1-1 program throughout the organization. One percent of profits, one percent of employee time and one percent of Salesforce products are donated to different charities. [10]

John Mackey and Raj Sisodia debunk the myth of profit maximization. The income from a business should not become an end in and of itself. Indeed, companies need profits to grow and continue operating; they are the source of new business and innovation opportunities. However, it is not difficult to see that income is a consequence of purpose: it belongs to a company's life cycle. It is the oxygen that allows them to breathe. Therefore, just as people do not live in order to breathe, companies should not conceive of profits as their reason for being.

People, the planet and benefits have to be better aligned. "The purpose of the corporation is to do things that address the problems confronting us as customers and communities, suppliers and shareholders, employees and retirees. In the process it produces profits, but profits are not the purpose of corporations *per se*. They are the product of their purposes.", explains Colin Mayer, former dean of the Saïd Business School, belonging to the University of Oxford [11]. "We agree that the objective of a company is to make money. But the purpose of companies must be much more ambitious. A company should hold to transparency to generate trust and attract investment, and profitability, factors that, in short, give it the power to change things and contribute to the growth of the societies where it operates. Companies also have an obligation to future generations, and they are not doing well. The terms of their governance are not on the right track. "[12]

## SDG (Sustainable Development Goals)

Since 2015, companies, governments, civil organizations, and other stakeholders have a common language to work through sustainability. The 2030 agenda recognizes companies as an engine of innovation and the main actor in global development.

The SDGs call for joint action to end poverty, create dignified lives and opportunities for all people and respect the natural limits of the planet [13]. These sustainable development goals are applicable to both developed and developing countries.

The United Nations explains that Sustainable Development Goals (SDGs) were built on the success of the Millennium Development Goals (MDGs). These new goals seek to go further to end poverty in all its forms. The new plans present the uniqueness of urging all countries, whether rich, low- or middle-income, to take steps to promote prosperity while protecting the planet. They recognize that initiatives to end poverty must go hand in hand with strategies that promote economic growth and address a series of social needs, including education, health, social protection and employment opportunities, as well as the time spent fighting against climate change and promoting the protection of the environment." [14]

*The SDGs: (Annex Table*)

Large, medium, and small companies are required to work on the SDGs. They must first understand them and then analyze their value chain and define their priorities. The 17 SDGs and 169 targets are not equally relevant for all organizations. Companies must identify their opportunities:

• Where can you have the most impact among the 17 SDGs you have set?
• What business opportunities can these sustainable development goals bring?
• How can all the value chain operations be integrated to reduce the environmental impacts reflected in the objectives, thereby increasing social benefits?
• What relationships will be established with stakeholders, and how will joint work be fostered to achieve these objectives?
• What alliances can be forged with other competing companies, NGOs, universities, or governments?

For example, the tourism sector has a vital role in these goals. SDG 1, "No poverty," can be performed by recruiting local personnel in those communities most in need or helping groups at risk of exclusion. Offering decent wages and promoting local purchases to small businesses, artisans, among others, are also alternative ways to contribute. SDG 4, "Quality education," can be worked on by creating alliances and business training programs that give people job opportunities within the tourism sector, and likewise provide opportunities for job development and continuous training of workers. SDG 7, "Affordable and clean energy," can be worked on by betting on clean energy, either on the property or by hiring green energy distributors; creating efficient natural resources consumption is another excellent contribution.

It should be noted that the SDGs must become part of the corporate culture. This matters a lot because, in this way, one avoids falling into 'greenwashing' vices concerning the objectives. This phenomenon could already be happening in companies, as is the case of some large hotel chains that have limited themselves to relating their common CSR strategies to the SDGs, but without going beyond the usual practices: they do not prioritize these objectives, nor do they set ambitious goals.[15]

Accenture and the United Nations Global Compact have monitored the implementation of the SDGs among companies. They have interviewed more than 1,000 executives from 21 different industries in 99 countries and confirmed that the business contribution to the goals, since they were launched in 2016, is not being enough. In 2019, only 21% of CEOs confirmed that they were making a substantial contribution to the SDGs.[16]

Entrepreneurs and corporate leaders worldwide now have a roadmap to change the business narrative and jointly contribute to social and environmental development. In 2017, Antonio Guterres, Secretary-General of the United Nations, stated at the UN Private Sector Forum that "if the business community does not fully embrace the SDGs, the impact on people, poverty and the planet will be minimal." "Without your leadership, our project will simply fail," he concluded.[17]

## Case study: a hotel that makes money from an altruistic principle

281

We all know the story of many entrepreneurs who have become rich and who, at specific moments, have donated large sums of money to social causes. For example, businessmen like Amancio Ortega, the founder of Inditex, indeed have merit, and their goodwill should be recognized when they donate millions of euros for health or other humanitarian programs. But there is another generation of social entrepreneurs, such as Marten Dresen, who acknowledge that companies can be more ambitious in their social and environmental impact. **Philanthropy is essential and necessary, but it is not enough. The sustainability challenges we face will not be solved through donations, no matter how generous, but through sustainable development goals that organizations achieve. This goal must be part of their DNA.**

The Good Hotel is a premium hotel chain with three hotels located in Guatemala, Amsterdam, and London and sustainable growth is projected in other destinations. These hotels seek to generate a unique value proposition through their product and service to their customers. So far, its business model is similar to most hotels. However, The Good Hotel also aims to set a new business paradigm: building a new standard and raising the bar in their industry.

How?

This organization has decided to generate training programs in catering and hotel management for long-term unemployed workers or affected social groups; the goal is to bring out the best in these people by offering help. However, The Good Hotel is not an NGO: it is a profit-seeking company that has to convince its customers first. This means that their product and service have to be exceptional. You cannot contribute to the SDGs or sustainability if you cannot first provide value to clients.

The training program they have designed for local hotel schools and other institutions is an intensive three-month theoretical-practical course. The demands are challenging, and students have to work hard to earn their degrees. For this reason, when they finish the training, they leave very well prepared to face a new career in the hotel or restaurant sector. Also, once they have graduated, the organization does everything possible for the students to enter the labor market; either in the same company or in others with which they collaborate. Altruistic impulses do not define these people's hiring, but they have received substantial training that allows them to bring value to any organization in the industry.

But its social contribution does not end there; the Good Group also contributes funds to other NGOs, among them, its foundation *Niños de Guatemala*. Likewise, they have prioritized strategies for sustainable actions with the environment.

Marten Dresen is the founder of these hotels. Before starting his career as an entrepreneur, he volunteered in Guatemala. His social actions went far; he obtained funds to open two schools in the country: "Nuestro Futuro" and "El Porvenir." The mission of both NGOs is part of the commitment to provide education in places where previously this opportunity did not exist. The future goal is to eradicate poverty in these areas. In addition to his humanitarian spirit, Dresen always showed a vocation for business. "When I graduated from university, it was clear to me that I wanted to be an entrepreneur," he says. [18]

Marten soon understood that he could generate even more social impact through a new business paradigm that did not put the profit first, and a business model that exceeds the common CSR or philanthropy proposals.

**Businesses can make money by doing good. However, the social enterprise also must be aware that both the value proposition and the management discipline are equal priorities.** This Dutch entrepreneur's goal is to create a unique product, but that in turn provides an excellent service experience through its people, and that customers are willing to pay more for this product. Only then will we be able to invest more in people in the long term. "Not all clients who come to Good Hotel know our history [social mission], so the product and quality we offer them have to be unique. Later, interacting with our staff, they can get to know what is behind it. That's when the magic happens," he concludes. 19

## ALTRUISM AND BUSINESS: 8 CHARACTERISTICS THAT MARK THE WAY FOR A SUCCESSFUL LINKAGE

What do Intrepid Travel, The Good Hotel, IKEA, Soneva, Scandic Hotels, Toms, Patagonia, Ben & Jerry's, Warby Parker, Natura, Toms of Main, Interface, Whole Foods Market, and Method all have in common? **All are brands that are highly admired by their customers because they provide a first-rate product and service while pursuing a higher purpose. The exciting thing is that, even when their purpose is not focused only on profits, these companies still report high profits.**

The good news is that these more socially oriented companies show their peers that it is possible to do business with another paradigm. They also teach that there are no constant sacrifices that have be made between stakeholders and shareholders.

The most authentic companies, with their purpose, share eight characteristics and working areas:

# #1. DNA = Culture

The founders and executives of these companies are the first to be committed to social and environmental initiatives. In some cases, these values were already part of their belief system, but others acquired them along the way. For example, entrepreneurs such as Ben Cohen, Jerry Greenfield (Ben & Jerry's), Yvon Chouinard (Patagonia) and Blake Mycoskie (TOMS) founded their companies prioritizing their social and ecological actions. But other entrepreneurs, such as Ray Anderson, founder of the industrial company Interface, gradually became apostles of change.

**These entrepreneurs could be defined as conscientious, ethical, or responsible leaders. In turn, they could be attributed to the title of Chief Sustainability Officer (CSO), in addition to CEO, since they are the first to promote sustainability in their companies.**

Some organizations prioritize their social purpose and others look to their environmental purpose. But generally speaking the triple balance between people, planet, and benefits is more balanced. This means that they will not sacrifice other interest groups to make more money in the short term. Therefore, sustainability is present in all business decisions.

# #2. Not perfect, but continually improving

Even the most sustainable companies are not entirely sustainable: they are not perfect, but their commitment to continuous improvement is more robust; they include ongoing goals to reduce their environmental impacts and increase social ones.

As we have explained in other chapters, excellence must be viewed as a continuous journey. The same goes for purpose. In fact, like the rest of the processes in a company, social and environmental sustainability should always be open to improvement. The kaizen philosophy also applies to this area; all employees are responsible for contributing ideas to improve processes.

**There will always be new challenges in overcoming mistakes, as well as creating opportunities and successes. In any case, clients and public opinion value these efforts more because these companies' message is powerful and connects with all stakeholders.**

This phenomenon reflects that these experiences are more credible than those of other companies; they have a different story and narrative. In short, their sustainability proposals are more ambitious and have the power to better impact consumers. Therefore, their message is more credible, relevant, and useful.

## #3. Value is impacted throughout the value chain

The commitment of these companies to sustainability does not remain simply a part of their operations but includes the entire life cycle of their products (LCA); they consider the impact they generate from all fronts: design, selection of materials, manufacturing, supplier management, distribution, and customer consumption, among others.

For example, in the case of a hotel, it must not only attend to its responsibility to reduce energy and water consumption and the generation of waste in its operations. A hotel sustainability strategy should include location, construction materials, type of suppliers, the impact of operations on the local area, the management of clients, the local community, etc. In this way, it works holistically, linking all areas of the company.

## #4. A higher transparency

Customers and consumers are often skeptical of companies' sustainable propositions, mainly because they are not transparent. Often, CSR or Sustainability reports are a copy-and-paste of previous years, or they only limit themselves to narrating a decalogue of correct actions, not counting the challenges and problems they encounter in their commitment to continuous improvement.

Transparency and honesty are two sides of the same coin. I mentioned before that most sustainable companies are not perfect, but they are more credible. Why? Among several reasons, the main one is because they are more transparent. **An organization with these characteristics shares information generously and continuously. They show the good and the bad.**

Patagonia is an example of transparency. Jill Dumain, its Director of Sustainable Strategy, describes it very clearly: "Everyone who works in the environmental area knows that if you are not talking about what is wrong, you are not telling the whole story." Similarly, Yvon Chouinard, founder of the company, explains that what matters most is that employees show the public that they are working to solve their problems: "If you are dishonest and try to hide your problems, they can always turn against you." [20]

In 2007, Patagonia launched its *Footprint Chronicles*: from its website, they share information about the materials that make up their products and their traceability, considering all the social and environmental impacts of their value chain. The objective lies in sharing the positive elements - renewable energy, recycling materials, organic cotton, fair trade certification, among others; and also the negatives - toxic chemical components in polymers, such as polyurethane (PU) or perfluorooctanoic acid (PFOA), etc.

## #5. More engaged employees

The first investment that a company has to make in its goal of sustainability begins with training. This type of company invests thoughtfully in training; they also manage to retain their employees. First, the idea is to train people and, once they learn, to begin to empower them.

For example, Scandic Hotels and IKEA began their paths to sustainability by training their executives first and then the rest of the employees. Both Scandic and IKEA enlisted the help of an organization called The Natural Step (TNS). This institution brings together scientists, environmental experts, and companies committed to research, education, and advice for development in advising companies on their search for sustainability.

TNS provides training for organizations that hire them. First, they teach the basics of sustainability. Later, they develop training with employees through workshops that promote the search for sustainable alternatives. Under this scenario, Scandic got 1,500 helpful suggestions for environmental and social improvement from workers who completed the TNS program 21. The recommendations were classified as follows:

(1) Short-term suggestions; feasible actions and activities that could be carried out immediately - actions that hardly required investment, such as best corporate practices.
(2) Ideas that need to go deeper.
(3) Ideas that need more investment.

**Experience shows that when employees are trained on environmental and social issues, their commitment increases. Even more so, if workers see first-hand how their actions can improve lives, they have indeed improved through the value chain.**

Employee commitment to the organization increases with this type of action. A company that pursues a higher purpose is also a better organization to work for. People's intrinsic motivation is manifested through the mission: "I work for a company that wants to help, in addition to making money."

## #6. Green Marketing

The most admired and most credible brands can engage the customers in a conversation. They keep them informed through all their communication channels. Traditional advertising and marketing are not as effective as they tend to focus on business objectives.

Green marketing differs from traditional marketing. Standard marketing practices don't work to communicate and share values with customers. Conversely, green marketing communicates principles and values. It seeks to inform, inspire, and educate consumers towards more responsible ways of consumption. It is not what is said or what is claimed to be believed that counts for the consumer, but the actions that are demonstrated.

This type of marketing could also be defined as ethical or values marketing.

The most credible organizations can afford a kind of moral 'superiority' to educate their customers towards more responsible consumption. These companies do not engage in the usual 'greenwashing' because their communication is authentic and transparent. Messages seek to raise awareness in public opinion.

## #7. Not just 'green,' but a first-class service and product

Do not fall into what is defined as "green myopia."

What is green myopia? This phenomenon refers to when a company neglects the user's unique value proposition, supposedly in exchange for prioritizing sustainability. Customers want brands to be more responsible, but above all, they ask for exceptional benefits. If a brand tries to attract customers only through its sustainability actions, it will fail miserably.

As John Grant clarifies in his book *The Green Marketing Manifesto*: "*Green* itself is actually not a functional product benefit. It does nothing for me directly, unless you count saving the planet that I am standing on." And he keeps saying: "A green product does not answer the ultimate UPS (unique selling proposition): What's in it for me? However, green products often do have secondary benefits; they can be more efficient, durable, affordable, or basic, or they can be healthier, better made, etc." [22]

For example, Scandic Hotels knows that a sustainability proposition is not enough on its own to deliver more value to customers. "Today, guests expect more than just a bed," says Anders Ehrling, CEO of the hotel chain. "We have to be able to respond with excellence to all variables -service, food, and design- to exceed user expectations," he reflects. [23]

Therefore, businesses could incur green myopia if their value proposition focuses on sustainability *per se*. **Sustainability matters, but it has to be part of the whole system. It will always be possible to integrate it into the experience in the best of cases, just as Soneva does.** This small hotel group has incorporated its sustainable initiative into its luxury value proposition, presenting it as something 'rare' and 'exclusive.' Its hotels are located in pristine locations and designed to merge with the environment. Soneva offers value by offering a unique product in a unique area. Sustainability is a secondary benefit throughout the customer experience.

## #8. A mission to inspire the rest

Social, conscious, and ethical entrepreneurs lead by example and demonstrate that they can be more profitable and competitive, also pursuing a social and environmental purpose. They inspire their employees first, and then their customers. But their work doesn't end there.

They are the first to participate and tell their story, their case study, to demonstrate that sustainability works. **These social entrepreneurs also show activism: seeking to inspire others.**

In the words of Ben Cohen and Jerry Greenfield: "The most powerful tool has a business's disposal is its voice. When businesses talk, people listen, politicians listen, the media listens. Yet, typically what businesses are talking about and advocating are issues that are in the business´ own self-interest, such as making more money. "[24]

That is why they are the first to open their doors, participate in forums and conferences to carry their message to other entrepreneurs. Additionally, they lead the initiatives to create alliances with competing companies, governments, and other institutions to better respond to users and the community's technical and social challenges.

**For these "social" entrepreneurs, the most excellent satisfaction comes from their contribution to creating a better world, adding their grain of sand.** This, for them, is more satisfying than financial gain *per se*.

## B-Corp companies

The aforementioned Good Hotel case could fall within the B-Corp philosophy, a good candidate to be certified under this seal. Other companies like Patagonia or Ben & Jerry's are already B-Corp. In Latin America, this is known as System-B or company-B.

The B-Corp movement was born with a purpose: to transform companies into a positive force capable of providing many solutions to people's daily problems. According to the present, this trend represents a necessary evolution of business; use the enormous potential that business has for changing things. B-Corp companies do not want to be the best in the world, but to do the best for the world.

Businesses certified as B-Corp meet the highest standards of sustainability, social impact, environment, transparency, and legality 25. In this way, organizations use their full potential to generate well-being for the community. Being B-Corp is not easy, but the visibility of this certification's logo is a significant boost to the brand. The companies in this category declare a social and environmental mission; they have been legally committed to both areas in the long term. Additionally, they have integrated these values into their organizational culture and have designed their corporate governance to make it possible.

**There are many environmental and social certifications, of greater or lesser prestige, as well as rigor, but few contemplate the sustainability of an entire business.** Furthermore, most limit themselves to implementing environmental actions and neglecting social factors. When they include the social area, they do so in a limited way and do not contemplate the company's employees. A company's social impact has to start with its employees.

B-Corp is a holistic certification that requires meeting 80 points out of 200. It seems easy, but very few companies get off the starting line. Usually, it takes them a while to get going.

Ultimately, the important thing is that companies create their sustainability strategies, meet the characteristics and demands that this challenge requires and, finally, establish a clear objective. Becoming a B-Corp company can be a worthy and significant goal for many organizations.

## The rule of 3: skepticism, goals, and balance

As has been seen, organizations' main obstacle in their quest for sustainability lies in skepticism -a widespread phenomenon- and managers, employees and customers show it. Therefore, fighting this vice is the first step. For this, the most crucial weapon that companies have lies in the highest purpose.

To the extent that companies avoid putting economic benefits at the center of their strategies and instead develop a holistic model that involves profit, the environment, and social justice as inseparable values, they can knock down the wall of mistrust.

As the numbers show, the problem is that these provisions are shared by company managers but are not reflected in actions. Therefore, this approach must permeate the DNA of organizations, blending with their cultures. It is not easy to achieve, although it is not impossible. Some companies are doing very well and represent clear examples. Likewise, there is a marked path: these eight characteristics in achieving sustainability are signals that can reduce uncertainty and provide results.

Finally, you must have a horizon: the B-Corp certification, for example, is an excellent title to stimulate the strategies and actions of companies. Besides, the benefit they generate to organizations' brand image is proven (this certificate cannot be obtained through superficial initiatives).

In short, trying to become a B-Corp company can be fertile ground for promoting transformative actions, since it will require breaking all the myths that exist in the relationship between altruism and business.

# Bibliography

## Chapter 1

1: Frankl, Victor. *El hombre en busca de Sentido* (Herder Editorial S.L. Barcelona. 1970)

2: Mackey, John y Sisodia, Raj. Conscious Capitalism (Harvard Business School Publishing Corporation. Boston MA. 2013.) p.41-67.

3: Gómez, Manuel V. El País. Kike Sarasola reprende a sus empleados en un vídeo por no querer reincorporarse de un ERTE. 2020 https://elpais.com/economia/2020-07-23/kike-sarasola-abronca-a-sus-empleados-en-un-video-por-no-querer-reincorporarse-de-un-erte.html

4: Barrywehmiller. Our Guiding Principles (s.f). https://www.barrywehmiller.com/our-culture/our-guiding-principles

5: TEDx. *Truly human leadership: Bob Chapman at TEDxScottAFB.* Youtube. 22:02. June 20, 2012. https://www.youtube.com/watch?v=njn-IIEv1LU

6: Mathieu, Cynthia & Neumann, Craig & Hare, Robert & Babiak, Paul. (2014). *A dark side of leadership: Corporate psychopathy and its influence on employee well-being and job satisfaction.* Personality and Individual Differences. 59. 83–88.

7: Stanford Graduate School of Business. Bill George: Leaders Need High Emotional IQ to Succeed. Video Youtube. 51:22. 21 November, 2011. https://www.youtube.com/watch?v=Xpe90T6_Dwk

## Chapter 2

1: Amabile, Teresa y Kramer, Steve. *The Progress Principle: Using Small Wins to Ignite Joy, Engagement and Creativity at Work* (Harvard Business Review Press, 2011), p.20.

2: Hill, Linda A. y Lineback, Kent. *Being The Boss: The 3 Imperatives for Becoming a Great Leader* (Harvard Business Review Press, 2011), p.7.

3: Sirota, David y Klein, Douglas A. *The Enthusiastic Employee: How Companies Profit by Giving Workers What They Want* (Pearson Education, Inc. 2014. Kindle Edition).

4: Nolan, Tom. *The Nº1. Employee Benefit That No One's Talking About.* https://www.gallup.com/workplace/232955/no-employee-benefit-no-one-talking.aspx

5: De Pree, Max. *Leadership Is an Art* (Crown Publishing Group, New York. 2003. Kindle Edition), p.107.

6: Mackey, Harvey. *You Haven't Hit Your Peak Yet!* (Jon Wiley & Sons, Inc., Hoboken, New Jersey. 2020), p.19.

7: Huguet, Carles. Economía Digital (ED). *"El trabajador debe notar la presión de los objetivos para rendir".* 2017 https://www.economiadigital.es/directivos-y-empresas/amancio-lopez-el-trabajador-debe-notar-la-presion-de-los-objetivos-para-rendir_187628_102.html

8: Yerkes – Dodson Law. Wikipedia. Recovered on the 2nd May, 2020. https://en.wikipedia.org/wiki/Yerkes–Dodson_law

9: Mintzberg, Henry. *Managing* (Financial Times Prentice Hall, Pearson Education Limited. Edinburgh Gate, Harlow. 2009-2011), p.31.

10: Ibid.

11: Hill, Linda A. *Becoming the Boss*. 2007. Harvard Business Review https://hbr.org/2007/01/becoming-the-boss

12: Ibid.

13: Dweck, Carol S. *Mindset: The New Psychology of Success* (Ballantine Books Inc. 2007)

14: Ibid.

15: Bock, Laszlo. *Work Rules!* (John Murray Publishers 2015. Kindle Edition), Chap 5.

16: Ibid.

17: Garvin, David A. Wagonfeld, Alison B. Kind, Liz. (2015). *Google's Project Oxygen: Do Managers Matter?* HBS No. 9-313-110. Boston, MA: Harvard School Publishing.

18: Bock, Laszlo. *Work Rules!* (John Murray Publishers 2015. Kindle Edition), Chap 4.

19: Cuenllas, Arturo. *People Development at the Rezidor Hotel Group: A Case Study of A Successful Approach to Talent Management.* 2014. https://www.hospitalitynet.org/opinion/4066866.html

20: Hill, Linda A. y Lineback, Kent. *Being The Boss: The 3 Imperatives for Becoming a Great Leader* (Harvard Business Review Press, 2011), p.8.

21: Amabile, Teresa y Kramer, Steve. *The Progress Principle: Using Small Wins to Ignite Joy, Engagement and Creativity at Work* (Harvard Business Review Press, 2011), p.58.

22: Stack, Jack y Burlingham, Bo. *The Great Game of Business* (Profile Books LTD, Suffolk, Great Britain. 2013. Kindle Edition), Chap 2.

23: Crossan, Mary. Seijts Gerard y Gandz, Jeffrey. Developing Leadership Character (Taylor & Francis Group, 2016. Kindle Edition), Chap 1.

24: Mintzberg, Henry. *Managing* (Financial Times Prentice Hall, Pearson Education Limited. Edinburgh Gate, Harlow. 2009-2011), p.8-9.


**Chapter 3**

1: Heskett, James. *The Culture Cycle: How to Shape the Unseen Force that Transforms Performance* (Financial Times Prentice Hall, Pearson Education Limited. 2012. Kindle Edition) Chap 1.

2: McGregor, Douglas. *The Human Side of the Enterprise* (McGraw-Hill, annotated edition. 2006.)

3: The Economist. *Idea: Theories X and Y*. 2008. Artículo recuperado de: https://www.economist.com/news/2008/10/06/theories-x-and-y

4: McGregor, Douglas. *The Human Side of the Enterprise* (McGraw-Hill, annotated edition. 2006.)

5: ABC. *Ryanair hace que la Guardia Civil expulse a una pasajera que quería volar con una «bolsita»* 2012. https://www.abc.es/espana/comunidad-valenciana/abci-ryanair-bolsa-manises-201210310000_noticia.html

6: Cinco Días. *Otro verano de pesadilla para Ryanair: afronta huelgas en cuatro países.* 2019. https://cincodias.elpais.com/cincodias/2019/08/15/companias/1565859056_126767.html

7: Creaton, Siobhán. *Ryanair: How a Small Irish Airline Conquered Europe* (Aurum Press Ltd. 2007. Kindle Edition), p.62.

8: Covene. *Colleen Barrett // Creating A High Performing Culture through Servant Leadership*. Youtube. 33:16. 26 May, 2015. https://m.youtube.com/watch?v=27HnWTZE2c4

9: Mackey, John y Sisodia, Raj. Conscious Capitalism (Harvard Business School Publishing Corporation. Boston MA. 2013.) p.75.

**Chapter 4**

1: Rhoades, Ann y Shepherdson, Nancy. *Built on Values: Creating an Enviable Culture that Outperforms the Competition*. (Jossey-Bass. A Wiley Imprint. San Francisco. CA. 2011. Kindle Edition), p.14.

2: Ibid.

3: Rossman, John. *Think Like Amazon: 50 ½ Ideas to Become a Digital Leader* (McGraw Hill Education ebook. Kindle Edition, 2019)

4: El País. Aprendemos Juntos, BBVA. *¿Qué diferencia a la gente más feliz del mundo?* https://aprendemosjuntos.elpais.com/especial/se-puede-aprender-a-ser-feliz-tal-ben-shahar/

5: Polzer, Jeffrey T y Gardner, Heidi K. (2013). Bridgewater Associates (Multimedia Case). HBS 413702-HYM-ENG. Boston MA. Video 17.

6: Dalio, Ray. *Principles: Life and Work*. (Simon & Shuster. 2017. Kindle Edition), Chap 3.

7: Mackey, John y Sisodia, Raj. *Conscious Capitalism* (Harvard Business School Publishing Corporation. Boston MA. 2013.), p.186.

8: McCord, Patty. *How Netflix Reinvented HR*. 2014. Recuperado de: https://hbr.org/2014/01/how-netflix-reinvented-hr

9: Michelle, Joseph A. *The New Gold Standards: 5 Leadership Principles for Creating a Legendary Customer Experience* (McGraw Hill. 2008. Kindle Edition.), Chap 4.

10: Freiberg, Kevin & Jackie. Nuts! Southwest Airlines Crazy Recipe for Business and Personal Success. (Broadway Books, Broadway. New York. NY. 1996), p.287.

11: Kantor, Jodi y Streitfeld, David. *Inside Amazon: Wrestling Big Ideas in a Bruising Workplace.* 2015. The New York Times.
https://www.nytimes.com/2015/08/16/technology/inside-amazon-wrestling-big-ideas-in-a-bruising-workplace.html

12: McCord, Patty. *Powerful: Building a Culture of Freedom and Responsibility.* (Silicon Guild, 2017. Kindle Edition), Chap 8.

13: Dalio, Ray. *Principles: Life and Work.* (Simon & Shuster. 2017. Kindle Edition), p.88.

14: Hsieh, Tony. Delivering Happiness: A Path to Profits, Passion, and Purpose. (Business Plus, Hachette Book Group. New York. NY. 2010), p.181.

15: Michelle, Joseph A. *The Zappos Experience: 5 Principles to Inspire, Engage, and Wow* (McGraw Hill. 2012. Kindle Edition), p.56.

16: Mackey, John y Sisodia, Raj. Conscious Capitalism (Harvard Business School Publishing
Corporation. Boston MA. 2013.), p.89.

17: Garvin, David A. Wagonfeld, Alison B. Kind, Liz. (2015). *Google's Project Oxygen: Do Managers Matter?* HBS No. 9-313-110. Boston, MA: Harvard School Publishing.

18: Nordstrom. *Dimond Story.* Youtube. 2:56. 30 December, 2011. https://www.youtube.com/watch?v=LbkhEB6H8Xk

19: Alec Dalton. Line-up at The Ritz Carlton Corporate Office. Youtube, 14:24. 10 May, 2015. https://www.youtube.com/watch?v=CEJ4YShx2BQ

**Chapter 5**

1: Dertouzos Michael, Lester Richard K. y Solow Robert M. *Made In America: Regaining the Productive Edge* (Harper Perennial, New York.1990.)

2: Winslow Taylor Frederick. *The Principles of Scientific Management* (Suzeteo Enterprises. Originally published in 1911. 2014), p.6.

3: Drucker, Peter. *Drucker Esencial* (Editorial Sudamericano y Edhasa. 2003), p.82.

4: La Vanguardia. *"Eres un número, una silla, una persona que sólo coge llamadas."* 2017.

https://www.lavanguardia.com/economia/20170801/43248228334/sector-contact-center-teleoperadores.html

5: Sainato, Michael. *'We are not robots': Amazon warehouse employees push unionize.*2019. https://www.theguardian.com/technology/2019/jan/01/amazon-fulfillment-center-warehouse-employees-union-new-york-minnesota

6: Survey conducted in Organise. Organise is an online community in UK. Survey made between February and March 2018. https://static1.squarespace.com/static/5a3af3e22aeba594ad56d8cb/t/5ad098b3562fa7b8c90d5e1b/1523620020369/Amazon+Warehouse+Staff+Survey+Results.pdf

7: Bloodworth, James. *"I work in an Amazon warehouse. Bernie Sanders is right to target them."* 2018. https://www.theguardian.com/commentisfree/2018/sep/17/amazon-warehouse-bernie-sanders

8: **Footnote:** This comparison seems to me, still and all, unfortunate. Since there are real practices of labor slavery in other countries: See Global Slavery Index 2018: https://www.globalslaveryindex.org/resources/downloads/

9: Equipo de Investigación. *La Lucha de las Kelly's*. La Sexta. 2017.

10: Pink, Daniel. *Drive: The Surprising Truth About What Motivate Us* (Canongate Books, Main. 2010. Kindle Edition.), p.144.

11: Spector, Robert y McCarthy, Patrick. *The Nordstrom Way to Customer Service Excellence* (John Wiley & Sons, Inc. Hoboken, New Jersey. 2012. Kindle Edition), pos. 327.

12: Linker, Jeffrey K. *Las Claves del éxito de Toyota*. (Gestión 2000), p.35.

13: Davenport, Thomas H. *Motivar, Retener y Crear Valor en la Era del Conocimiento.* (Ediciones Deusto. HBS School Press. 2006.), p.23.

14: Drucker, Peter. *The Effective Executive* (Harper Collins Publishers. 2006. Kindle Edition.)

15: Tindell, Kip. *Uncontainable; How Passion, Commitment, and Conscious Capitalism Built a Business Where Everyone Thrives* (Gran Central Publishing. 2014. Kindle Edition), Chap 4.

16: Pink, Daniel. *Drive: The Surprising Truth About What Motivate Us* (Canongate Books, Main. 2010. Kindle Edition.)

17: Warner, Rodd y Barter, James K., PhD. *The 12 Elements of Great Managing* (Gallup Press, New York. 2006. Kindle Edition.) Pos 38.

18: Michelli, Joseph A. *The New Gold Standard*. (McGraw Hill, 2008. Kindle Edition.), p.155.

19: Ton, Zeynep. *The Good Jobs Strategy* (Lake Union Publishing, 2014. Kindle Edition.) Chap 6.

20: Amy Thomson. *The Human Effort to Sail The Cosmos on Sunlight*. 2019. Supercluster: https://www.supercluster.com/editorial/solar-sails?xid=PS_smithsonian

21: Wrzesniewski, Amy, Dutton Jane E. and Debebe, Gelaye. *Interpersonal Sensemaking and the Meaning of work*. 2003.

22: Rework. Job Crafting - Amy Wrzesniewski on creating meaning in your work. Video Youtube. 12:29. 10 November, 2014. https://www.youtube.com/watch?v=C_igfnctYjA

23: Robèrt, Karl-Henrik. *The Natural Step* (New Catalyst Books. 2008), p.102.

24: Bhatnagar, Jyotsna y Jaiswal, Shweta (2016). *Amazon as an Employer*. Ivey Publishing. No. 9B16C006

**Chapter 6**

1: Tuckman Bruce W., Jensen, Mary Ann C. *Stages of Small-Group Development Revisited*. Group & Organizational Studies (pre-1986); Berverly Hills Vol.2, Iss. 4, (Dec 1977), 419.

2: Catmull, Ed y Wallace, Amy. *Creativity Inc.: Overcoming the Unseen Forces That Stand in the Way of True Inspiration* (Transworld Digital, 2014, Kindle Edition) Chap 4, pos 1177.

3: Mackey, John y Sisodia, Raj. Conscious Capitalism (Harvard Business School Publishing Corporation. Boston MA. 2013.), p.238-239.

4: Ibid, p.89

5: Ibid, p. 92-93.

6: Rossman, John. *The Amazon Way on IoT: 10 Principles for Every Leader from the World's Leading Internet of Things Strategies* (Clyde Hill Publishing, Bellevue, Washington, 2016. Kindle Edition). Chap 5, p.67.

7: Hackman, Richard. *Leading Teams: Setting the Stage for Great Performances* (Harvard School Press. Boston. MA. 2002 ), p. 116-122

8: Tichy Noel. Mica Schneider Rating the Management Gurus. Business Week. 2001.

9: Raue, Steve; Tang, Suk-Han; Weiland, Christian y Wenzlik Class. *The GRPI Model: an Approach for Team Development.* White Paper Draft, p.6. Systemic Excellence Group. 2013

10: Roberto, Michael A., and Edmondson Amy C.. *Everest Leadership and Team Simulation.* Simulation and Teaching Note. Boston: Harvard Business School Publishing, 2008. Electronic. (Product number 2650.)

11: Rhoades, Ann y Shepherdson, Nancy. *Built on Values: Creating an Enviable Culture that Outperforms the Competition.* (Jossey-Bass. A Wiley Imprint. San Francisco. CA. 2011. Kindle Edition) Chap 5, p. 75 y 76

12: Stack, Jack y Burlingham, Bo. *The Great Game of Business* (Profile Books LTD, Suffolk, Great Britain. 2013. Kindle Edition), Chap 1, p.34.

13: Ibid, Cap 5, p.101.

14: Southwest Investor Relations. *Southwest Airlines Employees Earn $544 Million in 2018 ProfirSharing.* 2019. http://investors.southwest.com/news-and-events/news-releases/2019/02-13-2019-195947063

15: Stanford Graduate School of Business. *Alan Mulally of Ford: Leaders Must Serve with Courage.*Youtube, 52:19. 7 February, 2011.

https://www.youtube.com/watch?v=ZIwz1KIKXP4&app=deskt
op

16: Edmoson, Amy C.. *Learning From Mistakes Is Easier Said Than Done: Group and Organizational Influences on the Detection and Correction of Human Error.* The Journal of Applied Behavioral Science, Vol. 40 No. 1, March 2004, 66-90.

17: Willink Jocko, y Babin, Leif. *Extreme Ownership: How U.S. Navy SEALS Lead and Win* (St. Martin's Press, New York, 2017), Chap 8.

18: McCord, Patty. *Powerful: Building a Culture of Freedom and Responsibility.* (Silicon Guild, 2017. Kindle Edition). Chap 3, pos. 635.

19: Sutton, Bob. *Good Boss, Bad Boss: How to Be the Best...and Learn from the Worst* (Business Plus, Hachette Book Group. New York. 2012. Kindle Edition). Chap 2, p. 82.

20: Dalio, Ray. *Principles: Life and Work.* (Simon & Shuster. 2017. Kindle Edition) Life Principles. Chap 3, p.190.

21: Rock, David. *Your Brain at Work: Strategies for Overcoming Distraction, Regaining Focus, and Working Smarter all Day Long* (Harper Collings e-books, 2009.Kindle Edition) Chap 3, p.35-36.

22: Bethune, Gordon. From Worst to First: Behind the Scenes of Continental's Remarkable Comeback (John Wiley & Sons, Inc.), p.159-160.

23: Levy, Paul F. *Goal Play! Leadership Lessons from the Soccer Field* (Create Space Interdependent Publishing Platform, 2012. Kindle Edition), Chap 2.

24: Gittell, Jody H. The Southwest Airlines Way: Using the Power o Relationships to Achieve High Performance (McGraw-Hill, 2003), p. 102-105.

25: Janis, Irving. A first Look at Communication Theory (McGraw Hill, New York, 1991), p.235- 246.

26: Heffernan, Margaret. *Forget the Pecking Order at Work*. Ted Talk: Margarett Heffernan, 2015.

27: Kelly, Tom y Kelly David. *Creative Confidence: Unleashing the Creative Potential Within Us* (Crown Business New York, 2013), Chap 2, p.81

**Chapter 7**

1: Whitmore, John. Coaching for Performance (Nicholas Brealey Publishing, 2009. Kindle Edition), Chap 1, p.13

2: Rock, David, Davis, Josh y Jones, Beth. *Kill Your Performance Ratings: Neuroscience shows why numbers-based HR management is obsolete*. Strategy+Business. 2014. Issue 76.

3: Margolis, Joshua, McKinnon, Paul y Norris, Michael. (2015). *Gap Inc.: Refashioning Performance Management*. HBS No. 9-416-019. Boston, MA: Harvard School Publishing.

4: Harvard Health Publishing. *Giving thanks can make you happier* https://www.health.harvard.edu/healthbeat/giving-thanks-can-make-you-happier

5: Warner, Rodd y Barter, James K., PhD. *The 12 Elements of Great Managing* (Gallup Press, New York. 2006. Kindle Edition.) Chap 4.

6: Pan, Jose Manuel. *"En un hotel de lujo todo tiene que ser perfecto."* 2018. https://www.lavozdegalicia.es/noticia/mercados/2018/04/29/hotel-lujo-perfecto/0003_201804SM29P11998.htm

7: Wiseman, Liz. *Multipliers: How the Best Leaders Make Everyone Smarter* (Harper Business.. 2017. Kindle Edition.)

8: Heskett, James. The Ultimate Question in Management. Harvard Business School: Working Knowledge. 2011. https://hbswk.hbs.edu/item/the-ultimate-question-in-management

9: Keagan, Robert y Lacey, Lisa L. *An Everyone Culture: Becoming a Deliberately Developmental Organization* (Harvard Business Review Press. Boston, MA. 2016. Kindle Edition.). Chap 3, p.95-98

10: Ibid, p.1, 2-3, 84, 90, 105-106, 181-182

11: Scott, Kim. *Radical Candor: How to Get What you Want by Saying What you Mean* (Pan Macmillan, 2018)

12: Bressler, Martin & Von Bergen, Clarence. (2014). *The Sandwich Feedback Method: not very tasty.* Journal of Behavioral Studies in Business. 7.

13: Stone, Brad. *The Everything Store* (Transword Digital, 2013. Versión Kindle). Chap 9, pos. 3926

14: Catmull, Ed y Wallace, Amy. *Creativity Inc.: Overcoming the Unseen Forces That Stand in the Way of True Inspiration* (Transworld Digital, 2014, Kindle Edition), pos. 4307-4572.

15: Sutton, Robert I. *The Asshole Rule. Building a Civilized Workplace and Surviving One that Isn't* (Business Plus, 2007. Kindle Edition), Chap 4, pos. 1211-1221.

16: Maslow, Abraham H. *Maslow on Management* (John Wiley & Sons inc. 1998) p.166

17: Covey, Stephen R. *Los 7 Hábitos de la Gente Altamente Efectiva* (Paidós Booklet, Ed. 2013) p.246-247, 250-251.

18: Dalio, Ray. *Principles: Life and Work.* (Simon & Shuster. 2017. Kindle Edition) p.353

19: Rock, David. *Your Brain at Work: Strategies for Overcoming Distraction, Regaining Focus, and Working*

*Smarter all Day Long* (Harper Collings e-books, 2009.Kindle Edition) Cap. 12, p.190.


## Chapter 8

1: Firth, Robert. *The Aftermath*. iBookit.com. Chap 2. https://books.google.es/books?id=yOcaV4thi2EC&lpg=PT10&ots=y5beFbdvut&dq=dutch%20not%20recognizing%20fault%20in%20van%20zanten&hl=es&pg=PT10#v=onepage&q=dutch%20not%20recognizing%20fault%20in%20van%20zanten&f=false

2: Sierra, Julio. *Los pilotos consideran a Los Rodeos "un aeropuerto pesadilla."* 1977. https://elpais.com/diario/1977/03/29/espana/228438029_850215.html

3: Brackett, Marc. *Permission to Feel: Unlocking the Power of Emotions to Help Our Kids, Ourselves, and Our Society Thrive* (Celadon Books, New York. 2019. Kindle Edition), Chap 8, p.158.

4: Aldao, Amelia. *Why Labeling Emotions Matters*. 2014. https://www.psychologytoday.com/us/blog/sweet-emotion/201408/why-labeling-emotions-matters

5: Langer, Ellen J. Mindfulness: 25th Anniversary Edition (A Merloyd Lawrence book. Da Capo Press Books. 2014. Kindle Edition), pos. 117.

6: *Air Florida 90*. Wikipedia. From the 10th July 2020: https://en.wikipedia.org/wiki/Air_Florida_Flight_90

7. Crossan, Mary. Seijts Gerard y Gandz, Jeffrey. Developing Leadership Character (Taylor & Francis Group, 2016. Kindle Edition), p. 6

8: Cuddy, Amy. *Presence: Bringing your Boldest Self to your Biggest Challenges* (Orion Books, London. 2015. Kindle Edition) Chap. 5, p. 111.

9: Gary Vaynerchuk Fan Channel. Self-Awareness [Gary Vaynerchuk].Youtube. 23:33. 21 January, 2017. https://www.youtube.com/watch?v=VThmmnu19H4

10: George, Bill. *Discover Your True North: Becoming an Authentic Leader* (John Wiley & Sons, Inc. Hoboken, New Jersey, 2015. Kindle Edition), pos. vii- viii.

11: Bennis, Warren. *On Becoming a Leader* (Basic Books, 2009. Kindle Edition) pos.1124.

12: Kruger, Justin & Dunning, David. (2000). *Unskilled and Unaware of It: How Difficulties in Recognizing One's Own Incompetence Lead to Inflated Self-Assessments.* Journal of Personality and Social Psychology. 77. 1121-34. 10.1037//0022-3514.77.6.1121.

13: Platón. *Apología de Sócrates. Critón. Carta VII* (Espasa Calpe, S.A, Madrid. 1990), p.67.

14: Eurich, Tasha. *Insight: How to Succeed by Seeing Yourself Clearly* (Macmillan, 2017. Kindle Edition), p. 3 – 6

15: Fowler, Susan. *Reflecting On One Very, Very Strange Year at Uber.* 2017. Artículo recuperado de: https://www.susanjfowler.com/blog/2017/2/19/reflecting-on-one-very-strange-year-at-uber

16: Covington & Burling. *Statement on Covington & Burling Recommendations.* Uber Newsroom. 2017. https://www.uber.com/newsroom/covington-recommendations/

17: Bradley, Paul. *"We call TA that Boob-er:" The four most awful things Travis Kalanick said in his GQ profile.* 2014. https://pando.com/2014/02/27/we-call-that-boob-er-the-four-most-awful-things-travis-kalanick-said-in-his-gq-profile/

18: Swisher, Kara y Bhuiyan, Johana. *Uber CEO Kalanick advised employees on sex rules for a company celebración*

*2013     'Miami     letter'.     2017.*
https://www.vox.com/2017/6/8/15765514/2013-miami-letter-uber-ceo-kalanick-employees-sex-rules-company-celebration

19: Hatfield, E., Cacioppo, J. L. & Rapson, R. L. (1993). *Emotional contagion. Current Directions in Psychological Sciences,* 2, 96-99.

20: Goleman, Daniel; Boyatzis, Richard; McKee, Annie. *Primal Leadership: Unleashing the Power of Emotional Intelligence* (Harvard Business School Publishing. Boston, MA. 2013. Kindle Edition), Chap 1, pos. 203.

21: Kahneman, Daniel. *Pensar rápido, pensar despacio* (Debate, 2012. Kindle Edition).

22: Scharge, Michael. *Daniel Kahneman: Thought Leader Interview.* 2003. Business+Strategy. https://www.strategy-business.com/article/03409?gko=d1233

23: Ibid.

24: Dalio, Ray. *Principles: Life and Work.* (Simon & Shuster. 2017. Kindle Edition) Chap. 5, p. 235-266.

25: Medina, John. *Brain Rules: 12 Principles for Surviving and Thriving at Work, Home, and School* (Pear Press, Seattle. WA. 2014. Kindle Edition) p. 104-123

26: TEDxTalks. The Magical Science of Storytelling/David JP Phillips/TEDxStockholm. Youtube. 16:44. 16 March, 2017. https://www.youtube.com/watch?v=Nj-hdQMa3uA

27: Hurst, A; Pearce, A; Cammie E; Scott, P; Kotansky, H; Vesty, L; Schnidman, A; Garlinghouse, M; Pavela, A. *Putting Purpose to Work: A Study of Purpose in the Workplace.* 2016. PWC.

28: Amabile, Teresa y Kramer, Steve. *The Progress Principle: Using Small Wins to Ignite Joy, Engagement and Creativity at Work* (Harvard Business Review Press, 2011), p.50-.54

29: Brackett, Marc. *Permission to Feel: Unlocking the Power of Emotions to Help Our Kids, Ourselves, and Our Society Thrive* (Celadon Books, New York. 2019. Kindle Edition), p.69

## Chapter 9

1: Covey, Stephen R. *Los 7 Hábitos de la Gente Altamente Efectiva* (Paidós Booklet, Ed. 2013) p.381

2: Cigna. *360° Well-Being Survey Well & Beyond.* 2019. Cigna.com:
https://wellbeing.cigna.com/360Survey_Report.pdf

3: Ray Julie. *Americans' Stress, Worry and Anger Intensified in 2018.* 2019. Gallup.
https://news.gallup.com/poll/249098/americans-stress-worry-anger-intensified-2018.aspx

4: Viejo, Manuel. Uno de cada cinco españoles sufre síntomas de depresión y ansiedad por el coronavirus. 2020. El País.https://elpais.com/espana/madrid/2020-05-06/uno-de-cada-cinco-espanoles-sufre-sintomas-de-depresion-y-ansiedad-por-el-coronavirus.html

5: Instituto de Salud Pública y Laboral de Navarra. Estudio de la situación de salud durante el confinamiento. Actividad física. 2020.
https://www.navarra.es/documents/48192/4142282/ppt+coronarivurus.ppt/61f3d979-7cec-36cf-1d84-d12fc3300bd0?t=1588678024606

6: Dweck, Carol S. *Mindset: The New Psychology of Success* (Ballantine Books Inc. 2007)

7: Siegel, Ronald D. *The Mindfulness Solution: Everyday Practices for Everyday Problems* (The Guilford Press, New York. NY. 2010. Kindle Edition), Chap. 2, p.41

8: Ibid.

9: Kabat-Zinn, Jon. *Mindfulness for Beginners: Reclaimng the present moment -and you life* (Sounds True, Inc. Boulder. CO Kindle Edition), p.17

10: Tovar, Javier. ¿Qué diferencia hay entre la meditación y el mindfulness? 2017. EFE: Salud. Artículo recuperado de: https://www.efesalud.com/diferencia-meditacion-mindfulness/

11: Chamine, Shirzad. *Positive Intelligence: Why Only 20% of Teams and Individuals Achieve Their True Potential* (Greenleaf Book Group Press, Austin. TX. Kindle Edition) Chap. 4, p.55

12: Wallace, Alan. *The Attention Revolution: Unlocking The Power of The Focused Mind* (Wisdom Publications. Boston, MA. 2006. Kindle Edition) p. 2.

13: McGonigal, Kelly. *The Willpower Instinct: How Self-Control Works, Why it Matters, and What You Can Do to Get More of It* (Penguin Group. 2012. Kindle Edition). Chap 1, p. 27-28.

14: Elaine, Mead. *The History and Origin of Meditation.* 2020. PositivePsychology.com. Artículo recuperado de: https://positivepsychology.com/history-of-meditation/

15: Goleman, Daniel y Davidson Richard J. *The Science of Meditation: How to Change Your Brain, Mind and Body* (Penguin. 2017. Kindle Edition), p.14

16: Wisdom 2.0. *Well being is a Skill: Richard Davidson.* Youtube. 25:27. 30 March, 2015.https://www.youtube.com/watch?v=EPGJU7W0N0I&list=RDCMUCEhI4Grr46IolhzGhZ3agNw&index=1

17: Goleman, Daniel y Davidson Richard J. *The Science of Meditation: How to Change Your Brain, Mind and Body* (Penguin. 2017. Kindle Edition) Chap. 14, p. 307-310.

18: Sakai, Jill. *Study reveals gene expression changes with meditation.* 2013. University of Wisconsin-Madison.

https://news.wisc.edu/study-reveals-gene-expression-changes-with-meditation/

19: Bradt, Steve. *Wandering mind not a happy mind.* 2010. The Harvard Gazette. https://news.harvard.edu/gazette/story/2010/11/wandering-mind-not-a-happy-mind/

20: Killingsworth, Matt. *Want to be happier? Stay in the Moment.* 2012. TEDxCambrige. https://www.ted.com/talks/matt_killingsworth_want_to_be_happier_stay_in_the_moment/transcript

21: d'Ors, Pablo. *Biografía del Silencio* (Siruela. 2012) p. 38

22: Böckler, A., Herrmann, L., Trautwein, F. et al. *Know Thy Selves: Learning to Understand Oneself Increases the Ability to Understand Others.* J Cogn Enhanc 1, 197–209 (2017). https://doi.org/10.1007/s41465-017-0023-6

23: Goleman, Daniel. *Focus: The Hidden Driver of Excellence* (HarperCollins. 2013. Kindle Edition), p.34-35, 54, 58

24: Villar, Cote. El pánico escénico que sufren Pastora Soler, Adele, Scarlett…El Mundo. LOC. 2014. https://www.elmundo.es/loc/2014/12/03/547dcdec22601d274c8b457c.html

25: Taren AA, Gianaros PJ, Greco CM, et al. *Mindfulness meditation training alters stress-related amygdala resting state functional connectivity: a randomized controlled trial.* Soc Cogn Affect Neurosci. 2015;10(12):1758-1768. doi:10.1093/scan/nsv066

26: IEA de PARIS. Tania Singer (Max Planck Institute): "Plasticity of Empathy and Prosocial Motivation (...)" Video Youtube. 35:30. 27 de junio, 2017. https://www.youtube.com/watch?v=TOa-sPMDNGg

27: Singer, Tania y Bolz, Matthias. *Compassion Bridging Practice and Science* (Max Planck Society. 2013. eBook)

28: Bohm, David. *Sobre el Diálogo* (Editorial Karidós. 2019)

29: Wallace, Alan. *The Attention Revolution: Unlocking The Power of The Focused Mind* (Wisdom Publications. Boston, MA. 2006. Kindle Edition) p. 23.

30: Covey, Stephen R. *Los 7 Hábitos de la Gente Altamente Efectiva* (Paidós Booklet, Ed. 2013) p. 112-125.

31. Wisdom 2.0. Wisdom and Compassion in Business/Scott Shute. Video Youtube. 14:00. 2 de julio 2018. https://www.youtube.com/watch?v=5BriWYCdFhA

32: Benioff, Marc. Trailblazer: *The Power of Business as The Greatest Platform for Change* (Currency, New York. 2019. Kindle Edition). 172-183

33: Collins, Jim. Good to Great: *Why Some Companies Make the Leap...and Others Don't* (HarperCollings. 2001) p. 17-40

**Chapter 10**

1: United Express Flight 3411 incident. Wikipedia from 13th July 2020.
https://en.m.wikipedia.org/wiki/United_Express_Flight_3411_incident

2: Thomas, Lauren. *United CEO says airline had to 're-accommodate' passenger, and the reaction was wild.* 2017. CNBC. https://www.cnbc.com/2017/04/10/united-ceo-says-airline-had-to-re-accommodate-passenger-and-twitter-is-having-a-riot.html

3: Wollongong, Robert; Barton, Rachel; Quiring, Kevin; Ishikawa, Masataka. *What today's consumers want isn't what you think.* 2017. Accenture Strategy. https://www.accenture.com/_acnmedia/pdf-68/accenture-global-anthem-pov.pdf

4: Manyika, James; Lund, Susan; Chui, Michael; Bughin, Jacques; Woetzel, Jonathan Batra, Parul; Ko, Ryan; Sanghvi, Saurabh. *Job lost, jobs gained: What the future of work will mean for jobs, skills, and wages*. 2017. McKinsey&Company. https://www.mckinsey.com/featured-insights/future-of-work/jobs-lost-jobs-gained-what-the-future-of-work-will-mean-for-jobs-skills-and-wages#

5: Roman, David. *"El ritmo implacable de la automatización" (y el futuro del empleo)*. 2017. MIT Technology Review. https://www.technologyreview.es/s/6783/el-ritmo-implacable-de-la-automatizacion-y-el-futuro-del-empleo

6: Food Retail. *Auchan también apuesta por el supermercado sin cajeros*. 2018. https://www.foodretail.es/retailers/auchan-supermercado-sin-cajeros-paris-milan-brescia_0_1229877012.html

7: Contreras, Manu. 2018. Clipset.com. https://clipset.com/alibaba-abre-el-primer-hotel-automatizado-con-inteligencia-artificial-n-y-robots-en-china/

8: Zhong, Lina y Verma, Rohit. *Robots: Hotel customers like them (mostly)!* 2018. Cornell SC Johnson College of Business. https://business.cornell.edu/hub/2018/03/22/robots-hotel-customers-like-them-mostly/

9: Holt,Steve. *Full Service: Automation in restaurants is changing the food industry*. 2018. GreenBiz. https://www.greenbiz.com/article/full-service-automation-restaurants-changing-food-industry

10: Meyer, Danny. *Setting the Table: Lesson's and Inspiration from One of the World's Leading entrepreneurs* (Marshall Cavendish Business. 2010), p. 65.

11: Michelle, Joseph A. *The New Gold Standards: 5 Leadership Principles for Creating a Legendary Customer Experience* (McGraw Hill. 2008. Kindle Edition.), Cap 8, p. 175

12: Welch, Jack. Winning [Ganar]. Las claves para el éxito del ejecutivo más admirado del mundo (Vergara. 2005), p.26

13: Reichheld, Frederick F. *The One Number You Need to Grow.* 2003. Harvard Business Review. https://hbr.org/2003/12/the-one-number-you-need-to-grow

14: Senge, Peter. La Quinta Disciplina (Granica. 2007), p. 260-61

15: Hsieh, Tony. *Delivering Happiness: A Path to Profits, Passion and Purpose* (Business Plus, New York. NY. 2010) p. 165-167

16: Carlson, Jan. *Moments of Truth: New Strategies for Today's Customer-Driven Economy* (Harper. 1989), p. 2-3

17: Mackey, John y Sisodia, Raj. Conscious Capitalism (Harvard Business School Publishing Corporation. Boston MA. 2013.), p. 72-73

18: Sirota, David y Klein, Douglas A. *The Enthusiastic Employee: How Companies Profit by Giving Workers What They Want* (Pearson Education, Inc. 2014. Kindle Edition).

19: Fleming John H; Asplund, Jim. *Human Sigma: Managing the Employee-Customer Encounter* (Gallup Press, New York. 2007. Kindle Edition), Chap. 8 y 9, pos. 1181-1483.

20: Toister, Jeff. *Getting Service Right: Overcoming the Hidden Obstacles to Outstanding Customer Service* (Toister Performance Solutions, Inc. 2019), Chap. 6, pos.1616-1719

21: Amabile, Teresa y Kramer, Steve. *The Progress Principle: Using Small Wins to Ignite Joy, Engagement and Creativity at Work* (Harvard Business Review Press, 2011) p. 89-90

22: Fleming John H; Asplund, Jim. *Human Sigma: Managing the Employee-Customer Encounter* (Gallup Press, New York. 2007. Kindle Edition), Chap 5, pos. 858-921

23: Sam Walton y Huey, John. *Made In America: My Story* (Bantam Books. 1993)

24: Jorrín, Javier G y Zuil, Maria. *La generación perdida: se duplica el número de jóvenes que deja de estudiar para trabajar.* 2019. El Confidencial. https://www.elconfidencial.com/economia/2019-06-30/futura-generacion-perdida-dejado-estudios-trabajar_2096110/

25: CTFORUM. *Danny Meyer on the Six Qualities He Looks for in Employees.* Youtube. 4:16. 24 March, 2017. https://www.youtube.com/watch?v=Ei3nbq7pAqg

26: Little, Brian R. *Me, Myself and Us: The Science of Personality and the Art of Well-Being* (Public Affairs, New York. 2014. Kindle Edition), Cap 1. p. 33-34

**Chapter 11**

1: Compromiso Empresarial. Edward Freeman: "La ética consiste en hacer cosas por los demás y por uno mismo." 2005. https://www.compromisoempresarial.com/rsc/2005/09/edward-freeman-la-etica-consiste-en-hacer-cosas-por-los-demas-y-por-uno-mismo/

2: Castillo, Jorge. Hotel RIU irá a juicio por daño ambiental. 2015. https://www.nacion.com/el-pais/hotel-riu-ira-a-juicio-por-dano-ambiental/HYZSB7UF2REBPBWZ3MD4J3WBHE/story/

3: Elkington, John y Zeitz, Jochen. *The Break-Through Challenge: 10 Ways to Connect Today's profits with Tomorrow's Botton Line* (Joseph-Bass. 2014. Kindle Edition). Chap 1, p.37-38

4: Elkington, John. *Cannibal With Forks: The Triple Bottom Line of 21st Century Business* (John Wiley &Son Ltd. 1999)

5: Leader's Quest. Harnessing Private Sector Purpose to Achieve the Global Goals. A report prepared for the Bill & Melinda Gates Foundation. 2020.

https://leadersquest.org/why-purpose-matters/purpose-stories/gates-report-leaders-quest

6: Hurst A; Pearce, A; Cammine, E; Scott, P; Kotansky, H; Vesty, L; Schnidman, A; Garlinghouse, M; Pavela, A. *Purpose at Work*. Global Report. 2016. https://business.linkedin.com/content/dam/me/business/en-us/talent-solutions/resources/pdfs/purpose-at-work-global-report.pdf

7: Barton, Rachel; Morath, Jürgen; Quiring, Kevin; Theofilou, Bill. *Generation P(urpose): From fidelity to future value*. 2019. Accenture Strategy. https://www.accenture.com/us-en/insights/strategy/generation-purpose

8: O'Brien, Diana; Main, Andy; Kounkel, Suzanne; Stephan, Anthony R. *2020 Global Marketing Trends*. Deloitte Insights. https://www2.deloitte.com/content/dam/Deloitte/uk/Documents/consultancy/deloitte-uk-consulting-global-marketing-trends.pdf

9: Fox Business. Capitalism as we know it is dead: Salesforce co-CEO. Youtube. 10:29. 17 October, 2019. https://m.youtube.com/watch?v=_I5AJyCXYkl

10: Salesforce. Pledge 1%. (s.f.) Salesforce.org: https://www.salesforce.org/pledge-1/

11: Mayer, Colin. *Prosperity; better business makes the greater good* (Oxford University Press. 2018. Kindle Edition) Chap 1, p.40

12: Carrizosa, Susana. Colin Mayer: "La ambición de directivos y accionistas pone en riesgo la empresa." 2019. El País. https://elpais.com/economia/2019/07/17/actualidad/1563353884_303450.html

13: GRI, United Nations Global Compact y wbcsd. SDG Compass: La guía para la acción empresarial en los ODS. https://sdgcompass.org/wp-content/uploads/2016/06/SDG_Compass_Spanish-one-pager-view.pdf

14: UN: Academic Impact. Objetivos de Desarrollo Sostenible. https://academicimpact.un.org/es/content/objetivos-de-desarrollo-sostenible

15: Jones, Peter y Comfort, Daphne. *Sustainable Development Goals and the World's Leading Hotel Groups.* 2019 Athens Journal of Tourism -Volume 6, Issue 1, p.1-14. doi=10.30958/ajt.6-1-1

16: United Nations Global Compact y Accenture. *The Decade To Deliver: A Call To Business Action.* The United Nations Global Compact —Accenture Strategy CEO Study on Sustainability 2019.https://www.accenture.com/_acnmedia/pdf-109/accenture-ungc-ceo-study.pdf

17: United Nations. *Secretary-General, at Private Sector Forum, Pledges Action to Embed Sustainable Development Goals into International Economic Policy, Harness Climate Finance.* 2017.https://www.un.org/press/en/2017/sgsm18690.doc.htm

18: Holistic. *Marten Dresen session.* Companies Doing Good Froum. Skopje. Yotube. 29:11. 28 December, 2016. https://www.youtube.com/watch?v=_iOQymRn6vl&t=281s

19: Ibid.

20: Högskolan i Boras – University of Boras. Transparency at Patagonia: What we've done and what we haven't done.Youtube. 30:01. 18 December, 2014. https://www.youtube.com/watch?v=mG1iqU8RBhU

21: Cuenllas, A. Scandic Hotel: Case Study in Sustainability. Hospitality.net. 2014. https://www.hospitalitynet.org/opinion/4064048.html

22: Grant, John. The Green Marketing Manifesto (John Wiley & Sons, Ltd. 2007), p. 123-125

23: Hotel Management International. Green roots: sustainability at the heart of Scandic. 2013. https://www.hmi-online.com/features/featuregreen-roots-sustainability-at-the-heart-of-scandic/

24:Cohen, Ben y Greenfield, Jerry. *Ben&Jerry's Double-Dip. How to Run a Values-Led Business and Make Money, Too* (Simon & Shuster Paperbacks, New York. NY. 1997)

25: Honeyman, Ryan. *The B Corp Handbook: How to Use Business as a Force of Good* (Berrett-Koehler Publishers, Inc.,Oakland. CA.2014), Chap 1, pos. 33

A Higher Purpose: 3 Rules of Conscious Leadership

Printed in Great Britain
by Amazon

66674423R00185